Lost Souls

The Possession at Winchester Grove

Corey Michaels

Archway Publishing books may be ordered through booksellers or by contacting:

Archway Publishing
1663 Liberty Drive
Bloomington, IN 47403
www.archwaypublishing.com
1 (888) 242-5904

ISBN: 978-1-4808-8432-8 (sc)
ISBN: 978-1-4808-8431-1 (e)

Library of Congress Control Number: 2019917145

Print information available on the last page.

Archway Publishing rev. date: 11/07/2019

In memory of George Miller
1865–1883

For Petey and Tink.

I put my hand into the flame,
Burning, but I feel no pain.
Don't speak, don't speak my name.
Hold on to this life of chains.

Foreword by Anne Delaney

There are no coincidences in life. Everything happens for a reason—perhaps to prepare us for something bigger, better, or even make us stronger before the storm. And I believe that it is all part of God's plan. I believe we are all born with free will. If we venture off our life path and we do not accomplish what we are meant to learn or teach others, I believe we are able to begin again. That is, until we get it right. Along the way, we learn or teach life lessons, and I believe God gives us the ability to resolve things when we veer off course.

Déjà vu supposedly occurs when we feel as though we have been in a particular situation or place once before. Whether it's a smell, familiar place, or even a perfect stranger that reminds you of someone you know or once knew. I believe at that moment we must stop and acknowledge our surroundings. Perhaps a fork in the road may be upon us at that very moment. You may have to decide which path to take in order to correct a mistake or make a wrong right again. This may be an opportunity to change your life or perhaps even someone else's life course. No, there are no coincidences in life. Things happen for a reason. And the story you are about to read has lots of reasons.

Lost Souls was inspired by actual events. Names and locations have been changed to protect the identity of those involved.

Acknowledgments

A special thank you to my children for allowing me to share our story, my research companion for helping me find my faith again, my sister for giving me spiritual insight I could never see before, and, last but not least, my parents for believing there's more out there.

April 22, 2010, Journal Entry

Four thirty in the afternoon couldn't arrive soon enough. I called Anne once I arrived home to make sure the group was still coming. I was anxious, to say the least. I knew what was going to transpire, but I would remain hopeful that there was still another way.

April 22, 2010, 5:30 P.M.

Father Joseph: In the name of the Father, and of the Son, and of the Holy Ghost. Amen. Most glorious prince of the heavenly armies, Saint Michael the archangel, defend us in our battle against principalities and powers, against the rulers of this world of darkness, against the spirits of wickedness in the high places. I want to speak to the entity that is tormenting this child of God.

Corey: *(Laughing.)*

Father Joseph: What is your name?

Corey: *(Laughing.)*

Father Joseph: By the power of God, I demand that you tell me your name.

Corey: *(Laughing.)* I have many names, Priest.

Father Joseph: I demand you to tell me your name. Why you are tormenting this child of God?

Corey: *(Laughing.)* She invited me in, Priest.

Father Joseph: Tell me your name.

Corey: I am many. I am many. I am many.

Father Joseph: Release her as she prays to have you removed from her body.

Corey: She prays for nothing and no one! She has no faith, Priest. *(Laughing.)* Ring around the rosy, pocket full of posy, ashes, ashes, you'll all fall down! *(Laughing.)*

Father Joseph: I know who you are. You cannot torment this child or her family anymore. She knows what you did, and you will enter into the eternal flames of hell for your deeds.

Corey: Hahahahahahahah! You have no control over her, Priest. She invited me in, and she has no faith in your so-called God.

Four Months Earlier

January 21, 2010, Journal Entry

Moving down on the river was probably the best thing I did when Renee and I separated. The kids seemed to like the water sports, and I enjoyed the peace and quiet. They were adjusting just fine, and it was the first winter alone with them in this big old house.

With the gentle blowing of the snowdrifts outside, I could hear the whirling of the wind as it blew off of the old sash windows—of course, reminding me to invest in some new windows in the spring.

The sigh from Bear was my indicator to wake up. Flipping over to avoid the sunlight now casting through my window, I stretched my tired legs across the bed as I curled up with my soft feathered pillow just another minute longer. And then another sigh exploded out of Bear. "Fine!" I said. "I'm up already!" Just then, Bear jumped up and charged me with a kiss on the nose. "Stop, Bear! That's so gross!" I yelled. She didn't seem to care. She knew what time it was. It was time for her to eat.

It was another night of tossing and turning as my reflection showed in the mirror. I was awakened by someone screaming in my ear to get out. It was a young man, and he was screaming for me to hide the children. Something was coming to do some damage. I had a gut feeling someone was not getting out alive this time. I quickly dressed myself and hurried downstairs. When I reached the bottom of the stairs, the scent of Polo sent a jolt of lightning to my chest. *No, this can't be!* I thought. Surely, this was just a dream. There's no way he could have found us. But as I walked slowly down into the foyer, I saw a shadow from the kitchen doorway. It was him all right and with a gun in his hand. It was Harley Hillcrest, and he was drunk. He had found us, and we were no longer safe. My children would be home from their dads soon, and I had to get him out of there.

I tried to rationalize with him that there was a better way to solve things, but there was no convincing a drunk. His intention was to get even for me leaving him. He had no intention of walking out alive.

Grabbing my arm, Harley violently pushed on the screen door, looking left and right to make sure no one would see him pulling me out of the house. Harley opened the door to his car and threw me into the front seat with him, then threw the car in drive and tore out of the driveway toward the old depot. Renee and the kids were just coming around the turn when they noticed his car and me inside it. The looks on their faces were as though they had seen a ghost. They knew I was in trouble, and Renee did nothing to stop it. Perhaps he thought I deserved it. I can see him now, smiling and laughing under his breath. But I didn't deserve this. Not even the worst grade-school bully deserved what Harley put us through. I screamed for Harley to stop, but he didn't listen. I tried to turn around to see the kids, but Harley's grip was so tight I nearly snapped my neck.

Harley began to rant about nonsense, and I just couldn't

understand what he was saying. "What are you doing, Harley?" I asked. But he didn't respond. I pleaded with him to stop the car, but he wasn't listening and just kept on ranting like a lunatic. We got about two blocks down the road when he began to lose control of the car. He was drunk, but it was not him behind the wheel of the car. It was something else.

Suddenly both doors locked, the shifter went into overdrive, and we were speeding down Washington Street. Harley looked at me in fear. The car was alive, and as the engine reeved, the radio station needle switched back and forth, and a sinister laugh amplified throughout the car. I was motionless and terrified. That laugh. That terrible, screeching laugh. I closed my eyes praying that this was all just a very bad dream. But it wasn't; this was no dream. The growling laugh I knew all too well. No, this was my reality.

We sailed through the snowbanks of the neighborhood, blowing every stop sign and red light along our path. The car swerved on and off the snow-covered pavement, traveling nearly a hundred miles an hour, and Harley had no control over it. "This is your fault! You brought this thing into my house!" he screamed. He blamed me for bringing bad luck into his family. But I didn't. It wasn't my fault bad things happened. They were just coincidences. That's all, coincidences. But he wasn't convinced, and frankly, neither was I. I knew something terrible was with me. And by the looks of it, it was all about to end right here and now.

The car continued down Washington Street until it abruptly stopped near the old Methodist church. Just then, both doors unlocked simultaneously. This was our chance to get out. Seeing an opportunity to escape, I grabbed the handle and continuously pulled on the door, but Harley took hold of my arm. I looked at Harley as his eyes widened so large he looked like he was in one of those alien abduction movies. Pure darkness oozed from his eyes. I screamed and tried to push Harley away from me, but I couldn't look away from what I was seeing. His eyes, his eyes were so menacing. I was afraid to look away only to look back and see an entirely different being holding me captive. No, this was no longer Harley that I was looking at. No, this was something much worse! The motor revved up, and the tires started spinning. The ride was far from over. The car took off, and before I knew it, the speedometer read fifty, sixty, seventy miles an hour, heading to the hill near the tracks. My stomach was in knots as the laughs over the radio continued and Harley held me down. The car sped up and became airborne over the hill and across the train tracks. The car slammed on the brakes and turned around, causing Harley to slide over on top of me, pinning me against the dashboard. I tried to push Harley off, but he was too big. We were now facing the train tracks, and the engine was racing. As if entering the running of the bulls, the rear wheels squealed, and a cloud of smoke filled the street, leaving rubber permanently marking the roadway. Harley was yelling and screaming, but what he was saying wasn't making any sense at all. It was as if Harley was cheering the car on. Still having a strong hold on my arm, I kept trying to reason with him to stop all of this at once. But Harley knew nothing of what I was saying.

Suddenly, the car stalled on the tracks. I knew what was coming next. It was just a matter of time. I heard the whistle to my left as I quickly turned to witness what would've been my last memory. This was the day that everything would fade to black. The train was just around the bend. I could hear it. Its whistle was getting louder and louder as it approached. And then, there it was—the Aberdeen train, and it was right on time.

Harley was transfixed on the wheel. Terrified, he wet himself. He had no idea what was coming for us. I yelled and screamed for him to snap out of it. Harley just sat there as if he was in a trance. Quickly, I grabbed the handle, opened the door, and jumped out. I screamed for him to get out, but he wouldn't move. Something was still in there with him. I screamed as I ran over to the driver's side door and pulled as hard as I could until finally the door swung open. Harley was still trapped and his body remained motionless. He turned to look at me, and his eyes filled with tears.

"Save him," they whispered.

I knew what I had to do. Despite my hatred toward Harley, I had to help him. "Harley, let's go!" I screamed. But he didn't hear me. "Harley, do you want to die in here? You have got to get out!" But Harley refused to move.

The train whistle whaled out three more blows as the conductor behind the glass waved his arms to get off of the track. I screamed as loudly as I could and grabbed the attention of some people passing by just south of the tracks. It was James Dixon and his wife, Eleanor, the antique dealer everyone loved to hate in town. It didn't matter to me. He knew Harley was in trouble, and James was the last person he would expect to help him.

Harley and James owned shops in town. Harley owned the Hillcrest General Store and sold everyday toiletries, goods, and groceries to the locals. The Hillcrest Store had been handed down by his great-grandfather, Peter Hillcrest. James, on the other hand, was a sixth-generation antiques dealer. He owned the Dixon Emporium off of Commerce Street. But unlike his ancestors, James and his partner, Leroy, were dirty.

The Dixon family arrived in the Winchester Grove in 1830. They purchased land along Commerce Street from Edmund Drake. Harley and James grew up in the business, and like their fathers and their fathers' fathers, they always had it out for each other. In fact, the whole town knew that they hated each other. They were the Hatfield and McCoys of Winchester Grove. And the local paper always had something to say about their hardships, dating back to the 1850s when a train derailed along the Kankakee River.

It all began during a weekend in the summer of 1853 when a few of the Hillcrests were on their way back from a convention in Chicago. The conductor, Harold Dixon, was new to the area. He began his run at the depot just outside of Chicago. Just as he approached Winchester Grove, a twist in the track required a deceleration to make it safely around the bend. Harold was already going too fast when he noticed the turn. He applied the brakes, but there was nothing else he could do to prevent what was to happen next. Screams filled the locomotive as she left the track and plummeted into the Kankakee River. All passengers on board died from impact or drowning. Three members of the Hillcrest family lost their lives that early morning in the accident, including Harold Dixon. Thus began the feud between the Hillcrest and Dixon families.

Locals say that Lake Superior never gives up her dead, and I believe that may also be true about other bodies of water. Harley told me about James and the articles that ran in the newspapers long ago. He had a binder full of newspaper clippings when it came to their feud. He kept them all, and it had me wondering if the river had something to do with their hardships.

About nine years ago, James ended up in the sheriff's office, claiming something had attacked Leroy while digging for artifacts on the island to sell in their shop. It was illegal, and they both new it, and it didn't stop them.

James rambled on about a ghost train that they witnessed fall into the Kankakee River. He claimed that while they were digging, they had both heard what appeared to be a locomotive coming across the Aberdeen tracks. When he heard the whistle blow, they looked at each other in disbelief, for there were no more locomotives on the Aberdeen line. It caught their attention, and they quickly turned around. The iron horse rolled through the prairie town, and within seconds, she was racing down the track toward the bend. Her engine flew off the track at such a speed the impact into the river was explosive, and flames shot out as the fuel leaked out across the river, leaving a fiery path of destruction in her wake. Leroy dropped his shovel and dove into the water to help them. Screams of despair filled the night sky, and James stood in awe at the sight. Women and children were engulfed in flames as they tried to swim away from the accident, but there was no saving them. He stated that a mist or shadow figures began to appear from the wreckage and attacked him and Leroy. James stated that Leroy got within five feet of a young child when suddenly the child turned into a grotesque monster and was in midair, flying right for him.

He claimed that women and children appeared as skeletons on fire and that they had come after them both. James managed to escape, but Leroy was gone.

Leroy turned around and began to swim back to the shore as fast as he could. He cried out for James, but James was still in shock from the whole sight. The child was then joined by others, and within minutes, Leroy was being dragged back to the burning locomotive by several women and children emitting firestorms from their bodies. Leroy has been missing ever since and some believe James had something to do with it.

James stood there, reflecting on the ordeal with Leroy long ago. He remained unsure of what would happen if he tried to help Harley. I screamed for James to help me and to snap out of it. James shook his head as if to gather enough courage to move forward; he managed to break free from his own spell. James pulled Harley to safety just before the train crossed the tracks, carrying Harley's car until finally falling off the bridge and landing in the Kankakee River. Harley's car was destroyed. The Winchester Grove Police Department was at the scene within minutes. I managed to give my testimony to the police department, stating merely that Harley was intoxicated and that there was nothing faulty with the vehicle, as Harley had said otherwise. To me, it was just the driver under the influence and nothing more. Harley told another story to the authorities that day. James silently walked away into the crowd and disappeared. Harley was jailed for a DUI and sent for a psych evaluation the following day.

I went to visit Harley a few days later while awaiting trial for his DUI. I told him to leave me and my family alone or things like this would continue to happen to him. I told him that I knew what he was contemplating regarding Renee. He looked rather surprised that I knew what his plan was. That's when he said something very, very foolish. "She's a witch, a witch, I tell you! She made this happen to me. She brought dead people in my house. She has visions of people dying. She is a witch!" he screamed. Harley began to lash out with rantings of a crazy person, and soon everyone in town heard about it. The incident even made the papers. There was no mention of me in the article for once. I was quite pleased this time that my name did not appear in the public's eye. We have been through enough these past few months, and it is time to start over. It is time to forget about Harley Hillcrest.

January 29, 2010

I have had enough. We cannot live like this anymore. I am fearful that this thing will take over me. I am afraid for my children. I don't know who to confide in anymore. The night terrors are getting worse. I have many sleepless nights. This house is making things worse. I don't know what to do anymore. I know I need help. I will remain hopeful that Dr. Raymond can help me. Help us.

February 1, 2010, Therapy Session

Dr. Raymond: Good afternoon, Ms. Michaels. My name is Dr. James Raymond.

Corey: Good afternoon, Dr. Raymond.

Dr. Raymond: I would like to tell you that I record all of the sessions for reference and progress in your therapy sessions. Are you comfortable with that?

Corey: Yes, that is fine.

Dr. Raymond: Okay, great. Are you ready to begin?

Corey: Yes.

Dr. Raymond: Corey Michaels, February 1, 2010. So, Corey, I understand you work at the Tapier Orphanage?

Corey: Yes, I have worked there for over fifteen years now.

Dr. Raymond: Okay. That's great! Let's go ahead and talk a bit about the reason why you are here. Yes, let's start with your personal history. You claimed to have night terrors or premonitions going back to an early age?

Corey: Yes, I documented most of them in a journal. I started writing them down back when I was in high school. Some of them are dreams. In fact, I have had several dreams that are the same that I have had for years.

Dr. Raymond: I know there are several reasons for your visit, and we will need to take one step at a time. I understand that you are fearful of certain things.

Corey: Yes, I am. Ever since I was a child, I have had distinct dreams about dying. The strange thing is how I die in them. All of them involve water and falling from a great height. To this day, I fear drowning, yet I know how to swim. I am also fearful of heights, but I enjoying flying. It's the strangest thing.

Dr. Raymond: Let's talk about the premonitions you indicated in your paperwork. Do you recall when you had the first premonition?

Corey: Yes, I was about nine or ten. I was playing in the park in my neighborhood with a friend when it happened.

Dr. Raymond: Tell me about it.

Corey: There was a children's park across the street from our house. A lot of the neighborhood kids would assemble there—ya know, to play hide-and-seek, swing on the sets, merry-go-round, and stuff. Back in the day—I mean long before I was born, like in the twenties—a school once stood there. But the school burned down ten years after it was built. Instead of rebuilding the school, they built a children's park there. It has been there ever since. Anyway, the park is at the top of a huge hill, and next to it is a large grove of trees. Teenagers used to drink back there, and there was talk of devil worshipping when I was younger. We never went back there though. We were all too scared to go beyond the grove.

Dr. Raymond: So, what happened on this particular day with your friend?

Corey: Martin—my friend's name is Martin. Anyway, we met at the swing sets like we always did. We were just standing there trying to figure out what to play. Then suddenly, I just got up and starting walking toward the grove.

Dr. Raymond: Did you think this was out of the ordinary?

Corey: Yeah, I mean, we were all terrified of what was behind the grove. We never, ever went back there.

Dr. Raymond: What happened when you got into the grove?

Corey: I don't recall actually walking into it. I just remember feeling as if someone or something was drawing me near it. I couldn't hear anything; I couldn't see anything. I just had a feeling there was something there for me.

Dr. Raymond: So what happened once you arrived at the grove of trees?

Corey: I just stopped and stared into them. Martin said he was calling for me, but I wouldn't answer. He told me it was if I were frozen or in a trance. I remember feeling anxious like something was coming. Ya know, like when you are on a roller coaster and you are at the top, just about to go over the edge? That is how I felt. I knew there was something coming. I felt it. The next thing I knew there was this huge black dog running right for me.

Dr. Raymond: A dog came out from the grove and attacked you?

Corey: Yeah, I saw it coming from within the grove of trees. I saw the tall grass sway back and forth as if there were some hidden path he was traveling. But I could not move. I could not run away.

Dr. Raymond: What happened when the dog came out of the grove toward you?

Corey: I quickly put up my right arm to protect my head and neck from being bitten.

Dr. Raymond: Did the dog bite you?

Corey: Yes, he bit my elbow and left me with a gaping hole in my arm and bruises up and down my legs. See?

Dr. Raymond: But you were able to escape?

Corey: Yes, Martin's father came running out when he heard him screaming.

Dr. Raymond: Did you yell for help?

Corey: I don't recall. I don't even recall crying after it was all over with. I just remember his father carrying me into the house. I don't remember much else.

Dr. Raymond: Okay, and you had similar experiences throughout your childhood?

Corey: Yes, in fact, the family used to make fun of my premonitions or feelings that I would have. They thought I was weird for telling them to be careful over the years. I would have vivid dreams about bad things happening to people around me.

Dr. Raymond: How did your family react to them?

Corey: Like I said, they thought I was weird and usually ignored me. That is until the accident.

Dr. Raymond: The accident?

Corey: Yeah, a friend of mine lost three of his friends back when I was in high school.

Dr. Raymond: And you predicted this?

Corey: Yeah, but no one ever believed me. Then when it happened, this friend of mine barely spoke to me again.

Dr. Raymond: So, this friend of yours, did he or she know that you had a vision or dream about an accident?

Corey: Yeah, I phoned him the morning before it happened. His name is Logan.

Dr. Raymond: What happened when you told Logan about your dream?

Corey: He didn't believe me. He insisted I was dreaming. Then when it happened, well, he just moved away, and I haven't seen him since the memorial.

Dr. Raymond: According to your questionnaire, you stated that for some time the premonitions or dreams went away, correct?

Corey: Yes, the last one I had before they returned was in the summer of '93.

Dr. Raymond: So from '93 until now, you did not have any premonitions or dreams?

Corey: Well, I had dreams, but the premonitions started up again in 2007.

Dr. Raymond: So now the premonitions have returned along with your anxiety attacks, correct?

Corey: Yes.

Dr. Raymond: Your questionnaire stated that you are not taking any medications. How are you dealing with the anxiety attacks without medication?

Corey: I am using breathing techniques I learned from a program I purchased from an infomercial. I have learned how to read the anxiety attacks.

Dr. Raymond: What do you mean, read the anxiety attacks?

Corey: It's when I know a premonition is coming.

Dr. Raymond: Do you dream about events happening as well?

Corey: Yes. In fact, lately I keep having the same dreams night after night.

Dr. Raymond: Would you like to talk about these dreams?

Corey: They are not pleasant dreams. They are rather disturbing.

Dr. Raymond: Tell me about your dream that frightens you the most.

Corey: Well, it's about my soon-to-be ex-husband. His name is Renee. I dream that he is driving our children home from school, and he gets into an auto accident. Just before the car hits the median, everything fades to black. I have this dream almost every night.

Dr. Raymond: That is very interesting.

Corey: Wait. There is more. Just before everything goes black, I see this dark figure above the hood of the car. It's as if someone was there watching it happen. But I can't see who it is.

Dr. Raymond: Does this figure appear as a woman or a man?

Corey: I can't tell. I guess it could be a man because of how big it appears. I mean, it looks like a black shadow, but it could be a shadow from the trucks coming from the opposite direction. I just don't know what it is. It's big though, and it moves like smoke. Then it all fades to black.

Dr. Raymond: Does the dream awaken you?

Corey: Yes, I mean, my heart is racing when I wake up, and I am usually in tears.

Dr. Raymond: Perhaps that is what the dream is about. Being unable to save them from your separation. Corey, whose decision was it to separate?

Corey: Mine. I was the one that left, but it's a long story, and I am not here to discuss my relationship. I am here because the dreams won't stop. I am losing sleep, and the anxiety is too much to handle.

Dr. Raymond: I understand. However, you are dreaming about the man you are divorcing and the bond that is being torn between your children.

Corey: I guess. I mean, even after the divorce is final, he will still be a part of my children's lives. So why would I dream about them all disappearing due to a violent accident?

Dr. Raymond: Perhaps it's the way you are interpreting the divorce or separation of the family as a whole. Corey, it is my belief that what we experience from day to day greatly influences what we dream about. I am willing to talk to you about your relationship and how it affects your dreams. I can help you analyze what the dreams mean in connection with what is going on in your life. It may explain a lot.

Corey: That's not what I am here for. I want to understand why the dreams keep reoccurring. Some of them have familiar faces—family and friends. The others, I see people that I have never met before. I don't know who these people are in my dreams.

Dr. Raymond: Can you tell me specifically what is so different about the people in your dreams?

Corey: Their clothing, their hairstyles. They even talk differently. Some are in uniform. Uniforms I've seen in military photographs.

Dr. Raymond: Do you recognize the uniforms? I mean, do you know what war the men were in? They are all men, correct?

Corey: Yes, they are all men. I am a historian, ya know. I see a lot of photographs, research family histories and sites. I know a lot about our history here. The uniforms look like those worn during the Civil War. But I don't know why I am dreaming about a particular moment in time.

Dr. Raymond: Perhaps what you read and research also affects your dream state. Are you working on something right now that may be influencing you?

Corey: I do all the time. I mean, history has always fascinated me, especially unknown histories or stories that have been lost over time.

Dr. Raymond: Okay, you mentioned that you were having two similar dreams, correct?

Corey: No, not similar, very different. But I do keep having the same two over and over again though. One is about the car accident, and the other is the one in the woods.

Dr. Raymond: Tell me about the other one. The dream in the woods.

Corey: Well, I'm walking in the woods, and I come up to a building. It's secluded, and you can barely see the roof with the tree lining it. It's almost hidden. There is no road or trail to get to it. It just appears out of nowhere.

Dr. Raymond: Do you recognize the building?

Corey: It looks a little familiar, but I cannot place where I have seen it before. I have lived in this area my whole life, and I do not recall ever seeing this particular area in our history books.

Dr. Raymond: What happens when you get closer to it?

Corey: I can see the door opening as if someone is inviting me in. I walk closer until I am at the front of the house. I can hear a woman screaming, but I can't see what is going on. I walk a little closer to get a better view through a window. I notice a man standing over a bed, tapping a clipboard with his pen. He looks wicked, like that character Slender Man.

Dr. Raymond: Can you hear anything?

Corey: A woman sobbing. I walk into the room to see what is going on, and there is a pregnant woman lying on the bed. She is in labor. She is pleading with them to save her baby. When I get a full view of her, her legs, they are tied together. I look up at the man holding the clipboard, and he smiles this terrible smile and laughs. His laugh is the one I hear over and over again. It's a terrible, menacing laugh. Evil. And those teeth and that stringy hair. I know that face. I've seen it before. I don't like it. This face is in my dreams.

Dr. Raymond: What do you mean you have seen the face before?

Corey: I have had terrible dreams about something in my bedroom at night.

Dr. Raymond: There is a connection between what you have experienced and what you dream about. It's just a matter of putting the pieces together, like solving a puzzle. It is possible that you may have subconsciously stumbled upon some histories from your research that may be influencing your dreams. Regardless, we will get to bottom of your trouble, and I will do the best I can to help you.

Corey: So, you think from my research, I am creating some sort of fiction or dark scenarios of people that lived there?

Dr. Raymond: It is possible that you are trying to create scenarios for what you have discovered at other sites.

Corey: Dr. Raymond, I couldn't make this stuff up if I were awake. I am not dreaming when this occurs. I am fully awake when I see the face.

Dr. Raymond: What is it that you see?

Corey: I don't know! I am afraid to talk about it.

Dr. Raymond: Corey, understand that I am here to help you.

Corey: It's something terrible. I just don't want to talk about it right now.

Dr. Raymond: Okay, okay, I see. Well, let's continue with your questionnaire then, shall we? I see that you have two children.

Corey: Yes, that is correct. Mason and Sara.

Dr. Raymond: I see that you are a published author as well.

Corey: Yes, I wrote a book about an old poor farm in my county. It took me a few years to write, but it was something that I really wanted to do.

Dr. Raymond: That is quite an accomplishment. You should be proud.

Corey: Dr. Raymond, you have no idea what the book has done to me and my family. From the moment I first stepped on the property, something changed in me. I felt different. You would think that I would be proud to be published, but I'm not so sure now. It's a chapter in my life I wish I could erase, but I can't.

Dr. Raymond: Why do you feel that it's a part of your life that you wish to erase?

Corey: I believe it brought something in with it. I am afraid what the family would do in the event the story ever got out. Not to mention losing my credibility as a historian.

Dr. Raymond: Are you worried that people won't believe you?

Corey: Well, yes. Certain people may want to see me locked up. I could lose my children and all credibility for my research.

Dr. Raymond: So you believe that writing the book is to blame for what you are experiencing with your dreams and premonitions?

Corey: I know it did, and I'm afraid. Things are getting worse.

Dr. Raymond: You claim that these dreams and premonitions began as a young child though, correct?

Corey: Well, yes, but lately the same dreams have been occurring, and the premonitions are more frequent now.

Dr. Raymond: Okay, well, let's take one step back. Are you afraid that Renee will take your children from you?

Corey: Yes. I can feel it. I know what they are trying to do.

Dr. Raymond: They, who?

Corey: Renee and his family.

Dr. Raymond: What do you mean?

Corey: It doesn't matter. I know what they are planning to do.

Dr. Raymond: How do you know? Have you tried talking to Renee about what is going on?

Corey: Are you kidding me? He would have me locked up. I know what they want to do. I know they are planning something.

Dr. Raymond: So, how often do you have your children?

Corey: They go to their father's every other weekend.

Dr. Raymond: How are things going with your children in regard to the divorce?

Corey: It is tough on them. I am trying, but things are cloudy in my life right now.

Dr. Raymond: What do you mean, cloudy?

Corey: There is a lot of uncertainty. I mean, I don't know what I am doing half the time.

Dr. Raymond: Do you feel as though you are able to be a parent to them during this time?

Corey: Whose side are you on here?

Dr. Raymond: I am not on anyone's side. I am asking if you feel well enough to provide for them during this time.

Corey: I am their mother. I would never let anything happen to them.

Dr. Raymond: Are your children receiving therapy as well during this time?

Corey: They are seeing a counselor after school to help with the separation.

Dr. Raymond: That's good. Tell me a little bit about them. Let's start with this past weekend, and perhaps we can work backward. Okay?

Corey: Okay.

Dr. Raymond: Were the children with you this past weekend?

Corey: Yes, I took my children to church yesterday morning.

Dr. Raymond: That's a good thing, Corey. How did it go?

Corey: His family was there, but they ignored me. In fact, they never even acknowledged I was there. They took my kids with them to sit in the pews and didn't even look up at me.

Dr. Raymond: So you attend the same church.

Corey: Yes.

Dr. Raymond: I know this is difficult for you. It still may take some time for everyone to heal. For some, the wounds are still fresh. Everyone deals with separation and divorce differently. You cannot change how others react to divorce.

Corey: Yes, but I know they will never forget. Nor will Renee ever be willing to forgive for me for what I have done. If they only knew what was going on, perhaps they would understand. Perhaps they would believe that there is a reason for all of this. What I have been subjected to is real, but I know if they find out, they will take my kids away from me. They would never believe me with everything that is going on right now. I need to figure this all out first.

Dr. Raymond: Corey, it is obvious that there are some things regarding your separation that you need to talk about. I can sense that your separation may be a key factor.

Corey: No, I would rather talk about other things. I mean, that is what I am here for, right? To talk about my dreams and premonitions.

Dr. Raymond: Okay, I understand. Perhaps if it should affect your sessions, it would be wise to discuss it. Just letting you know that it may become an issue for concern later. Okay?

Corey: Okay, yes. Later would be fine.

Dr. Raymond: I often hypnotize my clients to help them process certain events that may have transpired that they no longer remember. The brain is a very powerful organ, and when traumatic incidents occur, our brains have a firewall, if you will, for locking in memories. It's a safety mechanism to protect us from breaking down emotionally, sometimes physically. As children, even as adults, sometimes we experience situations that can create a mental crisis. As I mentioned before, our brains are capable of suppressing thoughts, emotions, and even physical stresses that we experience. It's a defense mechanism.

If a person witnesses a traumatizing event, the brain has the capability to block the memories out. It is only through hypnosis that we are able to bring back those memories or events that transpired. Those events may have been difficult to deal with when they occurred. Everyone handles stress differently. You are no exception. Will you allow me to hypnotize you?

Corey: Yes. I have never been hypnotized before. What do you plan to do?

Dr. Raymond: I plan to ask you a series of questions pertaining to your dreams, your emotional state, and perhaps help unlock memories of an incident that would help analyze why you are having these dreams. We may also tap into the reasoning behind certain phobias or fears you have as well.

Corey: So, will I know what is going on? Will I remember what happens during the hypnosis?

Dr. Raymond: Yes, you will remember everything we talk about. Okay. Are you ready?

Corey: Yeah. I'm ready.

Dr. Raymond: Okay, Corey, I want you to relax. Listen to my voice and close your eyes. Take some deep breaths in and out. Relaxing deeper and deeper. Clearing your mind of any negative thoughts. Take some deep breaths in and out. In and out. Your heartbeat gradually slowing down. Taking deep breaths in and out. With every exhale, your muscles begin to feel heavy and relaxed. Feeling more and more relaxed with every breath in and out. Continuing with your breathing in and out. Slowly relaxing. Deep breath in and out. I am going to count backward from five to one. When I get to one, you will be fully relaxed. Five, drifting deeper and deeper as your body begins to feel relaxed and heavy. Four, drifting deeper and deeper with every breath in and out, drifting, drifting, deeper and deeper. Three. Every muscle slowly beginning to feel heavy and relaxed. Drifting deeper and deeper, heavier and heavier. Two, drifting deeper and deeper, muscles feeling heavier and heavier, and one, fully relaxed. Corey, can you hear me?

Corey: Yes.

Dr. Raymond: Are you relaxed?

Corey: Yes.

Dr. Raymond: Are you comfortable?

Corey: Yes.

Dr. Raymond: Can you tell me your full name?

Corey: Corey Virginia Michaels.

Dr. Raymond: Okay. Corey, can you tell me why you are here today?

Corey: To help with my bad dreams. I don't sleep very well.

Dr. Raymond: Let's start with when the dreams began, shall we?

Corey: Okay.

Dr. Raymond: Do you remember when you started having the bad dreams?

Corey: Yes, it was the summer of 2006.

Dr. Raymond: Okay, I want you to go back to the summer of 2006. I want you to imagine a long, lightly lit hallway. Can you imagine the hallway?

Corey: Yes.

Dr. Raymond: Okay, good. Now at end of the hallway is a door. I want you to walk toward that door slowly. As you walk toward the door, you can see there are several doors on each side of you. Each door represents special times in your life. School days, vacations, family gatherings, fun things, and good memories. I want you to walk past them, slowly moving closer and closer to the door at the end of the hallway. As you slowly walk by, each doorway is slightly cracked open so you can see what is behind it. I want you to continue on though.

I want you to continue moving toward that door at the end of the hallway. Are you getting close to the door?

Corey: Yes, I can almost touch it.

Dr. Raymond: Okay, good. When you reach the door, I want you to open it slowly, and when you do, I want you to tell me where you are. Can you open the door and tell me what you see behind the door?

Corey: Yes. I'm at home with my husband. We bought a ranch in the country.

Dr. Raymond: That's good. What town?

Corey: Waterford Glen. Outside of City Limits.

Dr. Raymond: Unincorporated, Waterford?

Corey: Yes.

Dr. Raymond: Can you tell me what day is?

Corey: Saturday.

Dr. Raymond: What are you doing on this day?

Corey: I am planning to visit the poor farm. *(Sobbing.)*

Dr. Raymond: Why are you upset?

Corey: Something is happening to me.

Dr. Raymond: What do you mean?

Corey: Something is trying to get into my head. Something is wrong with me. I can feel something is coming. I don't feel like myself anymore.

Dr. Raymond: What is different about you?

Corey: My head feels cloudy. I can't make the right decisions. I feel so alone in this house. I don't belong here. I feel homesick.

Dr. Raymond: Why do you feel homesick?

Corey: I don't want to be here. I'm afraid.

Dr. Raymond: Why are you afraid?

Corey: I don't feel right anymore. I don't feel like myself.

Dr. Raymond: Did you try to talk to Renee about what you are feeling and experiencing?

Corey: Yes, he keeps telling me that things will get better.

Dr. Raymond: How does that make you feel?

Corey: It made me even more upset. *(Sobbing.)* Renee said I would be okay. He promised it would be okay. But the dreams continued. He tried, but it just wasn't the same. *(Sobbing.)* Everything changed in me. It was too late.

Dr. Raymond: What do you mean things changed?

Corey: I changed. My whole aspect on life changed. It's as if I went to sleep, and when I woke up, I was a different person. He couldn't protect me. He tried, but he was not strong enough. He was weak from his own demons.

Dr. Raymond: What was Renee supposed to protect you from that made you change?

Corey: The darkness. It wasn't his fault. He tried to understand. He tried to rationalize, but things around me were fuzzy, and I was changing so fast. I wasn't the same person anymore.

Dr. Raymond: Tell me what was so different about you and why you felt a darkness.

Corey: I felt alone and depressed. Then I became fascinated with the Victorian era. It was as if I belonged in that era. I wanted to move. I changed.

Dr. Raymond: There is nothing wrong with being interested in a certain period in time or actively playing the role during that era. Is that what drew you to researching for your book?

Corey: I don't know. I was just drawn to the cemetery grounds. I did something foolish. I was warned not to meddle, but I still called out to them. *(Sobbing.)*

Dr. Raymond: Meddle with what?

Corey: The spirit world. The lady in Gettysburg warned me.

Dr. Raymond: What lady in Gettysburg?

Corey: A lady we met while vacationing. She warned me. She told me I could call out to them for help, but I needed to prepare myself spiritually first.

Dr. Raymond: Whom did you call out to?

Corey: Them. The reason I am here. The reason why all of this is happening. The trip to Gettysburg was only the beginning. She knew why I was there. She told me there were soldiers from the battle following me around, trying to get my attention.

Dr. Raymond: You are talking about the research for your book, correct?

Corey: Yes.

Dr. Raymond: Do you believe that the characters in your book were communicating with you?

Corey: Yes. I pleaded with them to guide me.

Dr. Raymond: How did they communicate with you?

Corey: Through my dreams. Sometimes visions. Like old movies playing. Then there are the voices.

Dr. Raymond: Who comes to you in your dreams?

Corey: I don't know who they are. They just tell me things. I can't see their faces sometimes. Sometimes all I see is a shadow.

Dr. Raymond: Okay, Corey, let's talk about that first night when the bad dreams began. Can you talk about it with me?

Corey: I'm afraid.

Dr. Raymond: It's okay, Corey. You are safe here. Nothing will happen to you. Please, tell me about your dreams.

Corey: We went to bed that night, and I was still feeling down. I lay down beside Renee and hugged him before he closed his eyes.

Dr. Raymond: When did you fall asleep?

Corey: I don't know. I don't remember. *(Feeling agitated.)*

Dr. Raymond: It's okay, Corey. Can you tell me what happens after Renee falls asleep? What are you doing?

Corey: I'm covering my eyes.

Dr. Raymond: Are you asleep?

Corey: No. I don't feel right. Something is wrong.

Dr. Raymond: Tell me what is wrong.

Corey: I'm afraid.

Dr. Raymond: Corey, there is nothing to be afraid of. You are safe at home. Tell me what happened as you lie in bed.

Corey: I'm afraid to open my eyes. It's in the room. It's here! It's here!

Dr. Raymond: Open your eyes and tell me what you see.

Corey: Oh God, no, please no! Make it go away. God, please make it go away.

Dr. Raymond: What do you see, Corey?

Corey: I am on the ceiling.

Dr. Raymond: You are on the ceiling?

Corey: Yes, I can see myself from the ceiling. I cannot move. I am afraid I am going to fall.

Dr. Raymond: Can you call out to Renee?

Corey: No, it won't let me.

Dr. Raymond: What won't let you?

Corey: This thing. This black thing. It is pressing me against the ceiling.

Dr. Raymond: What is it doing to you?

Corey: *(Screaming.)*

Dr. Raymond: Corey, what is happening to you right now?

Corey: It is holding me up against the ceiling. *(Screaming.)* I am falling. I am falling from the ceiling. Something is in my bed! *(Screaming.)*

Dr. Raymond: Where is Renee?

Corey: *(Screaming.)* Please help me!

Dr. Raymond: Where is Renee?

Corey: He's right there. He is not moving. Renee, wake up! Wake up!

Dr. Raymond: Tell me what is happening.

Corey: The black thing. It's hovering on the ceiling and looking down on me. It's breath—it's disgusting! I can smell it. *(Gagging.)* It is getting bigger, and it's coming! It's coming for me! *(Screaming.)*

Dr. Raymond: Ask it what it wants.

Corey: *(Screaming.)*

Dr. Raymond: Corey, what does it want from you?

Corey: It's pressing against me. It's holding me down. Oh my God, the smell! *(Screaming.)* Help me! Please help me!

Dr. Raymond: Can you call out to Renee?

Corey: *(Screaming.)*

Dr. Raymond: Corey, can you call out to Renee?

Corey: It's hurting me! Get it off me! Get it out of my head! *(Screaming.)* Let go of me! Please, God, help me! Oh God, please help me. Make it go away! Make it go away! It wants me to see it. I can't look away. I can't close my eyes.

Dr. Raymond: Why can't you look away?

Corey: It wants me to look. It wants me to look in the mirror! It's coming for me! God, help me, please!

Dr. Raymond: Relax, Corey. Take some deep breaths. It's okay. Relax and tell me what it is doing to you at this moment.

Corey: It is pressing on my chest! I ... can't ... breathe. I ... don't want ... to ... look! *(Voice changes.)* Look at me, look at me, and look at me!

Dr. Raymond: Corey? Corey, are you still with me?

Corey: *(Voice different from client.)* Look in the mirror now. Do it!

Dr. Raymond: It's okay. Go ahead and look in the mirror. Tell me, what do you see?

Corey: No, I am afraid. Please don't make me look in the mirror. Please, God, no! *(Screaming.)*

Dr. Raymond: It's okay. Look in the mirror. Tell me what you see in the reflection.

Corey: I can't. I am afraid to look. Please don't make me look.

Dr. Raymond: Corey, you need to confront it. Look in the mirror and tell me what you see.

Corey: No! Please, God, make it go away. Make it go away!

Dr. Raymond: What happens when you look in the mirror? Tell me what you see in the reflection.

Corey: Oh God! *(Screaming.)* Why? Why?

Dr. Raymond: What do you see, Corey?

Corey: *(Screaming.)* No, please, no! *(Screaming.)*

Dr. Raymond: Tell me what you see in the reflection.

Corey: *(Screaming.)* Its teeth are gray and sharp, like shark teeth. *(Screaming.)* It won't stop laughing at me.

Dr. Raymond: I know this is difficult, Corey, but you have to be strong and face your fears. I need you to tell it to leave you alone. Tell it to go away.

Corey: It won't let me. It's my fault. I invited it in. I can't move. Please, Renee! Renee! Please wake up!

Dr. Raymond: At the count of five, I want you to awake feeling relaxed and comfortable. One, two, three, four, five. Corey, open your eyes. Here, have some tissues.

Corey: *(Sobbing.)* What is happening to me? Dr. Raymond, am I going insane? I mean, what is wrong with me?

Dr. Raymond: Corey, take some deep breaths in and out. In and out, that's right. Now, you stated in your initial medical statement that you have suffered from night terrors since 2006. I know this is difficult, but I will need you to talk about them more as to when and how often they occur. I believe with hypnosis it will be easier to get to the bottom of what is going on with your mental state. Corey, have you ever heard of sleep paralysis?

Corey: No, but you said that I am not going insane.

Dr. Raymond: What I meant was I have to determine if what you are experiencing is indeed sleep paralysis or something else.

Corey: And that something else is what?

Dr. Raymond: It is too early to diagnose you based off of one regression session. You will need to be regressed several times before I can determine the form of treatment.

Corey: Okay, how much longer will this take?

Dr. Raymond: It depends with each individual. It takes time. I need you to be patient.

Corey: Dr. Raymond, I feel as though I am losing my mind. I mean, I don't know what is going on in my life right now. Everything is like a blur. Certain memories pop up, and I don't know if they actually occurred or if I was dreaming. I need to find out what is going on with me. I have two children I need to protect.

Dr. Raymond: Corey, you have to be patient with the process. Sometimes, the regressions can make you remember things that you are not ready to deal with. If you show signs of distress or appear to be harmful to yourself or others, I may have to take a different approach for your safety.

Corey: What does that mean? Are you going to have me locked up?

Dr. Raymond: Like I said, if you appear to show signs of distress from the regressions, then a full psychiatric evaluation will be necessary. Corey, have you ever talked about your experiences to anyone? Other than your husband of course.

Corey: Yes, I actually waited about two weeks before I finally got enough courage to talk about it openly to a priest.

Dr. Raymond: And how did the priest take the information?

Corey: He expressed compassion but told me that God would not send negative thoughts or dreams to anyone. He said that premonitions were sent by the devil. And once I heard that, I became terrified.

Dr. Raymond: What were you afraid of?

Corey: Becoming the next Linda Blair!

Dr. Raymond: Well, the *Exorcist* was exaggerated for television. I believe what you may be experiencing is treatable.

Corey: Dr. Raymond, these past few months have been anything but controllable.

Dr. Raymond: Do you believe that you have the ability to see things because of your dreams?

Corey: Yes, I know that I do. I just don't know why. I mean, I find myself doing things that I would not normally do. It is frightening me.

Dr. Raymond: There are a few possibilities here, but as I said, you need to be regressed more to determine what in fact is causing your experiences. Do you understand now why it is important to be patient with the regression therapy?

Corey: I know, I know.

Dr. Raymond: I want to see you again next week. Can you make it at four o'clock on Monday afternoon?

Corey: Yes.

Dr. Raymond: Okay, great. And, Corey, we will get to the bottom of your troubles.

Corey: I don't think I have much time.

Dr. Raymond: Why do you say that?

Corey: I just know.

February 1, 2010, Journal Entry

When I arrived home tonight, I seemed to unlock a memory from my past of when things started to change. It was the first physical incident that occurred when Renee and I were first married back in

1996. He had gone away for a week on business, and I was alone with our dog, Blackie. After work one night, I had settled into my normal routine. Read the paper and ate dinner. I remember retiring early that night after falling asleep on the couch. I woke to the sound of footsteps on the second floor. Immediately, the anxiety consumed me as I looked across the room for someone to jump out at me. Blackie, my lab, sensed it too. She darted out from the kitchen and began ferociously barking at the ceiling.

I tried to rationalize by thinking it was just the wind, but not a window was open in the house. Blackie was in full-force attack mode, and my anxiety was getting worse. I saw the black mist form in the corner of the ceiling where Blackie was barking. It was getting darker and darker, and within seconds, it had consumed the entire southeast corner of the ceiling. Thinking that I was having a bad nightmare, I remained still to gather my thoughts. I figured that if I remained still, it would go away; I closed my eyes and held my breath. I was terrified. When I opened my eyes, it was still there. This thing was getting bigger and bigger and coming right for me.

Blackie continued to charge at the black mist until it had had enough. Blackie was hit from the left side and thrown against the wall. She cried in agony as she tried to get up to protect me. I remained fixed on the mist and unable to yell out. The mist reached the couch where I was sitting and took control from then on. It pushed my torso back into the couch and pinned me in. My heart was beating so fast. I tried to gather strength to fight back. I felt as if the next breath would be my last, as I found it difficult to breathe. It had control of me. My body lifted off of the couch and began to rise up to the ceiling. I was unable to move as I watched the floor around me get farther and farther away. I heard the mist whispering in a sinister voice as if it was more than one person. Perhaps several people began to argue as to what was to become of me.

My body was then pressed against the ceiling as some force was whipping at my back and legs. I felt the wetness of blood soaking my shirt as the beatings stripped my clothing with each hard blow.

I could feel my legs burning as if they were on fire. It was terrifying knowing some invisible force was beating me. What was happening to me? I felt as though I was being punished for some heinous crime I had committed. I was in my own prison. Trapped in my own home and being beaten by something I could not see.

I recall waking up the next morning with a terrible heaviness in my head. I looked around the room to see where Blackie ended up in all of this mess. She lay in the corner of the kitchen trembling. Not realizing the extent of my own injuries, I tried to get up to check on her and fell to my knees in agony. My torso and legs were bloody and bruised. I had taken a terrible beating and was in terrible pain.

Renee wouldn't be back for another two days. I called him to tell him that Blackie was limping and that something was wrong with her. When he arrived home a few days later, we took her to the vet to be looked at. Dr. Lee, our veterinarian, was amazed at the extent of her injuries. She immediately inquired about how she was injured. I couldn't exactly explain the truth to them just then. I told her that she had fallen down the stairs. It seemed logical and believable. They bought it too. It was better for them to believe that she had fallen rather than what actually happened.

Blackie wore a cast for the next six weeks from her injuries. I hid the truth from Renee and my family. No one knew what was going on with me. I didn't even know exactly. I just felt it was easier to ignore the truth than face the reasoning as to why it was happening to me. After all of these years, Renee never knew what truly happened that week he was gone.

February 25th, 2010, Regression Session

Dr. Raymond: Corey Michaels, February 25 regression session. Good afternoon, Corey. I am sorry that I could not make our last meeting. Have you had any issues since we last met?

Corey: Yeah, you can say that.

Dr. Raymond: Why don't we talk about it?

Corey: Well, I remembered something I experienced a long time ago with the mist. I haven't thought about it since it occurred.

Dr. Raymond: Perhaps you blocked it out for a reason. What did you remember?

Corey: Something attacked me years ago. Renee was away on business, and my dog and I were attacked. I remember being lifted off of the ground and pressed against the ceiling in my own house. I was pinned, and I could not break loose. Something had beaten me up pretty bad.

Dr. Raymond: Did you tell Renee about this when it happened?

Corey: No. In fact, I never told him.

Dr. Raymond: Why did you not tell him what was happening to you?

Corey: I was afraid that he would think I was crazy. I was afraid that he would leave me.

Dr. Raymond: Did this happen often, I mean, physical evidence?

Corey: No, but on occasion, I have awoken to bruising and cuts on my body. I know what you are thinking. I am not doing this to myself. How the hell could I?

Dr. Raymond: Corey. I am not claiming that you are. There is a logical explanation.

Corey: Really? And what might that be?

Dr. Raymond: We talked in our last session about sleep paralysis. Are you familiar with sleep paralysis?

Corey: No. I'm not.

Dr. Raymond: Sleep paralysis is closely related to the natural part of rapid eye movement when you sleep. You can experience it when you are falling asleep or while waking up. Many people experience it.

Corey: So what you are saying is that I am dreaming all of this stuff? Perhaps maybe even did this to myself and my dog?

Dr. Raymond: Not exactly. Let me explain a little further. It occurs when you are transitioning from a deep sleep to the awakening state. During this time, many experience hallucinations. You feel a deep sense of fear, and often times, the person may feel as though they are being menaced by something in the room. This can also occur throughout one's lifetime. This could explain why it happened at a young age. It is more common than you think, Corey.

Corey: I am not sleeping when this happens. I am awake.

Dr. Raymond: People who experience this may also feel as though they are having an out-of-body experience. A feeling of floating above the ground. This would explain why you felt as though you were lifted up to the ceiling.

Corey: I don't buy it. Something was in that room with me. Something made those scars and hurt my dog. I didn't do this. I don't believe this is what is happening to me.

Dr. Raymond: Corey, please just listen, and perhaps it may explain a few things. It has been well documented when people experience similar situations as you have described. Due to the amount of stress you are and have been under, it would not be unheard of to accept this prognosis.

Statistically, people who have experienced such terrors as you have described, they often feel and see the same things as you. They experience fear as if someone were in the room with them. They feel as though they cannot breathe, as if someone or something is weighing them down. They feel threatened. This can all be attributed to sleep paralysis. When it occurs, centers of the brain act differently—almost confused because there is no actual movement, and the individual is left feeling as though something is taking over. Projecting fear.

Thirty-six percent of the general public have experienced this but in their adult years. There is also a connection with anxiety disorders. The regulation of melatonin is lower during the REM stages of sleep. If your levels are elevated during this stage, you may experience all of the symptoms that you are describing, as if someone were taking over your body, and paralysis. It's not an evil entity. It's a sleeping disorder often contributing to the levels of serotonin, which causes anxiety attacks.

Corey: I don't believe it! I know what I saw. I know what it did to me and my dog. This is no anxiety or sleep disorder. Something was and still is terrorizing me.

Dr. Raymond: I want you to try something tonight. People suffering from sleep paralysis have found that taking melatonin tablets before bedtime usually eliminates the symptoms. Try it out for a few weeks. Melatonin is a natural substance, much like a vitamin, so you don't need to worry about any side effects. I want you to pay close attention to when you go to sleep at night. Document what position you are in when you close your eyes and when you wake up. Keep track of your sleeping habits and note any changes in your stress levels at work and at home. Keep it all in a diary and bring it back with you when I see you again. In the meantime, I would like you to see your family physician for some blood work to rule out any other medical conditions you may have. Is that okay with you?

Corey: Sure. But I am telling you now nothing is going to show up on my test results. I can assure you. I have been over this before with my last physician before I booked my first appointment with you. Nothing is wrong with me physically. You'll see. And I refuse to take the medication for the anxiety attacks too.

Dr. Raymond: I understand. Your physician indicated your refusal to take them in his report.

Corey: It doesn't help. It only makes me more vulnerable to the terrors.

Dr. Raymond: Okay, Corey, why don't you sit back on the couch? Let's try another regression session. Would that be ok?

Corey: Ok. Yes.

Dr. Raymond: Alright. Let's start by closing your eyes. Take some deep breaths in and out. Relaxing deeper and deeper. Clearing your mind of any negative thoughts. That's right, deep breaths in and out. In and out. Your heartbeat gradually slowing down. Taking deep breaths in and out. With every exhale, your muscles begin to feel heavy and relaxed. Feeling more and more relaxed with every breath in and out. Continuing with your breathing in and out. Slowly relaxing. Deep breath in and out. At the count of four, you will be completely relaxed but fully conscious of my questions. I want you to imagine yourself drifting deeper and deeper as your body begins to feel relaxed and heavy. Every muscle slowly beginning to feel heavy and relaxed. Feeling heavier and heavier. At the count of four, you will be fully relaxed but able to answer my questions. One, two, three four. Are you comfortable, Corey?

Corey: Yes.

Dr. Raymond: I want to talk about the dreams you have been having. Can you talk about the dream of the girl in the woods?

Corey: Yes.

Dr. Raymond: Tell me about your dream.

Corey: I'm walking through a field full of tall timbers. It's foggy, but I can see a light up near a small clearing.

Dr. Raymond: What happens when you get to the clearing?

Corey: I can hear a woman screaming. She's in pain.

Dr. Raymond: Where is the screaming coming from?

Corey: There is a cabin near the clearing. I can see the light from inside. It's dim, but I can see shadows of people moving around.

Dr. Raymond: Can you look inside the cabin?

Corey: It's foggy; I can barely see the light. I can hear her screaming. I'm afraid to look inside.

Dr. Raymond: It's okay, Corey. You can look inside. Tell me what you see.

Corey: She is in pain. The men, they are just standing there watching her scream.

Dr. Raymond: What men?

Corey: I don't know who they are. She is in so much pain.

Dr. Raymond: What are the men doing? Are they helping her?

Corey: No, they are covering her mouth so she does not scream. No! No! Stop, please stop!

Dr. Raymond: Relax and take some deep breaths. Tell me what is happening to the woman.

Corey: Don't take my baby! Please, don't take him away from me! Harley, no! Please, don't let them do this to me.

Dr. Raymond: Harley? Who is Harley?

Corey: It hurts! God, please help me! I'm sorry! I'm so sorry! No! Please, God, help me!

Dr. Raymond: Corey, what is happening? Who is Harley?

Corey: Please, please, save him! Save him! Don't let them take him away, I beg of you! Please, God, help me!

Dr. Raymond: Note: Patient seems to be suffering from some sort of external trauma. Both wrists are immediately bruising, yet no one and no nearby objects are visually touching her. Looking at her ankles, I am noting there is recent scarring and appear to be bruised. Judy, please grab the medical kit!

Judy: Oh my goodness. Shall I call for an ambulance?

Dr. Raymond: No, that won't be necessary, but I am going to need you to set up some tests for Ms. Michaels. And, Judy, I need you to get Anne on the phone immediately. Corey, at the count of three, I want you to awaken, fully relaxed and remembering everything. One, two, three. Corey?

Corey: Yes? Oh my God! What is happening to me? *(Sobbing.)*

Dr. Raymond: Corey, I need you to get a full physical once you leave here today, okay? Judy is setting up the appointment now.

Corey: I have already seen a doctor. Remember? You have his statement.

Dr. Raymond: I need a full physical to make sure that there is nothing being overlooked medically. I have to make sure your chemical balances are where they should be.

Corey: Okay, but I can tell you now that nothing is going to show up on any tests that you order.

Dr. Raymond: This is very important. What you just experienced is something we need to talk about further, but I need you to see your physician.

Corey: I told you, there is nothing going to come out of being looked at by my doctor. Look at my wrists and my ankles. Did I do this to myself? Tell me! Did I?

Dr. Raymond: In order for me to continue with your therapy, you need to get a full evaluation. A few scans and some more blood work. Okay?

Corey: Are you kidding me? Did I or did I not do this to myself? You know it, and I know it. Something evil is trying to hurt me! *(Sobbing.)*

Dr. Raymond: Corey, please try to relax. I will help you get through this. I will need your help though.I want to be able to see your results by tomorrow. This is important, Corey.

Corey: Fine.

Dr. Raymond: Judy is ordering your lab work, and I will see you in my office at eight o'clock tomorrow morning.

Corey: Fine.

February 26, 2010, Regression Session

Dr. Raymond: Corey Michaels, February 26 regression session. Good morning, Corey.

Corey: Good morning, Dr. Raymond.

Dr. Raymond: How are we today?

Corey: Okay. I mean, look at my wrists. Do they look ok to you?

Dr. Raymond: I received your test results from your physician. Your levels are where they are supposed to be for a woman of your age. However, your physician noted that you refused to remove some of your clothing for further testing. Can you tell me why you refused?

Corey: I didn't think it was necessary. That's why.

Dr. Raymond: Corey, I have been in this field for a long time. You have nothing to hide here. There is no judgment being placed on you. I need you to be honest with me. I have your medical report. I know that there is some physical abuse. Do you want to talk about it?

Corey: And confuse things even more? No thanks.

Dr. Raymond: Corey, I can help you, but you have to trust me. Tell me, does it involve your husband? Did he beat you?

Corey: Renee, lay a hand on me? No! Never!

Dr. Raymond: I know you were subject to physical abuse. Would you like me to turn it over to the authorities?

Corey: You are going to confuse things worse than they already are. I don't want to discuss this.

Dr. Raymond: Then I believe our sessions will conclude here. I cannot help you, Mrs. Michaels. I do wish you the best of luck.

Corey: Wait. I thought you were going to help me.

Dr. Raymond: I can't help those who are not willing to trust me. You need to tell me what is going on in your personal life as well. I know what you are going through to a certain extent, and it is evident that you have been physically abused. Are you going to tell me who did this to you?

Corey: Yes, no, it's difficult to explain.

Dr. Raymond: I know that you were beaten by someone. If you decide to refrain from telling me who did this to you, I cannot help you.

Corey: Renee would never lay a hand on me. He didn't do this to me.

Dr. Raymond: Then who did and why did you refuse to file a report?

Corey: I didn't have a choice in the matter.

Dr. Raymond: You always have a choice. Now, who did this to you?

Corey: The mist.

Dr. Raymond: The mist did this to you?

Corey: Yes. Now do you understand why I couldn't file charges against anyone? I mean, they would have locked me up. They could take my kids away from me. I would never let anything hurt my kids.

Dr. Raymond: Why did you not tell me of this earlier?

Corey: You don't understand. A lot is going on right now. My life is chaotic. I just want it all to end. Do you believe me? I mean, have you ever dealt with something like this before?

Dr. Raymond: As a matter of fact, I have. Now, Corey, how recent are the scars?

Corey: A few weeks old.

Dr. Raymond: This is part of your therapy. If the abuse continues to happen, we need to look at additional therapy. You do understand that this is very serious?

Corey: What kind of additional therapy is going to help when I am being beaten by something that no one else can see?

Dr. Raymond: Let's just slow things down a bit. Let's try to relax. I would like you to take some deep breaths in and out. Okay, please try to take some deep breaths in and then out.

Corey: How can I? Something is happening to me, and not you or anyone else can help me.

Dr. Raymond: I can help you. However, we need to continue with this discussion. Let's talk about another topic to help you. Let's talk about your journals. Did you bring your journals in with you today?

Corey: (Sobbing.) Yes, I have some of the journals here. Oh, and I got divorced yesterday.

Dr. Raymond: Do you want to talk about it?

Corey: No. I just wanted to tell you that.

Dr. Raymond: Okay, so tell me what you have written in your journal.

Corey: Sure. I can tell you that every day was the same. Every night was the same. Dream after dream after dream. But last night, I dreamt something different, something bizarre.

Dr. Raymond: Okay, so this is another dream in addition to the others, correct?

Corey: Yes.

Dr. Raymond: So, you are still dreaming about Renee and your children?

Corey: Yes. The dream is the same.

Dr. Raymond: Well, you are still in the process of moving forward. However, Renee and the children may still be hurting. Perhaps when you see them days or weeks from now, when the smoke clears, you will no longer have the dream.

Corey: Perhaps … but I think it will stop when it actually happens to them. That's how it works with me. I see it, and then it happens. I have no control over the outcome. I don't know exactly when it's coming.

Dr. Raymond: Is that what you believe? That you have no control over your dreams?

Corey: Yes, because if I had control, I would change the outcome of the dreams. But I can't. I keep having the same dreams over and over and over again until it happens. The stronger the dream or the more often I have it, the sooner it happens.

Dr. Raymond: So, tell me about this new dream.

Corey: It was last night. I dreamt of a little boy standing on top of a slope. He is watching the town below change. It's as if he is motionless, and life is passing him by year after year as the scenery around him changes. I see the landscaping change: houses are being built, the grove is being washed out by weather, and buildings are being put up and then torn down. It's as if he is in a time warp. He doesn't look like he belongs there. He is so young, and he looks trapped there.

Dr. Raymond: Does the child do anything in the dream?

Corey: No. He just stands there and watches the slope change. I don't understand it.

Dr. Raymond: Are you able to see the face of the child?

Corey: No. He always has his back to me.

Dr. Raymond: How are things going at home with the children?

Corey: The kids are doing okay. Still trying to get used to our new lives and without living with their father. We recently bought a new house. Ya know, to get a fresh start.

Dr. Raymond: That's wonderful! How is your relationship with your children? Have they shown any indications of depression or disconnection of any sort?

Corey: Yes and no. I mean, my son doesn't understand why I wanted to separate from his father. But he doesn't seem disconnected or anything.

Dr. Raymond: It sounds like the dream of the little boy on the slope could be your son. Perhaps you are fearful of how he is going to accept the changes happening around him or that lay ahead between you and Renee. He may be feeling disconnected from the things around him. He cannot face you, nor can he do anything about what is happening around and in front of him. Have you ever thought of it that way?

Corey: No, I guess not. So you think I should try to talk to him more about the divorce?

Dr. Raymond: Perhaps. How is the after-school therapy going for them?

Corey: Well, she is more like a social worker provided by the school district. They have been seeing her for three months, but I don't see much of a change with them.

Dr. Raymond: Well, I am sure therapy is still quite new to them, similar to buying the new house. It's new and maybe still a little difficult to get used to. Perhaps you would like me to refer you to someone else the children could talk with?

Corey: Can I think about it for a few days and get back to you?

Dr. Raymond: Sure. So, how do the kids like the new house?

Corey: They are still getting used to it. We all are. Something's strange about it though.

Dr. Raymond: Well, it's a new environment. It's another change. I am certain the first few months will require some getting used to, as with any unfamiliar home. It's not out of the ordinary to feel uneasiness in a new home and excitement at the same time. It can be overwhelming for all of you.

Corey: That's not what I meant. The house seems to react to things.

Dr. Raymond: What do you mean?

Corey: Well, the other day I was talking to a coworker about getting a cat for my daughter. She's always been quite fond of animals, especially cats. I thought it would help keep her mind off of things. Ya know, kind of like a peace offering. Anyway, the following day I got up and was making breakfast when I heard a scratch at the back door off of the kitchen. I was quite spooked by it because we have a stockade fence in our backyard, and the dog was in the house still. It continued to scratch, so I opened the back door, and there it was. A dead black cat on my porch. Now how in the hell did that cat get there? And imagine if my daughter would have seen it? I quickly grabbed some paper towels and grabbed it by its hind legs and threw it in the garbage can. Is that strange or what?

Dr. Raymond: That is certainly something to be concerned with. However, what does the house have to do with it?

Corey: Well, it's just like weird things, ya know? I mean what are the odds that I would be talking about getting a cat, and then the following day, one appears on my porch—dead, mind you, but still a cat! And sometimes our dog acts weird, and stuff doesn't seem to work right, like appliances. The kids seem to be getting up a lot in the middle of the night too.

Dr. Raymond: What do you mean?

Corey: I can hear the kids walking back and forth in the hall upstairs at times while I am downstairs watching television. When I go upstairs to check on them, they are fast asleep already. And the dog, well, she just barks and barks at the walls sometimes, and I can't explain it. And the other night, she refused to come upstairs with us. She doesn't normally act this way.

Dr. Raymond: What else? Anything else make you uneasy about the house?

Corey: Well, lights turn on and off by themselves, doors open and close before I reach them, furniture gets moved around, items in the house disappear and reappear in places they shouldn't be. I can go on and on. That sort of stuff that creeps me out! It creeps us all out!

Dr. Raymond: Hearing that your divorce is final, there is surely a logical explanation for what you are experiencing in your home.

Corey: The divorce is one thing, but then I come home to this stuff. I am terrified that there is something more going on. It's as if something is building up for some grand entrance. I am telling you, something is going on. I am beginning to believe that something is wrong with our home.

Dr. Raymond: You have to rationalize with your surroundings and what is going on in your life. First, canines have the ability to sense when people are not well. They have become useful resources when working with patients that suffer from various conditions, such as epilepsy and seizers. As far as the lighting issues and doors slamming and opening, well, there could be bad wiring or drafts in the house.

Corey: I already had the house inspected for the electrical issues, and nothing came up faulty in the wiring. The house is pretty drafty, so I guess that could make the doors close, but open? I don't think so.

Dr. Raymond: See, there may be some logical explanations for some of the issues with the house.

Corey: I like how you said *some* issues. Do you believe in the paranormal, Dr. Raymond?

Dr. Raymond: I believe that there are some things that just cannot be explained. It is a big universe out there, and there is much we have yet to learn. But we are getting off the subject here. Tell me, have you ever experienced moments of blacking out or losing consciousness?

Corey: No, not that I can remember, but then again, how would I know if I had blacked out?

Dr. Raymond: Well, have you ever fallen asleep and awoken somewhere else?

Corey: Yes, a few times, but I believe it was due to anxiety.

Dr. Raymond: Tell me about those experiences.

Corey: Well, one evening I was watching the television while the kids slept nearby. The television shut off for no reason, and the lights began to flicker. I shrugged it off as an electrical short circuit in the television, for nothing else turned off. I got up to check the plug, and it wasn't even plugged in! I didn't know what to think. I mean, we were watching television most of the evening, and it was never even plugged in! At that moment when I realized that we were watching an unpowered television, well, that's when I lost track of time. It's as if I just dozed off and didn't worry about what I had just discovered.

When I awoke, I was lying on the floor in the corner of the upstairs bedroom. The kids were still downstairs. I wondered how I got up there. I looked down, and in my lap was my Bible. It terrified me that

I could not remember what happened from the moment I found out about the television to when I woke up in another part of the house.

Dr. Raymond: Could the cord of the television have been partially pulled into the wall outlet? If we think about this rationally, a few scenarios come to mind. It is possible that the television was still supplying power if the cord was partially unplugged.

Corey: No! It was completely out of the wall.

Dr. Raymond: Hmmm, interesting.

Corey: And what about me ending up in a different part of the house clutching my Bible? And why was I clutching my Bible? Was I afraid of something?

Dr. Raymond: Had you been drinking that evening?

Corey: No. I seldom drink.

Dr. Raymond: Have you ever experienced sleepwalking? That could explain how you ended up in another room.

Corey: Yes, but I don't recall ever sleepwalking before. I don't recall it ever. When I woke up the next day, it felt as if I had been drugged. I mean I felt hungover and doped up. Like I said, I don't drink, and I don't do drugs. It doesn't explain why I had my Bible with me either. And why would I feel like as if I had been drugged?

The rental house had a tricky staircase to get upstairs, and I often had difficulty stepping up off of the foyer due to the construction of the steep steps. I don't remember maneuvering the stairs if I was sleepwalking, for surely I would have broken my neck if I lost my balance.

Dr. Raymond: Perhaps we can ask these questions through another session of hypnosis. I want to talk a little bit about hypnosis and why I think it's important we continue with this form of therapy. You briefly spoke about your feelings of being different or having feelings of being homesick, yet you were home. So tell me, were you ever depressed as a child?

Corey: Well, sure. Every child goes through bouts of depression. If you don't get what you want. Getting picked on from their peers. That's normal. But, yeah, I had my moments.

Dr. Raymond: Did you ever feel like hurting yourself during those times?

Corey: No. Never. I loved life. I was never depressed long enough to even think about doing something stupid. I loved my family, my friends, life itself. But I still saw things that frightened me, and I was terrified to tell anyone. I was the first one to imagine something prowling around the basement steps or corner. I could feel the hair stand on my arms each time I walked into a dark room looking for the light switch. I was terrified of the dark. I still am.

Dr. Raymond: You stated in your last session that the first night terror occurred while you were married to Renee. But things were happening to you before you met him, correct?

Corey: Yes.

Dr. Raymond: This next question is different from the previous questions I have asked you. I would like to talk to you about your religious beliefs. Is that okay with you?

Corey: Sure.

Dr. Raymond: Do you attend a church regularly, Corey?

Corey: No.

Dr. Raymond: You stated on your questionnaire that you are Catholic. Is that correct?

Corey: Yes. I converted when my children were born. I wanted to be active in their religious upbringing, so I agreed to convert so we could receive Holy Communion as a family when they became of age.

Dr. Raymond: So you are not a practicing Catholic?

Corey: Correct. I thought I was doing the right thing when I became a Catholic, but ya know what? The Catholics don't believe in premonitions or foreseeing the future. To them, it's all demonic and unnatural. So as time went on, I went to the Catholic Church about my premonitions. I became confused about why I had them. The church told me that was unnatural and basically told me I had a vivid imagination.

Dr. Raymond: Did you ever discuss this with your parents or your husband?

Corey: With Renee I did, but my parents didn't go to church. My husband and I attended church on a regular basis, but my parents thought I was being controlled by his family for attending their church.

Dr. Raymond: But your parents never went to church?

Corey: No.

Dr. Raymond: Hmmm. So they didn't like the fact that you were trying to be more spiritual?

Corey: They never said whether it was good or bad. They just didn't like the fact that I was going with his family to church.

Dr. Raymond: Did it bother you that they did not condone you being in a Catholic church?

Corey: Yes. But I tried to do what was right. I tried to become more spiritual for my new family.

Dr. Raymond: Did you often struggle with approval of your parents?

Corey: Yes. Especially when I was dating Renee. It didn't get any better when I married him. It was a constant competition between my family and his. It was miserable.

Dr. Raymond: Was it depressing?

Corey: Yes. Very much so. I went without speaking to my parents for months at times due to the tension between us.

Dr. Raymond: So, you became depressed when you felt you were letting them down by going to church?

Corey: Yes. I know that it is stupid, but I knew I wanted to go to church, and I knew that my parents didn't approve. I was torn. I couldn't understand why it wasn't acceptable. I felt I was letting them down. I felt as though I had disappointed them. I wanted them to be proud of me. Instead, I upset them.

Dr. Raymond: Okay, Corey. I want to talk about your research and your discoveries while writing your book. I saw you in the newspaper over the weekend. You are getting a lot of attention for your research. How does this make you feel?

Corey: I don't know. I mean, they put me in the spotlight when the book came out, and when everyone learned about the people that are buried in the cemetery, well, people got all crazy about the close proximity to the subdivision. It was something that was always there. Anyone could have done what I did to find them. I still don't understand how it was so simple. I am glad that the research and the book is done, but I feel as though it may not have been the right thing to do all along. I know this book has something to do with what is happening to me now. I just wish everyone would forget about me ever writing the book. I wish the media would leave me alone.

Dr. Raymond: Yes, well, let's talk about the media attention.

Corey: Why? I mean, I keep having that same dream about the house in the woods. I want to know why I keep having the same dreams over and over again. And the premonitions, I keep seeing and hearing things. What does the media have anything to do with my dreams or premonitions?

Dr. Raymond: Corey, there are variables that I discussed in an earlier session. Depression and getting attention may be another key factor in your troubles. We need to discuss these things. I need to know to what extent these variables have affected your life. Perhaps you did not receive the proper parenting as a child, or something emotional was missing from your marriage that you longed for. Both of these could be factors.

Corey: I don't think they have anything to do with what I have and continue to experience. My parents were good to me. Renee was good to me. I had my issues just like the kid down the road, but it wasn't traumatizing. I mean, I don't think one single childhood bout with depression caused this to happen. It's a pretty intelligent theory, but it doesn't explain why I have had the premonitions my whole life, now would it? It wouldn't explain the dreams either. The dreams make no sense, and the premonitions, well, they eventually happen! All of the premonitions are in my diaries, and when the events happened, I documented that too. It's all in there.

Dr. Raymond: I see. Okay. So has anything changed in the dreams?

Corey: No, it's just the same thing over and over again. I don't know what it means.

Dr. Raymond: I want to continue with the hypnotherapy so you will be more relaxed and able to discuss what you have experienced. Would it be possible to talk more about events that transpired while you were writing your book?

Corey: Ya know, Dr. Raymond, each time I talk about the discovery in my lectures, something bad happens. I mean, that night, I have the dreams and the premonitions, and they just keep coming on stronger when I am lecturing about the book. I believe that writing the book may not have been the brightest idea after all.

Judy: Excuse me, Dr. Raymond. You have an emergency call on line 7.

Dr. Raymond: Excuse me, Corey. I will be right back.

Corey: Sure.

Judy: I am sorry, Ms. Michaels. Dr. Raymond has been called away on an emergency. He would like me to reschedule your appointment for next Tuesday. Is that all right with you?

Corey: Sure. I mean, it'll be awhile before he comes back, right?

Judy: Yes, I am afraid it will be quite late.

Corey: Okay, well. I guess I have no choice but to reschedule.

Judy: Thank you for understanding, Ms. Michaels.

Corey: Judy, does Dr. Raymond do this often? I mean, get up and leave?

Judy: Dr. Raymond is a well-respected therapist. He is very sensitive to all of his clients. Unfortunately, he has stretched himself rather thin these days by taking on additional clients. But have faith in knowing that if you need him outside of business hours, Dr. Raymond will surely make himself available to you.

Corey: Well, that's good to know in the event that I need him at the drop of a hat.

Judy: Well, Dr. Raymond is a special therapist. He is very unique and very good at what he does. He's a guardian angel to many that have crossed his path. And I mean that literally. Okay, well, let's reschedule that appointment.

Corey: What do you mean, literally?

Judy: You will learn to trust him, Corey. He has a gift. Let him help you. That's all I can say.

Corey: Okay, well, thanks.

March 5, 2010, Regression Session

Dr. Raymond: Corey Michaels, March 5 regression session. Good afternoon, Corey.

Corey: Good afternoon, Dr. Raymond.

Dr. Raymond: How are you today?

Corey: I am okay. I'm glad to see the snow is finally melting.

Dr. Raymond: Well, the weatherman wasn't joking when he said it was going to be a long winter, so let's hope for a warm spring.

Corey: No kidding! I am tired of the cold weather already.

Dr. Raymond: Corey, let's go ahead and get started. I wanted to tell you that I managed to read the first box of diaries you brought to our last sessions. And as any therapist, I also had to research a bit on my own to validate when the occurrences transpired.

Corey: Are you saying that you are questioning my journals?

Dr. Raymond: What I am saying is that I can validate certain things pertaining to your diary entries. Particularly the accident that involved your friend back in 1986.

Corey: You think I wrote the incidents first and then left a few pages blank? Is that what you think I did?

Dr. Raymond: No, I am not saying that is what you did. However, it is hard to prove when these entries were written so long ago. Because of not being able to validate when each entry was written and comparing it to if and when the event actually occurred, I have decided to take a different approach to your therapy.

Corey: What do you mean?

Dr. Raymond: Well, first, let me explain something about my practice. For more than thirty years, I have come across cases such as yours. I have learned that through hypnosis, my team and I have been able to successfully help hundreds of people that suffer as you do from night terrors. There is obviously something much deeper going on with us spiritually. But many fail to seek help with their awakening, as I like to call it.

Corey: So you agree that there is more than just the bad dreams I am dealing with. Do you think I witnessed something traumatizing?

Dr. Raymond: You may have indeed witnessed or lived through something unimaginable for you, at the time, to comprehend. In case studies, people suffering from very similar symptoms as you were are often diagnosed with sleep paralysis, multiple personalities, or schizophrenia. Patients are quickly medicated and on occasion institutionalized, depending on their severity. Now, I don't want you to get the wrong idea here.

Corey: You have me wondering where you are going with this.

Dr. Raymond: With hypnotic therapy, we may be able to find something about yourself that has been hidden in your memory and has influenced your decisions in life. The reason why I am telling you all of this now is because of a few observations during your regressions and one repetitive entry that I read in your diary.

Corey: I know the one you are talking about. It's the one with the little girl falling, isn't it?

Dr. Raymond: Yes, that is correct. Now, Corey, I have invited a spiritualist to sit in our session today. She will help me determine what you have been experiencing. There are many variables in the types of therapy I can provide for you. Mrs. Delaney can help categorize those variables based off of what you have told me. She and I will work together to help you cope with the memories that are recollected and perhaps offer guidance on the awakening process.

Corey: Why a spiritualist? I mean, what variables are in question? And what do you mean by awakening?

Dr. Raymond: Corey, this is all a part of the process. There are certain things that need to be observed before we can come to a resolution. What you believe is different from what I believe. I have techniques to assist with determining what is believable based on tangible facts. I can capture your memories through hypnosis, and we can discuss each session as it pertains to your state of mind and actions. Mrs. Delaney can help in other ways. But again, steps need to be taken to identify the root of your troubles. Whether it is physical, mental, psychological, spiritual, and perhaps even paranormal.

Corey: I am afraid I know where this is going. You know that I don't have sleep paralysis. You know that what I have experienced is not easily explainable. That is why you called this lady in, isn't it?

Dr. Raymond: As I said, I am not ready to rule anything out. Mrs. Delaney will help you on a spiritual level since I am unable to influence you one way or another on your religious beliefs. She is here to help you find your balance in faith. Judy, please send in Mrs. Delaney.

Dr. Raymond: Corey, this is Mrs. Anne Delaney. I think you will find her helpful with your therapy.

Corey: Hello, Mrs. Delaney.

Mrs. Delaney: Call me Anne, please. Dr. Raymond contacted me after your second hypnosis session due to the sensitivity of what transpired. I am a spiritualist and work with individuals like yourself that experience things that are not quickly identifiable—experiences such as premonitions, night terrors, feelings of anxiety in certain places or situations. Corey, there are reasons why things happen. There is also a very good explanation for why you are here and now.

I can help you, but you have to listen. I want you to understand what I do and feel comfortable in how I can help you. You see, some of us are born sensitive. And by sensitive, I mean more spiritually connected to the unseen.

Corey: Wait a minute. Wait a minute! What are you saying?

Mrs. Delaney: I am talking about your spiritual connection with the dead. I am talking about those that have passed before us. You see, some of us are born with special abilities to see, feel, or sense things. Others are blind to their gifts until they are awakened. By awakened, I mean they remember things through a traumatic event. This can happen when a person remembers a near-death experience. Sometimes, the part of the brain that stores our memories temporarily falls asleep, but these memories cannot be erased. It is when we are awakened through hypnosis, we are able to remember things. We are also enlightened and able to do, hear, and see things that we could not before.

Some people claim they are a totally different person all together. Others suppress the memories due to fear of having to deal with the reality of being different and having special gifts. And so often, many are diagnosed through their physicians as having schizophrenia or some other form of mental illness. Before you know it, those individuals settle for a lifetime of psychotropic medications and therapy or face being institutionalized for seeing and hearing things that others cannot. I was able to see things at a young age that I could not explain. Fortunately, my mother was the same way, and she showed me what to do with my gift.

Corey, you were born with this too. I believe you may have suppressed certain memories for a reason. And then, somehow, you were awakened. At some point in time, you chose to forget what truly happened and what started it all. I, among others, am here to help you find those memories and help you get back on your life path.

Corey: I don't understand. When and where did I venture off of the path? And what others are you talking about? I mean, how was I to know that I was heading in the wrong direction? What traumatic event did I witness? I have so many questions.

Mrs. Delaney: Slow down. Well, it's not easy when you are living in the moment, day by day. And of course, during one of the most vulnerable periods in your life, your divorce. But we are all given hints when our paths are going to be jeopardized. You were given hints too. And right now, from what I understand, you were being tested. Unfortunately, you were given a choice, but you took the wrong turn. Do you recall having déjà vu, Corey?

Corey: Why, yes, all the time. Ever since I was a kid.

Mrs. Delaney: Good, very good! This is where you need to pay attention.

Corey: But I read up on déjà vu and why it happens to people. It has something to do with the temporal lobes having seizures or something like that. It's like a malfunction in the brain. I have read case studies, and it can be triggered by a lot of things.

Mrs. Delaney: It's interesting you say that. Yet, it's those same studies that cannot explain why millions of people have reactions to what they experience and why a memory is triggered with the sense of familiarity. But, Corey, I and others believe differently. We believe that your spirit guides are speaking to you when you experience déjà vu. That's when your life path is approaching a fork in the road. A decision to change your life path will need to be made. In other words, your spirit guides will try to get you back on the right path.

Corey: I don't know. I mean, researchers believe that it has something to do with mental disorders, which may be something I may be dealing with. I don't know. And what do you mean by spirit guides?

Mrs. Delaney: Spirit guides are angels, loved ones, and even those we have never met that have passed on. They are assigned to us throughout our lifetime. They are that inner voice that speaks to us when we are about to do something that may require great thought.

Corey, there is so much more you can learn and do with your gift. You just need to know what to do and when to do it. The light of God surrounds all of us, and you must believe this. Try to imagine how a bulletproof vest protects those in the line of duty. We have a similar shield that can protect us; it's the white light emanating from God's love, and it is there to protect your soul. It is a protective shield you must wear to keep you safe from the negativity of the unseen. Anyone can do it, but not everyone is sensitive to their guides. You must make it a practice in your daily routine and put it on as those would in the line of duty.

Corey: Okay, well, I am sure Dr. Raymond told you that I am not very religious. I go to church with my kids every now and then, but I don't feel as though I am getting anything out of it anymore.

Mrs. Delaney: I understand. It happens to many of us. We lose faith when we no longer feel the presence of God in our lives. Especially when our lives hit a dead end or something terrible happens to us. We lose faith when we feel God has left our side even during the most troubled hardships. But find comfort in knowing that he is still with you and taking on the brunt of the pain and suffering that you are experiencing. God will never give you any more than what he knows you can handle.

Corey: I used to enjoy going to church. I really did, and then our priest, Father Bill, passed away, and I just could not find a reason to return. I could never find another priest that made me feel so uplifted like Father Bill.

Mrs. Delaney: Then perhaps you should seek another church. Do not give up until you find the faith that makes you believe again. Find your faith again, and your life will turn around. Your guides are with you to help.

Corey: So what do I do now?

Mrs. Delaney: Corey, it is very important that you place God in your heart. You don't need to attend church to feel the spirit of God. But you do need him in your life. Not just when you are being bullied. You need him always and in all ways of your daily life.

Corey: I know. I know.

Mrs. Delaney: So, are you ready to begin?

Corey: Begin? What are we doing? Some sort of a séance or something?

Dr. Raymond: No, we are not having a séance. You will learn to trust Anne. I know that you may have a lot of unanswered questions, but I believe this course of therapy may prove beneficial to you.

Mrs. Delaney: Dr. Raymond shared with me on your first session. Within time, you will understand why these things have happened to you throughout your life. They will continue to too. You have had this ability your whole life. It is only now that you are becoming strong enough to awaken your purpose. You have the ability to use it to your advantage and for the good. So, having said that, I will let Dr. Raymond continue.

Corey: Okay, but I am still quite confused about all of this. I mean, special gifts? Guides? Wrong life path? What I am experiencing is not a gift! I can tell you that.

Mrs. Delany: Corey, it is only when we accept that we are lost that we will find our true path. You must believe that you were drawn here by forces that cannot be seen. Your faith has already been tested, and your family bonds will be severed if you do not find your faith again. You have to believe that you are part of something much, much bigger. What you have is not a curse.

Corey: You are really starting to scare me. Is something else going to happen to me or my children?

Mrs. Delaney: You must find faith in yourself and in God, and when you do, all will be clear to you.

Corey: This is crazy. Dr. Raymond, is this really necessary? Is this where my therapy is going?

Dr. Raymond: Corey, please just listen to what she has to say.

Corey: But she is making no sense. I mean, come on. Really? I have bad dreams. What does this have to do with my purpose in life or my faith?

Mrs. Delaney: Within time, Corey. You will see soon enough. Dr. Raymond, why don't we go ahead and begin. Will that be okay with you, Corey?

Corey: Yeah, because I am really anxious to see where this is going.

Dr. Raymond: Okay then. I want to talk about your discoveries. I purchased a copy of your book last week when I read about you in the newspapers for an upcoming book signing. Very interesting stories in there. Did you research all of those people that are supposedly buried in the cemeteries?

Corey: Yes, all of them. It took a long time to put the story together, and even when I was done, there was still more that I could have written on them. Their stories were fascinating to me.

Dr. Raymond: You stated earlier that when you talk about them, things happen to you that are negative. Why do you say that?

Corey: Every time I talk about them, I either have a dream or a premonition. I don't think that I should be talking about them.

Dr. Raymond: Corey, you need to talk about it. Your book has just been published. People want to know what happened in history. Especially here and knowing so many records are missing from our county archives.

Corey: I didn't think it was going to be like this. I didn't think people would actually want to read about this stuff. I really just wanted to tell their story. I didn't think anyone would be interested. But the dreams, the dreams about people with unfamiliar faces doing really strange things, and somehow I'm a part of it. It's as if I am supposed to be there with them but in a different time. Sometimes, I can see myself in a mirror, and it's not really me. I mean, it's me, but I'm different.

Dr. Raymond: What do you mean by different?

Corey: I only get a quick glimpse and take a double take into the mirror. I'm wearing clothes that no longer exist, or should I say the clothes are no longer worn. It's as if I am in another time. A long time ago. And then just like that, I'm back in my regular clothes.

Dr. Raymond: Okay. That's interesting. Corey, do you mind if we continue with a regression session?

Corey: Yes, but I have to be honest with you. After listening to you both these past few minutes, I'm frightened of what might come out.

Mrs. Delaney: It's okay to be fearful. Within time, it will make you stronger. And within time, all of your questions will be answered, leaving you without fear and able to help not only yourself but so many others that are lost on their own path.

Corey: I hope you're right. Okay then. I am ready.

Dr. Raymond: I need you to relax and get comfortable. Close your eyes and clear your mind of any negative thoughts. Take some deep breaths in and out. That's right, in and out. Your heartbeat gradually slowing down. Taking deep breaths in and out. With every exhale, your muscles begin to feel heavy and relaxed. Feeling more and more relaxed with every breath in and out. Heavier and heavier as you breathe in deeper and deeper. Your muscles becoming heavier and heavier and relaxed with each deep breath in and out. Continuing with your breathing in and out. Slowly relaxing. Deep breath in and out. Now I want you to imagine a long hallway in front of you. Notice that there are several doors on either side. Each one appearing to be slightly opened where you can peek inside. Inside each doorway is a memory from your past. Some good, some bad. At the end of the hallway is a door. I want you to continue to walk toward it. Slowly relaxing and taking deep breaths in and out. In and out. Your muscles almost completely numb from the heaviness you feel in them. As you continue to walk closer toward the door, I want you to reach out for the doorknob and turn it slowly to the left. The door will open for which I want you to remember the first time you had a fear of falling. When the door opens, I want you to walk in and tell me where you are at the count of four. You will be completely relaxed but fully conscious of my questions. One, two, three, four. Corey, are you with me?

Corey: (Grasping chair.)

Corey: Ja. Ich sitze auf der Brücke mit meiner Mutter und meinem Bruder. Wir hängen unsere Füße über den Rand.

Dr. Raymond: Corey?

Mrs. Delaney: *(Whispering.)* Dr. Raymond, did you know she spoke another language?

Dr. Raymond: *(Whispering.)* No. She never indicated that she knew anything other than sign language. It sounds German.

Mrs. Delaney: Yes. Dr. Raymond, do you mind if I ask a few questions?

Dr. Raymond: Sure, go ahead.

Mrs. Delaney: Corey, sie sprechen sehr gut Deutsch. Wie alt waren Sie, als sie gelernt?

(I told her she spoke German well and inquired as to how old she was when she learned the language.)

Corey: Was meinen Sie damit?

Mrs. Delaney: She is inquiring as to why I am asking her this.

Dr. Raymond: Can you ask her why she has chosen to speak German during her regression?

Mrs. Delaney: Corey, warum haben sie sich dazu entschieden, uns auf Deutsch zu?

Corey: Ich kann sprechen nur gebrochen Englisch.

Mrs. Delaney: She said that she can speak English, but it is very broken. Corey, warum sprechen sie Deutsch? Warum haben sie sich dafür entschieden haben, in deutscher Sprache?

Corey: Mücken als fliegende Impfspritzen? Mein Name ist Ingrid. Möchten Sie mich zu versuchen mein Englisch? Warum ist es so du mich Mücken als fliegende Impfspritzen?

Mrs. Delaney: Dr. Raymond, she is wondering why we are calling her Corey. She said her name is Ingrid. She has broken English but is willing to try.

Dr. Raymond: Ingrid, can you tell me how old you are?

Corey: (Pausing.)

Mrs. Delaney: Ingrid, wie alt sind Sie?

Corey: Nine.

Dr. Raymond: Ingrid, we were talking about the first memory of falling. Do you remember ever falling?

Corey: We are on bridge. Laughing.

Mrs. Delaney: Was machst du auf der Brücke?

Corey: It is my day of birth. Feier.

Mrs. Delaney: Feier? (She said they were celebrating her birthday.)

Corey: Wir werden sie auf unsere Schuhe auch zu einem Song. Mein Vater kaufte mir ein neues Paar Schuhe. Wir Lärm machen mit Ihnen durch Klatschen Sie sie zusammen.

Mrs. Delaney: That sounds like fun. (She said her father bought her a new pair of shoes. They are hanging their feet over the edge of the bridge and singing a song.)

Dr. Raymond: That sounds peaceful. Who is with her?

Mrs. Delaney: Wer ist sonst noch bei euch?

Corey: Mother and brother.

Dr. Raymond: Ingrid, can you sing the song you are singing?

Mrs. Delaney: Es klingt sehr friedlich. Auf dem Wege, welcher Song ist es, dass Sie singen?

Corey: Ring um die Rosy, Tasche voller Ihre Lieblingssträußchen aus, Asche, Asche, sie alle nach unten fallen lassen.

Mrs. Delaney: She said they are singing, "Ring around the Rosey."

Dr. Raymond: So are you very high up on the bridge?

Mrs. Delaney: Sind sie sehr hoch oben auf der Brücke?

Corey: Far. Frightens me.

Dr. Raymond: So tell me, what frightens you about it?

Mrs. Delaney: Was erschreckt sie?

Corey: The darkness. It comes from behind me, and I fall. *(Sobbing.)*

Mrs. Delaney: You fall off the bridge?

Corey: *(Pausing.)*

Mrs. Delaney: Sie fällt von der Brücke?

Corey: Yes.

Dr. Raymond: What does she mean by the "darkness"?

Mrs. Delaney: Ingrid, kannst du mir von der Dunkelheit erzählen, von der du sprichst? Was ist passiert, wenn sie von der Brücke fiel?

Corey: The darkness pushed me, and I fell. I drowned.

Dr. Raymond: What do you mean, you drowned?

Corey: Der Fluss, es war nicht tief. Ich riß meinen Kopf aus der fallen. Von der Zeit meiner Mutter hat es bis zum River's Edge, ich war ertrunken. (Sobbing.) Ich stelle mir vor, dass ich im Wasser schwebende. Ich bin gestorben.

Ms. Delaney: She said that the river below was not very deep, and she had broken her neck. Her mother could not reach her in time to keep her from drowning.

Ms. Delaney: Ingrid, one more question. Can you tell me your birthday? Eine weitere Frage, Ingrid. Können Sie mir sagen, wann sie geboren sind?

Corey: June 18.

Ms. Delaney: Verzeih mir aber meine Mathe ist ziemlich schlecht. Das heißt, dass sie geboren wurden wann? (I asked her when she was born.)

Corey: Eighteen thirty-eight.

Ms. Delaney: Can you tell me when you died? Können Sie mir sagen, wann sie gestorben ist?

Corey: June 18, 1847.

Dr. Raymond: Okay, I would like to fast-forward a little. I want you walk back to the door and turn the doorknob to your right. At the count of four, I want you to go to the year you were writing your book. One, two, three, four.

Corey: *(Pausing.)*

Dr. Raymond: Corey? Are you still with me?

Corey: Yes.

Dr. Raymond: How long have you spoken German?

Corey: I don't know any other language.

Dr. Raymond: Did you ever learn another language, perhaps while in high school?

Corey: I learned to sign during my junior high years. I had a friend that was hard of hearing.

Dr. Raymond: Tell me what made you decide to visit the poor farm and write a book?

Corey: I was drawn to it. It was as if someone called out to me to write their stories.

Dr. Raymond: What do you mean?

Corey: I felt like each time I visited the grounds, there was a story to be told, and it drove me to research the property. It became an obsession.

Dr. Raymond: Corey, you often bring up someone from your book. It's a familiar name in the county that you wrote about. Can you tell me about him?

Corey: His name was Charles, Charles Cooper. He was the poor farm keeper.

Dr. Raymond: When did you first learn of Charles?

Corey: The fall of 2006. That's when I began to write about them individually.

Dr. Raymond: Why did you decide to write about the poor farm?

Corey: It was my job as a researcher to help the community find missing records.

Dr. Raymond: The community?

Corey: Someone inquired on some markers in a field, and I became fascinated with the mystery surrounding their meaning. It became my purpose. It became an obsession.

Dr. Raymond: What kind of markers?

Corey: Tombstones. It turned out that the markers were graves located on the poor farm grounds.

Dr. Raymond: What else did you discover?

Corey: The people that lived there were interesting. They all had stories to tell. It was missing from our history books. It was as if they never existed. I felt it was my job to tell their stories and to tell everyone how they played important roles in society.

Dr. Raymond: It felt good to find their stories then?

Corey: Yes, but some were very sad to write.

Dr. Raymond: Why is that?

Corey: There were children buried there, and there were no markers to identify them.

Dr. Raymond: Surely this bothered you?

Corey: Yes, I thought about how it would feel if I could not find my children in the event they should pass. It made me very upset that I could not find where the children were buried on the property.

Dr. Raymond: Were you able to find any records for the children?

Corey: No. Children were unimportant in those days, unless of course you had a son.

Dr. Raymond: So you decided to write about them and publish your findings for all to see?

Corey: Yes. But there were a lot of things missing.

Dr. Raymond: What was missing? What were you searching for?

Corey: I could not find everything that I needed on everyone. I wondered if they had family nearby. If they had children of their own or if they ever visited them.

Dr. Raymond: How did that make you feel?

Corey: It saddened me to think that many died alone. And it made me determined to search each and every entry in the ledgers as to their age, sickness, next of kin, ailment, and location of their burial. But I was left overwhelmed and even more saddened when I would hit dead ends, literally. I felt as if I were a failure as a researcher.

Dr. Raymond: What made you feel this way?

Corey: I felt that no one would read what I did find, and they would be upset if they knew that there were still documents missing.

Dr. Raymond: What you did find has helped many people find their ancestors. You have to feel some gratification for your research, no?

Corey: Yes, but by then, it was too late.

Dr. Raymond: What was too late?

Corey: What I had done was done. There was no turning back.

Dr. Raymond: What did you do?

Corey: I provoked them. I asked them to come. I invited them. The lady in Gettysburg, she warned me about them. I didn't listen. *(Sobbing.)*

Mrs. Delaney: Can you tell me about the lady in Gettysburg?

Corey: Renee and I had planned our seventeen-year anniversary there. We had wanted to go earlier in the year; however, I was suffering from a diseased gallbladder and ended up having emergency surgery earlier in the year, and it took some time to heal. I remember trying to plan the trip just before I had my last attack. It was all I could think about doing once I returned home from the hospital.

Dr. Raymond: Was your recovery long?

Corey: Yes. I ended up with a bad infection before the surgery. They had to wait several days before they would operate. When they did, the infection progressed. I spent two weeks in the hospital recovering.

Mrs. Delaney: Do you remember much during your illness?

Corey: Yes. I remember not being able to sleep. I woke up often during the middle of the night with a heaviness in my chest.

Dr. Raymond: What else do you remember?

Corey: I often woke up downstairs with my Bible.

Mrs. Delaney: Did you seek a physician?

Corey: Yes, I saw my physician on several occasions, but they could not find anything wrong.

Mrs. Delaney: So, when did they discover that you had a diseased gallbladder?

Corey: I ended up in the emergency room one evening, and the attending physician did an ultrasound on my gallbladder.

Dr. Raymond: When did you have the procedure to remove your gallbladder?

Corey: Three days later.

Dr. Raymond: How was your recovery?

Corey: Not very well.

Dr. Raymond: Why is that?

Corey: He nearly lost me on the table.

Mrs. Delaney: Corey, this is Anne. Can you tell me the last thing you remembered before you awoke from the surgery?

Corey: The lights.

Mrs. Delaney: The operating lights?

Corey: I think so. They were so bright.

Mrs. Delaney: Was this the only surgical procedure you have had?

Corey: Other than having my children, yes, but even then, I was never put under when I delivered them both.

Mrs. Delaney: Corey, can you go back to the day of your surgery and describe the room to me?

Corey: Yes.

Mrs. Delaney: Tell me about what the room looked like.

Corey: There are machines and tables with sharp objects on them.

Mrs. Delaney: What else do you see?

Corey: There is a bright light above my head.

Mrs. Delaney: Can you see the doctor?

Corey: Yes, there are two doctors looking at my chest.

Mrs. Delaney: What else do you see?

Corey: A nurse is putting red stuff all over my chest and stomach.

Mrs. Delaney: Can you tell me what the doctors are doing?

Corey: One of the doctors has a small probe, and the other is just watching him. He is pushing the probe into my stomach and moving it around. It's a camera. There is a screen, and I can see under my skin.

Mrs. Delaney: You said there were two doctors. What is the other one doing?

Corey: He is looking over everything that the first doctor is doing. He has a glow to him, like there is a light shining on him, but I don't see where it is coming from. He seems to be directing the other doctor, but he's not saying anything.

Mrs. Delaney: Can you describe what he is doing?

Corey: He is just standing there watching the first doctor. Wait. He is not wearing scrubs.

Mrs. Delaney: What is he wearing?

Corey: It's a uniform of some sort. Wait, he's not a doctor! He looks too young to be a doctor. He looks like a baby still. What is he doing in here?

Mrs. Delaney: Can you tell me who he is?

Corey: I don't know who he is, but he is just looking in the corner. He shouldn't be here. I don't understand what he is doing here? *(Screaming.)* Oh my God. It's here! It's here in the room

with me.

Dr. Raymond: What is there? What is in the room with you?

Corey: That thing! It's hovering on the tray in the corner. It's smiling at me with those teeth.

Mrs. Delaney: Corey, I want you to tell me what the doctor is doing.

Corey: Oh God, no! What is it doing here? What is happening to me? God, please help me!

Mrs. Delaney: What is the young man doing?

Corey: God, please help me. It's coming closer. He can't stop it.

Dr. Raymond: Relax, Corey. It's okay. Nothing can harm you. This is only a memory.

Corey: It's on top of me! Get it off, get it off!

Mrs. Delaney: What is on top of you?

Corey: That thing. It wants to hurt me.

Mrs. Delaney: Tell it to go away, Corey. Tell it that it has no control over you.

Corey: I can't. I can't move. There are alarms going off, and the doctors are panicking. What is happening to me? I can't breathe; it's on top of me. Why doesn't anyone do something? Get it off of me!

Mrs. Delaney: Where is the young man?

Corey: He is floating toward him. Oh, my God, he is flying!

Mrs. Delaney: What is he doing?

Corey: He is raising his arms at him. The doctor is rushing around pushing buttons on the monitors. What is happening to me? Help me, God, please help me. Don't take me away from my family.

Mrs. Delaney: Where is the young man? What is he doing while this is happening?

Corey: The black thing, it's inside me!

Mrs. Delaney: Where is the young man? Where did he go?

Corey: He's here with me. He is extending his hand to me. He is helping me get up. What is happening to me?

Mrs. Delaney: Corey, tell me what is the young man doing?

Corey: He is helping me off of the table. Wait! I can see myself on the table. How is this possible? I am above my own body. Oh my God, am I dead? God, please no! I'm not ready to die! Please, God, no!

Corey: It's so bright. The light is so bright. I can see others.

Mrs. Delaney: What others?

Corey: The people in my dreams.

Mrs. Delaney: What are they doing?

Corey: They are showing me scenes.

Mrs. Delaney: What are they showing you?

Corey: I was on the operating table. They found something hiding underneath my liver. They have to cut it out. They are trying to revive me, but there is so much blood.

Mrs. Delaney: So tell me, what are the others showing you?

Corey: They are showing me scenes on a field. I'm on the poor farm. They are all there.

Mrs. Delaney: Who? Who is all there?

Corey: My other families. Oh no! Don't let this happen. Please not my babies! Please don't let this happen to my children! Please, God, help me save them!

Mrs. Delaney: What other families?

Corey: Renee, Harley, all of them. They were all there, long ago. They said I used to live there with them. *(Sobbing.)*

Mrs. Delaney: What is it, Corey? What is happening?

Corey: They are all dead! All of them. I need to go back. I need to go back and fix things. I am not supposed to stay here.

Mrs. Delaney: Where? Where is the young man? Where did he go?

Corey: He is holding my hand. I needed to see. I have to go back and fix things.

Mrs. Delaney: What did you need to see?

Corey: Them dying. The reason why I am this way. No! Please no! Please don't hurt my babies.

Mrs. Delaney: Corey? Corey?

Corey: I can't stay. I have to go back and finish things. I have to find my way back home. If I don't, they will all die.

Dr. Raymond: Who will die?

Corey: Renee, my children, our families. They will all die terrible deaths.

Dr. Raymond: How do you know this?

Corey: They showed me what would happen if I didn't go back. I have to go back and fix it. I have to save them. I have to save them all. *(Sobbing.)* I want to go back. I don't want them to die.

Mrs. Delaney: This is your life path. You must return. You must fix things for those around you. I know it is difficult to return, but you must.

Corey: I can see the doctor, he is cutting something out of me. It's dark, and it shoots across the room. It was in there! It was in my liver hiding! Oh my God, it was inside me!

Mrs. Delaney: It's okay, Corey. It's all over now.

Dr. Raymond: It's okay, Corey. Relax.

Mrs. Delaney: Corey, have you seen the young man before? The young man that was showing you these things?

Corey: Yes.

Mrs. Delaney: When have you seen him?

Corey: Long time ago.

Mrs. Delaney: Can you describe him to me?

Corey: He is short, dark hair and dark eyes. He looks like something out of an old movie. His clothes look torn and out of date. He is covered with black dirt too. But he was all cleaned up when he was in the operating room with me.

Mrs. Delaney: How often have you seen him? Do you still see him?

Corey: Different times. Mostly in my dreams.

Mrs. Delaney: Did he tell you to do things?

Corey: No. He puts thoughts in my head.

Dr. Raymond: What kind of thoughts?

Corey: Things, sort of like a camera taking still shots. I see scenes from the past. People, places, and events over time. But they feel like I have lived through the events. Like memories I can reflect on.

Dr. Raymond: Now at the count of three, I want you to awaken fully rested and remembering everything that we discussed in the regression today. One, two, and three. How do you feel, Corey?

Corey: Exhausted.

Dr. Raymond: Well, you had quite the awakening.

Mrs. Delaney: Corey, what we may have witnessed this afternoon was a possible near-death experience. Your regression also shed some light on a few things as well. If I am correct, shortly after you had your gallbladder surgery, things became different. You became different, correct?

Corey: Yeah, that was right about the time. But something really changed in me when I began researching the poor farm. I don't know how to explain it. I just had to write about them. Are they the ones that are doing this to me? I mean, are they causing all of this negativity in my life?

Mrs. Delaney: I'm not quite sure yet, but obviously some unresolved issues have spilled over from the past into your present time. I think it may be up to you to resolve things, as hard as it may be to understand right now. And it may be possible that there are some old souls intertwined in it all.

Corey: So, what is it that they want from me?

Mrs. Delaney: Corey, it may not be a matter of what they want from you but rather what you can help them resolve so that they can move on.

Corey: What could I possibly help them with?

Dr. Raymond: Corey, if I may, I would like to play back the tape. It may shed some light on where you can go from here. I would like you to hear your responses to some of the questions we asked you. Is that all right with you?

Corey: Did I say something to be worried about?

Dr. Raymond: I think you may find it rather interesting to say the least. Let me get another recorder here so we can continue on with your session while we listen. Tape ends. New tape begins. (Rewind previous tape for review with client.)

Playback:

Mrs. Delaney: Corey, sie sprechen sehr gut Deutsch. Wie alt waren Sie, als sie gelernt?

(I told her she spoke German well and inquired as to how old she was when she learned the language.)

Corey: Was meinen Sie damit?

Mrs. Delaney: She is inquiring as to why we are asking her this.

Dr. Raymond: Can you ask her why she has chosen to speak German during her regression?

Mrs. Delaney: Corey, warum haben sie sich dazu entschieden, uns auf Deutsch zu?

Corey: Ich kann sprechen nur gebrochen Englisch.

Mrs. Delaney: She said that she can speak English, but it is very broken. Corey, warum sprechen sie Deutsch? Warum haben sie sich dafür entschieden haben, in deutscher Sprache?

Corey: Mücken als "fliegende Impfspritzen? Mein Name ist Ingrid. Möchten Sie mich zu versuchen mein Englisch? Warum ist es so du mich Mücken als "fliegende Impfspritzen?

Mrs. Delaney: Dr. Raymond, she is wondering why we are calling her Corey. She said her name is Ingrid. She has broken English but is willing to try.

Dr. Raymond: Ingrid, can you tell me how old you are?

Corey: (Pausing.)

Mrs. Delaney: Ingrid, wie alt sind Sie?

Corey: Nine.

End tape.

Corey: You have got to be kidding me. Was I really talking in German? I mean, why don't I remember this? I remember bits and pieces, but I don't remember this part.

Mrs. Delaney: Yes, and this could explain a few things. What I would like to know is more about the young man in your dreams.

Corey: I remember dreaming about a young man when I was younger, but these night terrors that I am having now? No, he is not present in them.

Mrs. Delaney: It's a lot for one to go through. I know.

Corey: May I have a glass of water?

Mrs. Delaney: Sure, let me get that for you. Can you tell me what happened when you returned home from the hospital?

Corey: Yes. Well, once I was feeling better after the surgery, I began to make arrangements to travel to Gettysburg. I wanted to go to research one of the characters in my book, Charles Cooper to be exact.

Dr. Raymond: Okay. Tell me about your time spent there. What did you do while you were there researching?

Corey: We stayed at a beautiful B&B and took advantage of all the touristy things with the battlefield.

Renee and I spent four days walking the battlefield and shopping around town. I was looking for information on the Mass. Twentieth Infantry in Gettysburg and was hoping I'd find a picture there of them. Charles Cooper was enlisted in the Twentieth Mass. He was the reason why I was there. The Twentieth Mass. played an important role in the Battle at Gettysburg, and I was determined to find something on them. We went to one antique shop after another and nothing. Pictures without names, faces without rankings. It was hopeless.

Mrs. Delaney: Did you know much about Charles before your trip?

Corey: No, I mean, I knew he grew up in Germany and that he had several brothers. But not much else really. I even researched the town his family settled in once they came to the States.

Mrs. Delaney: You have mentioned on several occasions about speaking with a woman in Gettysburg that made you quite upset. Can you tell me a little more about her?

Corey: Well, it was the strangest thing. One evening this lady came up to us while we were out walking.

Dr. Raymond: Go on.

Corey: The evening before we left, we decided to take one more stroll down the roundabout by the Lincoln Hotel. It's where all of the streets meet in one central location downtown. An old woman got our attention and was calling out from behind us. She was about sixty-five or seventy, dressed in an old Victorian dress, her hair up in a bun and a child wrapped around her hip. I thought it was her granddaughter, and I really paid no attention to the child.

She told us that she had been watching us around town. She told us that there were all kinds of dead people surrounding me and trying to talk with me. I didn't know what to think.

Mrs. Delaney: What else did the woman tell you?

Corey: She invited me into her antique shop to talk. She told me to leave Renee and that I could join him later. She said it was import-ant. We walked with her and the child down the street to an antique shop. I thought it was rather odd though. She never once spoke to the child. Nor did the child ever speak. He just stood there staring at me. Anyway, I walked inside the shop and followed her and the child to another room in the back. It was filled with antiques, and I wondered why we had missed this store earlier. The room was small and dim. Only a couple of chairs and a round table with a small lamp were on it. She said her name was Camilla and that she was a medium. She said she noticed me in the square the other day, and then I only had a few following me, but now there were many. I stood there in amazement. *Many?* I wondered.

She motioned for me to take a seat, and I gladly did next to the child. She told me that I had a gift. A gift that I refused to use. She said I was twisted in my faith because of what I was being taught and what I chose to believe.

Mrs. Delaney: Did you believe her?

Corey: No, I thought she was a little nuts. But then she started talking about my research. She could not have known any of that stuff. I hadn't published the book yet. Yet she still spoke of spirits following me around, trying to get my attention. She described many of them and even gave names and places that I was familiar with and that pertained to my research. I frankly could not explain how she could have known all of this stuff. My own city was unaware of this stuff!

Mrs. Delaney: What else did she tell you?

Corey: She said that I was not there by coincidence, that there are no coincidences—something I am getting quite used to now.

Dr. Raymond: How did you feel when she was telling you all of this?

Corey: I didn't want to believe her. It scared me to think that I had spirits following me around and meddling in my life. But it would explain a lot of things and especially how my mood often changed.

Dr. Raymond: What do you mean?

Corey: Well, the whole time we were there, I was depressed. I kept being drawn to the battlefield, and when I got there, I felt ill. It is one thing to feel saddened by its history, but this was different. I felt this heaviness in my chest, and I could not breathe at times. Wherever we walked, something on my body would ache but not like a muscle pull. They were sharp pains to the abdomen, tingling pain in my legs and arms. I could not explain it. I could not help but cry every time we were visiting the battlefield or where one of the hospitals stood. It was crazy. This was supposed to be a fun trip.

Mrs. Delaney: She told you something about yourself, didn't she?

Corey: Yes. She said a few things.

Dr. Raymond: What did she tell you, Corey?

Corey: She told me that I was sensitive to them. That I was able to sense their feelings and pain. That if I learned to use my gift, they would be able to communicate with me. I know, I know. Crazy, isn't it?

Mrs. Delaney: No, it's not crazy, Corey. She told you to do something too, didn't she?

Corey: Yes. How do you know these things?

Mrs. Delaney: Please continue.

Corey: She said that it is my duty to guide them. The lost ones have attached themselves to me because I showed compassion for them. She warned me not to return until I had found my faith again.

Mrs. Delaney: Why do you think she told you this?

Corey: I don't know. Something about being connected to the battlefield and something back home. She said I would be able to help others that cannot find the light. She warned me to find my faith before I sought any more answers about my research. She warned me not to go back there, but we did. One last time, we walked the fields of the battlefield, and I reached out for answers.

Mrs. Delaney: What do you mean?

Corey: I invited them to communicate with me. I wanted answers. I wanted to write my book, so I asked them to guide me. I didn't think I was doing anything wrong. She said they needed my help, and if I was going to believe any of this, I had to invite them to guide me. So, I did. I invited them in that very evening.

Mrs. Delaney: Corey, when you invited them in, something attached itself to you. In fact, I believe you may have several attachments due to your sensitivity as a child. Sensitive individuals like yourself that lose their faith can become empty vessels for malevolent spirits. Their souls become susceptible to invasion to the darkness. Hearing your regressions and recollections of premonitions, night terrors, and incidents that have happened to you since you were a child, I believe something long ago made a claim to you as well. It has been testing you all along.

Corey: In other words, you are saying that I am possessed, aren't you?

Mrs. Delaney: What I am saying is that you have an attachment, possibly more than one. These entities can come in and out of your life when they want. But they don't always do the damage quickly. The darkness has no concept of time, and for some, they will space their torture over time so you and those around you brush it off as bad luck or just coincidences. While all along they are pulling you away from God and pulling you deeper into the darkness until, well, they make your life a living hell. And if you don't pay attention to the subtle hints of your guides, it's easy for you to veer off course. But the negative ones, they can meddle with your life path. Truly, you have a gift, but when you lose your faith, the negative entities will take from you. You need to find your faith again. When you do, you can manage it and use it to help so many people find their way home. I can help you learn how to use it, and I can teach you how to ward off the negativity that may try to harm you in the future. This gift has been with you before you were writing the book. Corey, understand that being a sensitive has many advantages. It is not a curse. It is truly a gift. And when you learn how to use it, you will feel blessed by those you can help.

Corey: But you just said that something really bad has attached itself to me and my life. How can that be a good thing?

Mrs. Delaney: We are going to help you with that attachment. However, there are a couple of things we need to do first. I believe you opened a portal when you went to Gettysburg. That portal is linked to the dead at Gettysburg and your home where you returned from your trip. It is you that drew negative entities into your life. Your spirit needs to be cleansed of this. The portal on both ends needs to be sealed. You will be enlightened, and within time, you will feel much reward from the gift you will give to many.

Corey: Wait! Cleansing? What do you mean by a cleansing?

Mrs. Delaney: Corey, we need to cleanse you of the negative attachments.

Corey: Okay, so I am not crazy, am I? This stuff is real?

Dr. Raymond: Mental illnesses are treatable with medications and therapy. I can conclude by stating that you are not suffering from sleep apnea or any other mental illness. Anne is going to guide you outside of therapy, okay? I am afraid that our time is up. I would like to continue to see you. Perhaps next week for another session. Mrs. Delaney will be here as well. See Judy on your way out and set up an appointment for next Tuesday, okay?

Mrs. Delaney: It's okay. You are going to be all right. Take my advice. Stay out of that cemetery and stay out of any old houses for the time being, okay?

Corey: Believe you me, I have had my fill of cemeteries for the time being.

March 6, 2010, Journal Entry

I have been documenting my sleeping habits for the past few days. The dreams continue to wake me every night. I write them down as I am instructed, but I still think it's useless. The dreams are the same each night. I see Renee driving the kids into a median, splitting the car in half, killing them all, and of me walking in on the young girl giving birth and the terrible thing that was keeping her hostage. I try to change the outcome of the dreams each night, but I can't. I am forced to witness them over and over every night. I can't stand the gut retching feeling I have just thinking about it. Regardless, either outcome is not good.

We have been in the new house nearly three months now. It doesn't matter where I live. I feel as though something is following me. Lights turn on and off when I walk into a room. Appliances malfunction. Doors slam shut before I reach them. I have no safe haven to come home to anymore. I continue to see the shadows, and other times, I think I am hearing the voices or someone whispering right around the corner. And that laugh. That terrible laugh I keep in the back of my head that terrifies me so. What is it and where is it coming from?

I took an afternoon nap today. Something I haven't done in a long time. It felt good to rest until Bear woke me up barking. I fell off the couch, and there she was barking at something over me. She growled at me as if I were a stranger as I made an attempt to get up from the floor. I could not move. Bear snarled her teeth and lunged at me as if she weren't looking at me, rather something inside of me. She didn't recognize me. My own dog was turning against me. A dog I raised from a pup, sheltered from the elements, fed from the table, and played with in the river. This was not the dog that I had trained to be playful. This dog was ready to attack me.

I slowly rose from the floor while Bear continued to lunge and growl at me. I managed to get behind the couch where she couldn't reach me. I tried talking both softly and aggressively to her, but she wasn't listening to my commands. Then just as quickly as it occurred, she stopped. She looked up at me as if I was the strange one. Bear jumped on the couch to reach me and began crying like a lost puppy. I didn't know what to make of it. I got out from behind the couch and held her trembling body and pondered what had just happened to make her act the way she did.

March 7, 2010, Journal Entry

Bear continues to act strangely. I took her outside tonight for a swim, and she would not stop barking at the house. She stood in the middle of the backyard and just barked. I kept looking up at the house to see if someone was knocking on the door or pulling into the driveway, and nothing. No one was there but me. When she started to cry, I turned around to look at the house, and that's when I saw the lights in the upstairs bedroom turn on and off. It startled me quite a bit since I knew that no one was home. I was in awe. I tried grabbing Bear to come in, but she would not move a muscle. She just kept crying and whimpering. Finally she lay down in the grass.

I quickly tied her to her leash in the yard and walked toward the house—not before getting the bat out of the shed, however. I walked in through the kitchen door and proceeded to turn on every light in the house as I moved from room to room. When I got to the stairwell to head upstairs, all the lights on the main level turned off. I was in complete darkness, and the house began to take on a new personality of its own.

The living room heading to the upstairs became very cold. It sent a shiver down my spine. I could still see Bear through the patio doors and saw her stand up at attention. She began to bark again and would surely draw the neighbors to inquire if she kept it up. I paid no attention to her though. I had other things to tend to, and I knew she would be safe being tied up in the yard.

I walked into the kitchen and grabbed a flashlight from under the sink and headed back to the staircase. There was only one way in and one way out through the stairs. If someone was in the house, I would see them before they had a chance to run out.

I heard whispering in front of me as if someone were trying to hide from me, followed by the devilish laugh I often feared. The anxiety I was feeling was indescribable. Surely, I had caught someone in the house, and they were going to pay for breaking in. But that laugh was not coming from anything human. I had to be brave. I thought of Anne coaching me to find my faith again. I clutched one hand around the bat and the other on the flashlight, and then proceeded to walk towards the laugh.

By the time I made it to the landing at the top of the stairs, the laughing had stopped. It was dead silent. I walked from room to room, looking for someone hiding, but there was no one there. I tried flicking on the lights, and they wouldn't come on. I must have walked through the house three times and nothing. I headed downstairs to check the fuse box for a tripped breaker. Just as I was opening the door to the garage, the lights came back on. Bear continued to bark outside.

When everything seemed well again, I stepped outside to get Bear. She was still barking and staring at the house. I unchained her leash, and she went running to the patio door. I turned around and caught a glimpse of a dark shadow peering out of my daughter's window. I ran after Bear and threw open the door. Once Bear was inside, she ran straight upstairs as if she were chasing a squirrel. There was something up there and Bear sensed it. On top of the stairwell Bear stood howling at my daughter's door to her bedroom. I ran after her, upstairs and slowly opened the door to my daughter's room. No one was in there. When I gazed at the walls, I screamed, then covered my mouth in horror. Plastered on the walls were profanities towards my children. I was disgusted by the words and the smell was enough to make anyone vomit. This has got to end. I cannot take much more of this.

It took nearly three hours to clean up the mess and smell. Bear sat beside me exhausted but never let her guard down. I am not quite sure when I had fallen asleep, but I awoke to her barking upstairs. I quickly grabbed my bat and went racing upstairs again. I opened every door to every room. Her bark seemed to echo throughout the house. I panicked and went back through each room and looked in every closet until I finally found her. Bear was wedged behind a gate in my son's bedroom closet. There was no explanation as to how she got there. Someone or something lured her up there, and someone or something had wedged the gate as to keep her there. I could not explain it. It frightened me, and I no longer wanted to stay there alone in the house.

March 9, 2010, Journal Entry

My therapy sessions seem to be quite bothersome but eye-opening. I wondered if I had indeed uncovered a few secrets I kept buried inside. I couldn't explain in the beginning why I was drawn to the research and the cemetery. I was beginning to understand why I was able to find them so easily. Perhaps I wasn't alone after all. It is rather exciting to think that I may be guided by something extraordinary.

I am consuming so many theories from my regressions.

At two in the morning, I was awakened by someone walking in the hallway upstairs. Bear was already growling when I put my robe on. I rushed to open my bedroom door, and suddenly I felt a sharp pain to my toe. Something had cut me. I looked down, and there were all of my kitchen knives lined up in a row. I had a small laceration to my pinky toe, causing me to leave a trail of blood leading to the bathroom. I quickly ran some cold water on it and grabbed a Band-Aid from the medicine cabinet. I walked back down the hall and picked up the kitchen knives when I noticed that one of them was missing. I looked down the hallway but saw nothing. The house was silent, with the exception of Bear growling.

I quietly walked down the hallway and entered my daughter's room. She was fast asleep snuggling with her Hello Kitty pillow I had gotten her the past Christmas. I continued down the hallway to my son's room and discovered he was not lying in his bed. I opened the closet, his bathroom door, and still no Mason. I quickly ran downstairs, through open the dining room door, and there he was. Mason was standing, and all of the dining room chairs were facing him as if he was speaking to people I could not see. His eyes were closed. He had been sleepwalking.

Cautiously, I walked over to him and reached for his hand. I was frightened coming up from behind him. I knew not to startle someone that had been sleepwalking, but this was not like Mason. Neither one of my children ever sleepwalked before. As I came around him, I noticed he was holding a knife at his side. His eyes suddenly opened, but I was not looking into the eyes of my son. His eyes quickly filled with a dark film, and my gut sank once again with a feeling of unthinkable terror. Mason was not in there. It was something else in that room. Mason's arm quickly raised the knife over me. I stood there motionless, fear filling every muscle in my body. "Leave me be or you'll suffer like the rest!" he yelled, but it was not my son's voice. And then that hideous laugh. That terrible, terrible laugh that paralyzes me! I could not move. The darkness behind that voice swirled around me as if I were on the tilt a whirl at Great America. It was nauseating, and I couldn't help by close my eyes, knowing I wouldn't see what would happen to me next.

Mason just stood there with his arm extended as if he were trying to get revenge for something I had done to him. I kept trying to waken him, but he would not respond to my voice. Suddenly, the chairs pushed themselves back under the table. *What the hell was that?* I thought. Mason lowered his arm, placed the knife on the table, and turned to walk back upstairs. He walked right passed me without saying a word. *Could the divorce be doing this to him? No!* I thought. There is no rationalizing what just happened. I saw what I saw, and I heard what I heard. I should not be analyzing this. I just don't know what to make of all of this. And what others? I wondered. What does he know about my research? I am beginning to think that it was my fault, and perhaps Dr. Raymond is right about my children needing therapy. I am not sure if I should inquire in the morning with Mason as to what transpired. The last thing I want is to have him scared too.

March 10, 2010, Journal Entry

I don't remember how I ended upstairs this morning. I vividly remembered the dream though. I was walking along the shore of the river when I heard a screeching noise from the bridge above. My heart rate sped up, and I was looking for the source of the noise, thinking that someone had just swerved off the road. When I looked up at the bridge, where the noise was coming from, I could only see the top of the vehicle. The moonlight was so bright, and it glared off of the roof of the vehicle. I could barely make out whether it was a car or SUV. And then I noticed something odd. Something was coming up behind it. It was dark and thick, like a mist flowing over the river on a cold winter day. I could see it forming toward the end of the bridge. I was so transfixed on the mist that I nearly missed the vehicle leaving the roadway. It was only when the vehicle broke through the guardrail that I slightly turned to witness the vehicle plummet in the river below. My heart raced, and time seemed to stand still. I tried to run toward the vehicle, but I couldn't move. I looked down to discover that my feet were buried in sand up to my knees. I was trapped, and there was nothing I could do as the sand continued to crawl up my legs.

Struggling to get free, the vehicle continued to sink in the river. It was a lighter color SUV, and if it weren't for the moonlight, I never would have seen the driver struggle to get free themselves. Immediately above the SUV was the dark mist, and it made me angry. It was massive, and it felt aggressive. As it grew larger, it split off, and a part of it was heading my way. It was getting bigger and moving toward me and the vehicle that was slowly sinking into the river. I cried out, but no sound would leave my lips. The darkness was consuming the SUV, and soon it would consume me too. Growing larger and coming in faster and faster. It stopped within inches of my face. I closed my eyes as I began to feel lightheaded and nauseous. It was here. It was with me once again. And that laugh, that terrible laugh! Then I woke up. That's all I remember.

March 11, 2010, Journal Entry

I headed to the library to research what Anne had relayed to me in therapy. I ended up checking out a half dozen books on the various topics dealing with possession, mental telepathy, clairvoyance, and the paranormal. I'm fascinated by what other people have experienced or claimed that they have. Most of them had experiences as a child, like me. Should I feel excited, knowing that others have the same experiences? But then again this isn't like childbirth, and every other woman has a similar story as far as a difficult labor. No, I'm not so sure about sharing my experiences with others. I am still afraid. And I still don't know why this is all happening to me.

The kids returned home from their father's house this afternoon, and I was overjoyed to see them. We had planned to go out to dinner tonight to their favorite restaurant, a Chinese restaurant their father and I often frequented, Chopsticks. I warmed up the car as the children were getting ready inside when my daughter came running out of the house screaming. Something was wrong with Bear. I ran inside, and there she was, lying on the floor as if someone was holding her down. She was gasping for air, and for a minute I thought that she was choking on something. I told my son to run next door to get Beth. She is a veterinarian.

By the time Beth reached the driveway, Bear had sprung up, wagging her tail as if nothing had happened. Her eyes were red as could be, and her heart rate was at 165, a dangerous level for a dog her age. Beth took her vitals and suggested she take her to her clinic up the road. We followed behind her. She did some blood work, and to be on the safe side, she kept her for a few hours for observation and testing. So the kids and I went home and got ready for dinner. Chopsticks would have to wait until another night.

Beth phoned the house shortly after eight that night and stated Bear was fine and that she would be bringing her home with her after work. When nine o'clock came around and no Beth, I started to worry. The clinic was less than a mile away. I wondered what could be keeping her so long.

The kids and I decided to head up to the clinic, and that's when we saw the divers trying to get her out of her car. It was partially sticking out of the water. I presumed we had lost them both. Fortunately, Beth was alive, but she was hospitalized for hypothermia. Bear was missing, and I presume she drowned. We followed the ambulance to the hospital but were told that we could not see Beth. The kids are saddened that no one claimed to have seen Bear during the ordeal.

March 12, 2010, Journal Entry

It has been the longest day ever, wondering what happened to Beth and Bear. We received a call from Ben, Beth's husband, and we were relieved that he reported that she was able to receive visitors later today. I arrived at the hospital shortly after six o'clock this evening. She lay in her bed, still recouping from the ordeal. She was weak but able to talk and tell me what happened.

Beth stated she had placed Bear in the kennel in her vehicle, but something had startled her. She began barking out of control. She tried to calm her down, but she began to thrash about so much that the gate to the kennel became loose and then swung open. Bear continued to bark aggressively, and at one point, she turned around, thinking that someone was coming up behind her. But when she turned around, she saw nothing, nothing but a few dark clouds lying close to the ground. But Bear continued to bark a chilling bark. Just then, Bear jumped out at her and began running back toward the clinic, back into the dark mist.

Beth ran a short distance after her, but she couldn't catch up to her. She got halfway down Van Buren Street, and Bear just disappeared. "She just vanished! I went after her, but I saw something.

Something had darted out onto the road. It started to come after me. It was dark, shapeless, and cold. So dark and cold. Beth said she ran back to her car when she felt a heaviness come over her. She struggled to turn around and run back. Her breathing became shallow, and her legs felt as though she had just completed her first 5K.

Beth continued to look back, as she felt the darkness was gaining speed on her—getting bigger and heavier, faster and growing more mad! Beth finally made it back to her vehicle, jumped in with the already running engine, then sped off. As she looked in her rearview mirror, she could see the darkness continuing to grow closer no matter how fast she drove. I could sense the fear in her voice as she fought back tears of true terror.

Beth doesn't remember much after that. What really startled me was how it made her feel "dark and cold." She claimed that whatever it was that darted out onto the road was shapeless and dark. Almost as if it were a mist, she said.

Bear is still missing. The children are horribly saddened she hasn't returned home.

March 13, 2010, Regression Session

Dr. Raymond: Corey Michaels, March 13 regression session. Good afternoon, Corey. I understand you have a few things to talk about today.

Corey: It's my son. He was sleepwalking and ended up with a knife in his hand.

Dr. Raymond: Is this something your son has done before?

Corey: No. Mason has never done something like this before. I am really frightened for my children.

Dr. Raymond: We discussed earlier on about the possibility of therapy for your children. Are you in favor of letting me talk to them?

Corey: I am. But I don't think my son and I were alone when this happened. I think something was in that room with him. Here. I wrote about it in my journal. Read it. Another thing happened that really startled me. The other evening, something wrote vulgar words with feces on my daughter's wall. Something terrible is going on, and I believe it is doing this to get back at me. I just know we have to do something before one of my children get hurt.

Dr. Raymond: Okay, before you leave, let's set up some appointments for me to meet with your children. We can discuss this further once Anne arrives. Would you like to talk about what you dreamt about since your last session?

Corey: Yes, more night terrors. I dreamt someone close to me would be injured by the mist, and it happened. It happened again!

Dr. Raymond: Tell me about your dream.

Corey: It was terrifying. And something terrible is going to happen soon to others. We have to stop it. We need to do something now. We don't have much time. Something needs to be done.

Dr. Raymond: Corey, remember you need to be patient with the process. You have to trust me.

Corey: Listen, Dr. Raymond, I know something is going on with me, and I know from experience something is going to happen to someone if I don't do something about it. A friend of mine was in a terrible accident this week. She is still in recovery, and I know it had something to do with the mist and my dreams. I dreamt about it before it happened only just the other day, and this past week, it actually happened!

Dr. Raymond: Ok. Tell me what happened to your friend?

Corey: She had my dog with her, and she was acting out of character. She took her in for tests. She was on her way home with her. She ran off the bridge and drove into the river. I know it had something to do with the mist. I saw it in a dream!

Mrs. Delaney: Sorry, I am late. Is everything okay? I got a phone call from Judy. Corey, are you okay?

Corey: No, I am not okay. Something terrible is going to happen, and we have to stop it before it does. Mason is sleepwalking with knives, and our dining room was arranged as if he was having company. Then I dreamt something would happen involving a car driving off a bridge into the river, and it actually happened to a neighbor of mine.

Mrs. Delaney: Dr. Raymond, may I have a word with you?

Dr. Raymond: Sure. Corey, please excuse us. We will be right back. Help yourself to some chocolates.

Corey: Really? Are you kidding me? Eat at a time like this?

Dr. Raymond: I'm sorry. Let me have a quick word with Anne, and we will be right back.

Corey: Fine.

(Tape stops.)

(Tape continues.) Dr. Raymond: Okay, Let's talk about this premonition you had. Are you able to relax?

Corey: No, I can't relax. You believe me, don't you?

Dr. Raymond: Ok, let's start by laying back and taking some deep breaths in and out. That's it, ok let's talk about what happened.

Corey: I first felt it when I came home from work last night. I started feeling anxious. I tried to make it to the table, but I fell against the counter. I saw it. I saw the whole thing. It was a house out in the woods.

Dr. Raymond: The cabin in the woods with the young woman?

Corey: No! This was different.

Dr. Raymond: Okay, tell me what you saw.

Corey: As I get closer to the house, I can see this thing hiding in the corner of the house. It looks like a small troll. It's jumping up and down on the gas line. It is chewing on the metal and smiling back at me. It's the mist, and it's laughing at me with that terrible smile. I don't like that smile. It is forcing me to look at what it is doing. I can't wake up and I can't scream. I stood there and watched it go up in flames. I watched them die. Do you understand me? I watched them die!

Dr. Raymond: Why do you think this is going to happen?

Corey: Because it will. That's the way it always happens. I dream it, and it happens. Just like with Beth and my dog the other day. It happened, and I saw it, but I did not know who it was going to happen to at the time. But this is different. I know who this dream will happen to.

Dr. Raymond: Who is this going to happen to?

Corey: Someone in his family.

Dr. Raymond: Whose family?

Corey: His. Renee's.

Mrs. Delaney: Surely there has to be a way to tell them.

Corey: They don't believe in this stuff. I don't know how to tell them. I just got divorced. I don't think anyone in his family is willing to talk to me right now. You have to understand something. I'm divorced now; there is no need for me to call any of them. They don't want to have anything to do with me other than to take my kids away. If I tell them now, they will have me locked up. You don't understand. I know I have to tell them, but I know the consequences if I do.

Dr. Raymond: Okay, Corey, I want you to lay down and relax. I want you to think about relaxing. Take some deep breaths in then out. In then out. Take some long, deep breaths. Imagine you are drifting on a boat and floating farther and farther away from shore. Farther and farther, further and further. Relaxing every muscle in your body, beginning with your shoulders, moving farther down across your abdomen … moving farther toward your arms, fingers, all along taking long, deep breaths in and out. In and out. Every muscle feeling heavier and heavier as we move down to your hips, slowing relaxing and feeling heavier and heavier as you relax. Falling deeper and deeper into a relaxed state. Moving slowing down your legs, knees, feet, and toes. Feeling heavier and heavier as your body becomes more and more relaxed with every breath you take. At the count of three, you will be fully relaxed. One, two, three.

Corey: *(Out of breath.)*

Dr. Raymond: Where are you, Corey?

Corey: *(Sighs.)*

Dr. Raymond: Corey, are you with me?

Corey: Yes.

Dr. Raymond: Corey, I want you to go back to the other day. You talked about having a dream about someone going over a bridge and into the water below.

Corey: Yes.

Dr. Raymond: Did you know the person that this happened to?

Corey: Yes, it was my friend Beth.

Dr. Raymond: Tell me what happened to your friend.

Corey: She was driving home from work. She had Bear with her. She drove off the road.

Dr. Raymond: Did you know that this was going to happen?

Corey: Yes.

Dr. Raymond: What else can you tell me about the dream?

Corey: I am walking alone toward the edge of the river. I can hear a vehicle approaching the road above me.

Dr. Raymond: Can you see anything?

Corey: I can see the dim lighting from the headlights approaching, but I cannot see the vehicle.

Dr. Raymond: Tell me, what do you see when the vehicle approaches the bridge?

Corey: There is a dark mass alongside of the road, swaying back and forth. Almost like it's waiting for something. It's cold and it terrifies me when I stare at it.

Dr. Raymond: Can you tell me what happens when the vehicle approaches the darkness?

Corey: It swerves off of the road and into the river.

Dr. Raymond: The vehicle swerves off the road?

Corey: Yes. It lands in the water below.

Dr. Raymond: What do you do when this happens?

Corey: Nothing. I cannot move. I cannot help.

Dr. Raymond: Are you afraid?

Corey: Yes.

Dr. Raymond: What are you afraid of?

Corey: The mist that is on top of the sinking vehicle. It won't let me help. I cannot scream for help. I am stuck in the sand along the riverbed.

Dr. Raymond: What else do you see?

Corey: That face. Those teeth. Chattering like a wind-up toy. It's frightening. I don't like it staring at me.

Dr. Raymond: Corey, I want you to go back to when you were a child. Do you remember the door at the end of the long hallway?

Corey: Yes.

Dr. Raymond: I would like you to walk down the hallway towards the door at the end. But before you get there, I want you to open the door that will lead you back to the day when you were playing with your friend Martin. Can you do that?

Corey: Yes.

Dr. Raymond: What year is it?

Corey: *(Chuckling.)* Seventy-nine.

Dr. Raymond: Can you tell me where you are?

Corey: At home with Mom. She is baking cookies for my Christmas party.

Dr. Raymond: How old are you, Corey?

Corey: Nine and a half.

Dr. Raymond: Corey, you are almost ten years old then, right?

Corey: Yep. Mom lets me eat some of the batter sometimes. It gives ya worms, ya know.

Dr. Raymond: That is true. Corey, I would like to talk to you about Martin, your friend. Do you want to talk about Martin?

Corey: I'm not allowed to play with him anymore.

Dr. Raymond: Why not?

Corey: 'Cause I got hurt.

Dr. Raymond: Does that bother you?

Corey: No.

Dr. Raymond: No? Why is that?

Corey: 'Cause when we play, I see things.

Dr. Raymond: What kind of things do you see?

Corey: Stuff.

Dr. Raymond: Can you describe what kind of stuff you see?

Corey: Bad things happen when I sleep. I have trouble sleeping sometimes.

Dr. Raymond: I want you to think about the day in the park with Martin. Can you talk to me about what happened that day?

Corey: Yes.

Dr. Raymond: What happened?

Corey: We were talking at the swing sets, and I heard someone calling my name.

Dr. Raymond: Who was calling your name?

Corey: I don't know. It was like they were whispering. I could not tell who it was.

Dr. Raymond: They? Was there more than one person calling you?

Corey: Yes.

Dr. Raymond: Did they tell you to do something?

Corey: Yes. They want me to walk into the grove.

Dr. Raymond: Do you know who they are?

Corey: No.

Dr. Raymond: Were you frightened about walking into the grove?

Corey: No. I wasn't scared.

Dr. Raymond: What happens when you walk to the grove?

Corey: It's coming! It's coming! Run! Run! Run!

Dr. Raymond: What is coming?

Corey: It! It's coming for me!

Mrs. Delaney: What is it? What is coming for you?

Corey: It's a black thing. It's coming! It's coming! Run! Run!

Dr. Raymond: Corey, I want you to walk back to the grove with Martin. Can you walk back toward the swings?

Corey: No! I can't move! It's here! It's here!

Mrs. Delaney: What's here? What is it?

Corey: It's not a dog! It's not a dog!

Mrs. Delaney: What is it, Corey?

Corey: *(Sobbing and screaming.)*

Mrs. Delaney: What is happening? Corey, tell me what is happening.

Corey: It wants me! It wants me!

Dr. Raymond: What wants you?

Corey: That thing! That black thing from inside the grove. George told me to run, but I was too scared to move.

Dr. Raymond: Who is George?

Corey: He is my friend.

Dr. Raymond: So, how did George know that the dog was coming out? Could he see the dog from where he was standing?

Corey: No.

Dr. Raymond: So, how did George know that he would come out?

Mrs. Delaney: Can you describe George to me?

Corey: Yeah. He's got dark hair and dark eyes. He's short like me.

Mrs. Delaney: Can you tell me what he is wearing?

Corey: He looks weird. His shoes have holes in them, and his clothes are all dirty and torn.

Mrs. Delaney: Corey, does George play with Martin too?

Corey: No.

Dr. Raymond: Why is that?

Corey: Martin says he can't see George. He's a secret.

Dr. Raymond: Why is he a secret?

Corey: George said that he died a long time ago. He said that if people knew about him, I could get in trouble. I didn't want to get in trouble.

Dr. Raymond: Corey, where was George when you were at the park with Martin?

Corey: He was watching me from the top of the slope. He warned me to stay away from the grove. He says he can't protect me in the grove.

Dr. Raymond: Corey, when was the first time you saw George?

Corey: I don't know. I don't remember.

Dr. Raymond: Do you remember the first time you saw something that you didn't quite understand or couldn't explain?

Corey: Yes. My grandpa came to my house one night to see me. He never comes over. Mom says he is very sick.

Dr. Raymond: How old were you when you saw your grandfather?

Corey: Seven.

Dr. Raymond: When did he visit you?

Corey: Christmastime. It was late one night. Everyone was sleeping. He wanted to see me before he went on his trip.

Dr. Raymond: What trip would that be?

Corey: I don't know. He said he was going somewhere to get better. He said he would not be in any more pain, but he wouldn't see me anymore. He made me cry. George was there too. He said that he would make sure that Grandpa was safe.

Dr. Raymond: Have you seen your grandfather since that night?

Corey: No, and I tried to tell Mom, but she didn't believe me. She said that Grandpa died that night. She told me I was dreaming.

Dr. Raymond: Did you believe that you were dreaming?

Corey: No. It was real. I saw him. But Mom wouldn't let me talk about it ever again.

Dr. Raymond: Corey, did your grandfather frighten you?

Corey: No. Grandpa told me to tell Mom that he would be okay. That it was time to let him go. I wasn't scared. George told me not to be afraid.

Mrs. Delaney: Can you take her back further, Dr. Raymond?

Dr. Raymond: Okay, Corey, I want you to go back further. I want you to relax, and at the count of three, I want you to tell me where you are. One ... drifting further, two, further ... three. Where are you now?

Corey: *(Sighs.)*

Dr. Raymond: Corey, where are you?

Corey: *(Sighs.)*

Dr. Raymond: Corey, where are you? Can you tell me what year it is?

Corey: Seventy.

Dr. Raymond: Nineteen seventy?

Corey: Yes.

Dr. Raymond: You were born in 1970, weren't you?

Corey: Yes.

Dr. Raymond: Do you remember being born?

Corey: Yes.

Dr. Raymond: What do you remember?

Corey: I can see light by my feet, but it's very dark by my hands.

Dr. Raymond: Are you able to move?

Corey: No. I'm trapped here. I can't get out. I'm trying to move to the light, but I'm trapped. They have to cut my momma open. I am stuck. I can see the doctor there. He looks like a nice man. My friend is there too. He held my hand and told me I would be okay.

Mrs. Delaney: Who is the young man? Do you recognize him?

Corey: It's George! My friend!

Mrs. Delaney: Further, Dr. Raymond. Please.

Dr. Raymond: Okay, I want you to go back further. Further still. At the count of four, I want you to tell me what year it is. One, drifting further, two, still drifting, three … and four. Corey, can you tell me what year it is?

Corey: Seventy-seven

Dr. Raymond: Nineteen seventy-seven?

Corey: No!

Dr. Raymond: Eighteen seventy-seven?

Corey: Yes.

Dr. Raymond: Who am I talking to? Can you tell me your name?

Corey: Lulu.

Dr. Raymond: Nice to meet you, Lulu. My name is Dr. Raymond.

Corey: Dr. Raymond? I am not sure we've met. Are you working with my father?

Dr. Raymond: Perhaps, but first I'd like to know a little bit about you. Can you tell me what's going on in your life right now?

Corey: It just hasn't been a very good year for me.

Dr. Raymond: Why is that?

Corey: We lost the house to the others.

Dr. Raymond: What house and what others?

Corey: The almshouse. The county came in and took it over.

Dr. Raymond: Are you a resident there?

Corey: No, I work here with my father. We moved here in '74 after the fever broke out.

Dr. Raymond: I've read about the fever. Were you sick with it?

Corey: No. My mother and brothers died from it here on the farm. Father and I were immune to it. The doctor told me it could be because of my condition.

Dr. Raymond: What condition do you have?

Corey: I am with child.

Dr. Raymond: How far along are you?

Corey: Seven months.

Dr. Raymond: What is it that you do on the farm?

Corey: I help them take care of the charges. I control the books.

Dr. Raymond: That's a very important job for a young lady to take on. Surely there must have been some differences that they would allow a young woman to control the records.

Corey: No one knows that I do. My father makes sure of it.

Dr. Raymond: So, what are in the ledgers?

Corey: Names of people that live here. Where they are from and who is responsible for them. A long time ago, some really bad people were assigned to watch over these people. They got greedy and didn't take very good care of them. They took payment for services to care for them, but the services were never performed on them as they should have been. I am in charge of making sure those practices are in place and our charges are taken care of. My father oversees everything I do.

Dr. Raymond: Does anyone else know about the ledgers?

Corey: My father reviews them annually for the county board meeting, but other than that, no one knows about them but my father and I.

Dr. Raymond: Can you tell me about the day they took over the farm?

Corey: I'm playing with the children in the field with the others. We are singing and dancing to a children's rhyme.

Dr. Raymond: What are you singing?

Corey: Ring around the rosy, pocket full of posies, ashes, ashes, we all fall down. *(Uneasiness … sobbing.)*

Dr. Raymond: What's the matter?

Corey: We had no idea they were coming. If we would have only known, we could have done something. I could have done something to save them!

Dr. Raymond: Okay. Let's slow down. Can you tell me what happened that day?

Corey: A wagon pulled up in the back of the laundry house. County officials stepped out one at a time, and they looked determined. I knew something was wrong! They should not be here. We all knew it. Steward James approached one of the officers to inquire as to who they were looking for, and he was shoved to the ground. That's when all chaos broke out. The staff went racing to gather everyone inside. The children were being trampled on by the adults, and the feebleminded were left wandering around the farm.

Dr. Raymond: Go on.

Corey: We're being escorted into the dining hall. But I can see them through the window. There is something in the wagon, but I can't see what it is. It's large, and something is covered over it. All of the staff are questioning why the wagon is here. But they are told to get back into their rooms or shoved against the wall for interfering with what appears to be some sort of raid.

Dr. Raymond: Do you know what they want?

Corey: Yes! There are five men carrying sacks from the wagon to the cemetery grounds.

Dr. Raymond: Can you see them? What are they wearing?

Corey: I can't see them.

Dr. Raymond: Tell me what is going on around you.

Corey: "Father, please, please no! Don't let them take me, please!" (Sobbing.)

Dr. Raymond: Your father is there?

Corey: (Sobbing.) Yes. He is holding them back.

Dr. Raymond: Who is your father again?

Corey: Father, please!

Dr. Raymond: Your father, is he allowing this to happen?

Corey: He has no choice. They barged in and took control. They said it would be better if it were cleaned out. He pleaded with them to bring more staff to assist them. They told him it was too late and if he wanted to save the family and others, to let them do their job.

Dr. Raymond: What is your father's name again?

Corey: Charles.

Dr. Raymond: Who were these men?

Corey: County men.

Dr. Raymond: Who? Which county men?

Corey: I can't say.

Dr. Raymond: It's okay. No one will harm you here.

Corey: *(Pauses.)*

Dr. Raymond: Lulu, are you there? What is happening now?

Corey: I can't. They won't let me.

Dr. Raymond: Why won't they let you?

Corey: They are holding me down. Father, no! Father, help me. I'm not sick. Let me go! Help me, God! Please help me.

Dr. Raymond: Lulu, what is happening to you?

Corey: Father, please don't let them take me! Father! Father! I can't breathe … They are holding me down. I can't breathe! Arggghhh!

Dr. Raymond: Where are they taking you? Lulu? Lulu? Relax. You are safe. Try to lay still and gather all the energy you can, and at the count of three, I want you to rewind to earlier in the day. Can you do that?

Corey: *(Sighs.)*

Dr. Raymond: One, drifting further, two … slowly drifting, three. Where are you now?

Corey: I'm in my office on the farm.

Dr. Raymond: What is going on at the poor farm?

Corey: The county came in this morning for the annual checkup. The disease was spreading in the county—first the Indians, now the city. My father sent for more nurses, but they cannot send any until this afternoon. St. John's Hospital has refused to take them because their beds are full too. My father was the only one that would take them in. But he needs help. They promised more help would come today. They lied to us! They lied to us!

Dr. Raymond: Where are the others?

Corey: They are in my father's office, discussing how many are affected and looking through their charts.

Dr. Raymond: Do you recognize them?

Corey: Yes, county officials. I can't see them, but I can hear them talking.

Dr. Raymond: What are they saying?

Corey: They are arguing with my father. They are telling him there is nothing more he can do.

Dr. Raymond: Can you peek in a window or crack open the door?

Corey: I can't. They will see me.

Dr. Raymond: It's okay. No one will see you.

Corey: If they see me, I'll be in trouble.

Dr. Raymond: Can you tell me what you see around you?

Corey: The staff is tending to their charges. They are getting ready to go outside.

Dr. Raymond: Who is going outside?

Corey: *(Sighs ... sobbing.)* The men in my father's office. I have to hide, or they will know I was listening in. I can see the doctor. He has a clipboard, and he is tapping a pen on it. Like he is nervous or something. He knows something. He has a secret! No one can find out! The doctor is walking toward my office.

Dr. Raymond: What is he doing?

Corey: He is telling Father to give him the ledgers. He is refusing to give them the ledgers. They are taking them away from him.

Dr. Raymond: Do you know how many records there are?

Corey: I have two ledgers. They have the names. *(Sobbing.)*

Dr. Raymond: How many names are there?

Corey: Sixty, maybe more.

Dr. Raymond: Sixty people?

Corey: He is coming. He is coming, and I have to hide!

Dr. Raymond: It's okay. Find a place to hide and let me know when you are out of his sight.

Corey: *(Out of breath.)*

Dr. Raymond: Where are you now?

Corey: I'm in the infirmary with the children.

Dr. Raymond: Where are the others?

Corey: The doctor is taking their charts and leaving.

Dr. Raymond: Where is he going?

Corey: I don't know. I don't know what he is doing. Father is walking toward me.

Dr. Raymond: Does your father tell you what is going on?

Corey: He says that they will return soon with more nurses.

Dr. Raymond: Did the doctor bring more nurses back to the farm?

Corey: No. He returned after supper, but he came with a wagon and more men. We were outside singing when they arrived and made us all return to our rooms.

Dr. Raymond: What did he do when they returned?

Corey: He is walking down to the hall and removing the infirm people from their beds. He's wheeling them in the hallway. Mothers and fathers, too ill to fend for themselves. Infants, toddlers, and even more ill children. The children are crying. They don't want to go … Please, God no, no, I'm not sick. Father, please, where are you? Don't take me away from my family. Help me please! Don't let them take me. Please! No!

Dr. Raymond: Okay, at the count of three, I want you to fast-forward to 2006. Relax. Nothing can harm you, and you are safe here. One ... two ... three.

Corey: *(Sighs.)*

Dr. Raymond: Where are you now?

Corey: No ... please, Harley, don't make me do this. Please, I beg you.

Dr. Raymond: Corey, who is Harley?

Corey: I am not supposed to tell.

Dr. Raymond: It's okay, Corey. You need to remember in order to get better. You need to be able to move on by remembering what happened to you.

Corey: But it hurts! It hurts. There is blood everywhere. Please, God, help me. *(Sobbing.)*

Mrs. Delaney: Corey, can you tell me where you are?

Corey: Kansas City.

Dr. Raymond: What are you doing in Kansas City?

Corey: I don't want to do this. Oh my God, it hurts! It hurts!

Dr. Raymond: What hurts, Corey? Why are you in pain?

Corey: I had to do it. He made me. I could not go back to Renee like this. I had to do it. *(Sobbing.)*

Dr. Raymond: What did you have to do?

Corey: My baby! *(Sobbing.)*

Dr. Raymond: What baby?

Corey: Harley's.

Dr. Raymond: Who is Harley, Corey?

Corey: No, no, no, leave me alone! Leave me alone! I don't want to do this. Please, God, help me save my baby! Please don't take him away, Harley! Harley!

Dr. Raymond: Note: Patient is again bleeding in the lower extremities. Anne, please grab the medical kit and call Judy in to help.

Mrs. Delaney: Oh my God, this is worse than I thought. We have to help her.

Dr. Raymond: Corey, on the count of four, I want you to awaken rested and relaxed. One, two, three, four. Corey?

Corey: Oh, God, no!

Dr. Raymond: Judy and Anne will take you into my bathroom to get you cleaned up.

Corey: *(Sobbing.)* What is happening to me? Please make this stop. I don't know how much more I can take of this. What is happening to me?

Dr. Raymond: We need to talk about Harley. You have brought his name up on two occasions, and you have been reluctant to discuss your marriage, and perhaps there is a reason for it.

Corey: *(Sobbing.)* Dr. Raymond, I know your intent is well. But this is something that I have never been able to forgive myself for. It's very difficult to talk about.

Dr. Raymond: I understand. The best way to cope is by talking about them and learning from these events. We can do that, and I can provide you with some additional options for helping you deal with your emotional state.

Corey: I know that I have to deal with it sooner or later, just not with everything else going on. I am just overwhelmed with all of this. I need some time.

Dr. Raymond: Okay, well, why don't you tell me a little bit about Harley?

Corey: When I was married, I reconnected with a childhood friend. The friendship quickly turned romantic, but I felt as if I could not turn back. I had no intention of ever committing adultery. But I did, and I regret it terribly.

Dr. Raymond: So, why did you wait until now to tell me about Harley?

Corey: When I first came to you and you wanted me to have an exam, that was shortly after he beat me. He had found out where we had moved, and he broke into my home. We were nearly killed by a train that day. But it was a year earlier, on our second get-together for coffee, that he raped me. I found out I was pregnant three weeks later. I was afraid that everyone would find out. I was ashamed of what he did to me, and I was scared to go to the authorities. I again hid it from everyone. I hid a lot of things. I was hoping that I could forget about him because the relationship had been over. I just wanted to forget about it. It was also quite confusing too because when I wasn't getting beaten by him, I was being beaten by something that I could not see.

Dr. Raymond: So, you believed it would have been difficult to file charges on someone when some of the beatings were from something else.

Corey: Yes, and it made things much, much worse. This is still very difficult for me to talk about. I have tried so hard to forget about the past, but the past is what keeps coming back, and I know I need to talk about it all or I may never understand why I did the things I did.

Mrs. Delaney: You understand now that those who you are close to experienced negative things as well?

Corey: Yes, I know, and yes, he did too.

Dr. Raymond: Meaning Harley?

Corey: Yes. I have seen what is to become of him. Part of me wants to warn him, and the other part of me says let him suffer. I know it's not the right thing to do.

Dr. Raymond: Please tell me the story of when you first met him.

Corey: It was the summer of 2007. I sat waiting to drop the kids off at daycare when I noticed him. I had grown up with him as a child. I circled around the block a few times before I gathered enough courage to approach him. I debated on whether or not to even say hello, but something in me said that I should.

I hadn't seen him in twenty years, and once I got the courage to step out of the car, it was like we hadn't skipped a beat. He stood about six feet tall, with a muscular build and full of confidence. I felt a sense of déjà vu when I walked up to him to speak. He was holding a clipboard and continuously flicking a pen on it—almost in an irritating manner that was annoying to me at first.

Mrs. Delaney: That is interesting! Déjà vu! If you recall, in your dream of the woman giving birth in the woods, there was a gentleman there with a clipboard and clicking a pen. If you remember, you mentioned it again while under hypnosis, describing the doctor that took Lulu's ledgers.

Corey: I know. That's why I need to tell you everything. I think Harley had something do to with some of the negative things in my life.

Dr. Raymond: So this is the first of you telling this to anyone?

Corey: Yes.

Dr. Raymond: Why did you not tell us about Harley sooner?

Corey: I just wanted to forget about him. I was afraid that if my family found out, they would look at me differently. I was afraid that they would disown me. I felt guilty because I chose to go out with him. It was me that made that choice to reconnect with him. I felt guilty I was leaving my husband at home. Something had drawn me to Harley. And after the rape, I was afraid he would tell everyone. I didn't want to hurt Renee or my children.

Dr. Raymond: Did you consider the consequences of meeting with him?

Corey: No. I mean, I had no idea he was planning on doing this to me. It just happened so quickly.

Dr. Raymond: Did you lead Harley on, perhaps in thinking that you were there for other than just coffee?

Corey: I don't know. I mean, he flirted but never did anything physical until that night.

Mrs. Delaney: Corey, I know this is difficult to talk about. You continued to stay with him for a reason. Do you want to tell us why you continued a relationship with him?

Corey: He said he would tell Renee if I left him. I knew if Renee found out, he would never forgive me, and I didn't want him to get hurt. And then when I found out that the pregnancy was the result of the rape, well, that would not sit well while Renee and I were going through marriage counseling. What would everyone think, knowing that I was pregnant by someone other than my husband? My husband wasn't able to have any more children. I was afraid that I would lose my family.

Dr. Raymond: Either way, it was Renee that got hurt though. You eventually left him to start a life with Harley. Did you feel that justified getting a divorce?

Corey: I felt as though Renee would never forgive me, nor would I ever forget about being raped. The child would be a constant reminder of the incident if I reconciled with Renee. So, I chose to stay with Harley because I was confused. He told me that if I left my husband, he would take care of everything. Foolishly, I believed him, and I packed some belongings and took a trip to get away from it all with him the following weekend.

He planned a trip to Kansas City and scheduled an appointment with a physician. I had no idea he made the arrangements to abort the child until he brought me there. I was in shock for him even wanting to abort the child. But I was afraid, and I was confused about what would happen to me if I didn't. I knew that he would leave me there if I didn't go through with it. I thought I could go back to Renee, but Harley threatened to tell Renee about the pregnancy if I did. Harley said he wouldn't tell anyone as long as I stayed with him.

To this day, I feel it was never my decision to leave; it was someone else's. Harley told me that Renee would never take me back and that if he knew of the baby, it would make things even worse.

Dr. Raymond: So, despite Harley raping you and making you abort your child, it was easier to move on with him than to be truthful with yourself on what was the right thing to do?

Corey: So I thought. I wanted to forget about the rape. I mean, Renee was my soul mate. I still loved him with all of my heart. But I messed up. There was no going back. No fixing it. I didn't want him to look at me any differently or his family. I didn't want to hurt him any more than I already had. I was afraid that he wouldn't love me anymore because I became a victim. I didn't want my family to think that I had it coming because I went out with Harley. But Harley encouraged me to leave him. I thought it would be easier to just start all over.

Dr. Raymond: How did your family feel about this?

Corey: Disappointed as usual. They were not supportive. They knew I was doing the wrong thing. I didn't listen. I didn't listen to anyone. My families disowned me and were not able to find a reason to accept Harley. He was right about one thing. He was the only one that was there to help me. Still, after what he put me through, I don't know why I stayed. The abortion should have opened my eyes.

I just wanted to move on and forget about everything, but Harley was always there trying to justify me staying with him. He said I had no one to turn to. He was right in that aspect. I had enough going on in my life, and I didn't want any more confusion. Yet I still felt lost. After the rape, I felt as though I had no choice but to stay with him.

Mrs. Delaney: While you were living with Harley, he experienced some things too, I imagine.

Corey: Yes.

Dr. Raymond: Tell me about your first experience with Harley. How did he take what was going on in your life?

Corey: While we were living in our first rental, I remember one evening seeing the shadows. I tried to explain my terrors to Harley, but he brushed them off as being stressed from the separation from my husband. He never accepted or wanted to believe anything we experienced while in the houses. Soon, he would believe though, and that's when he began to change himself. That's when we had to leave.

I began having the terrible nightmare about the garage and everything fading to black. It was almost immediately after I moved out of Renee's house. I was pulling my car into the garage at Harley's house, and as I shut the car off the garage door began to close. I saw a shadow come from behind the car. It was a tall figure, dark and massive. Its arm was extended. I turned to see what it was, and I heard a loud noise. Then everything went black.

Mrs. Delaney: Do you know why its arm was extended?

Corey: It was holding something. Something small, but it made a noise, almost ear-piercing. Everything went black after that, and I woke up shaking.

Mrs. Delaney: So what did Harley say about the nightmares?

Corey: He made me take the medications my doctor prescribed.

Mrs. Delaney: Did you take the medication as he requested?

Corey: For a while I did, yes. He encouraged me to keep quiet about any weird experiences or dreams. He told me I had to be distant from the family or they would have me locked up. He told me he would protect me and my kids, but if I left him, he would hurt Renee, and he would tell everyone that I was crazy.

Mrs. Delaney: So what happened that you became estranged from him?

Corey: Well, he changed. I mean, he was the total opposite of when I met him. Even after the rape. He was not religious by any means. He believed in God, but he never did things from the heart. He was wicked! He never cared for anything but himself. He could never forgive, and he never forgot things with people. He had issues with bringing things up from the past. He continued to bring up the abortion and how he would never allow his previous wife to have one. I didn't understand why he was saying such hateful things when he was the one who demanded I have one.

After about six months went by, things started to get really ugly. One night we were lying in bed when I received a phone call from a local paranormal group from St. Louis. It was out of the ordinary, but I listened on the line to what they had to say. They stated they were doing a story about my research and were anxious to meet me about the travels. I saw no harm in meeting with them the following week.

Her name was Carol, and her assistant was named Susan. Carol would be the one asking all of the questions as to what drew me to the research and the discovery of the area cemetery. When they arrived, they had tape recorders and went right into the interview. Knowing Harley was not a believer in the spirit world, I set up the meeting during his trip away from the house for work. When the group sat down, the lights began to flicker in the house, and they questioned it.

We talked for some time about the poor farm, but during the

interview, Carol became frustrated. She looked as though someone or something was distracting her from my answers. At first I thought it was my response to her questions. I thought perhaps my answers were not what she was expecting. I inquired when she appeared to be so frustrated that she blurted out, "Go ahead." Just then, the lights flickered, and the television came on. I sat there in awe.

Mrs. Delaney: So things were going on in your house, and she was a witness to these events?

Corey: Yes, but I didn't really take it all seriously at first. I didn't know much about the group. I thought they were just there to interview me for the paper.

Mrs. Delaney: Did she give you any information about what they did or how she could help you?

Corey: I never asked, and they never offered. Remember, I was terrified of what was to come out in all of this.

Mrs. Delaney: But she sensed things with you. Why did you wait so long to get help?

Corey: You still don't get it! I was afraid. I have always been afraid. You don't understand. In the beginning when this all started as a kid, I thought it was normal. The older I got, the more in tune it was, and I became frightened. Do you have any idea how hard it was to hide this from your family and still be considered a freak?

Mrs. Delaney: Yes, as a matter of fact, I do. I spent my childhood being bullied by classmates because of the visions I saw. I know exactly how you felt. Please tell me what else happened during their visit.

Corey: She told me that I was a sensitive. She knew how I solved the mysteries too. She explained that when I suffered from anxiety attacks when I was a young adult, it was my guides' way of communicating with me. She repeated everything that the lady in Gettysburg told me.

Just then, I broke down sobbing. I explained what I had experienced, how I had been raped by the man I was living with, how my married life ended terribly, how the premonitions began to affect my life, and how I invited it all in! I gave in. I told my whole story to complete strangers.

By the end of the conversation, I was not only in awe but anxious to learn more and why my life had changed so dramatically when everything was perfect for so long. But I never did. Things got worse, and I thought I had no control over my life anymore. Decisions were being made for me. I became weak, and then all hell came crashing down on me.

Mrs. Delaney: Most people, because of what they are taught in church, do not believe there are spirits among us that can do harm. I believe that Harley was subjected to one of those entities that harms you still today. When you have the gift, you attract good and evil. The good guide you to be the best person God wants you to be. In your case, your purpose is to help lost souls. The evil will force you to do things in your everyday life to occupy your time so you can't help the lost souls. It is up to your guides to help get you back on your life path. You were being tested. You lost your faith by temptations during this time. Do you understand what I am saying, Corey?

Corey: I guess so. I know now that whatever it was that was messing with Harley was there to keep me from writing the book. Harley was there to keep me from working things out with Renee. He kept me from a lot of things including the research and publishing of the book. But now that it's done, why are things still happening to me and those around me?

Mrs. Delaney: You're not done! In fact, you'll write another book telling this story to others. And I believe writing your history book was the beginning of their story. Something is still not being told about their lives. Something is yet to be discovered or resolved. You need to find out what that is, or you may never have peace. Because you opened a portal, the resolution may come from the poor farm itself, or the portals in Gettysburg, or even your previous home.

Corey: What else could there be? The records were discarded a long time ago. I don't even know what I need to look for, let alone look for portals. I mean, I have no clue what to do next.

Mrs. Delaney: First, listen to your guides or your intuitive thoughts. There has to be something else you need to expose on the poor farm.

Corey: I have done all that I can to find records, but there is nothing else I can do.

Mrs. Delaney: There is something still out there. You need to find it. Trust me. This thing has attached itself to you, and it wants something from you. You need to find out what it wants. And as long as the portal is open, more negative things will come through.

Corey: So you think this stuff will continue until then?

Mrs. Delaney: Yes, I do. Corey, did you know that Harley meant you harm from the beginning?

Corey: No. I had no idea. It was about that time that he began to become more aggressive though. So, I found myself trying to save money to move out.

Mrs. Delaney: My question is how Harley became influenced by an entity. Corey, did Harley ever go to the cemetery with you?

Corey: No. He would not allow me to work on the farm. I wanted to, but each time I told him my plans, he told me I was wasting my time and then would become violent with me. That is when he began to drink heavily too.

Mrs. Delaney: Did you continue to see the mist while you lived with him?

Corey: Yes but when he wasn't there. So, first I would have to deal with his abuse, and when he wasn't home, the abuse from an entity that I could not see. It was like living in a battlefield, and I had nowhere to hide from the knives being thrown at me. When I tried to talk to him about it, he ridiculed me for seeing or hearing things. He refused to believe me.

Dr. Raymond: Why didn't you just leave him and go to your family or a shelter for help?

Corey: Are you kidding me? My family disowned me. Remember? There was no way I was going to raise my kids in a shelter. I had to plan things out. I had to prepare. I had to hide everything that I did from him.

Dr. Raymond: Did your children witness his aggressive behavior?

Corey: His aggressiveness, yes. They witnessed him throwing me down stairs, swinging his arms in my face, and the verbal abuse. He was abusive to them as well—physically, mentally, and verbally, every single day. Sometimes the verbal abuse seemed to be worse than the actual beatings.

Mrs. Delaney: Tell me about what he experienced while you were with him.

Corey: Well, the night that Carol came to the house was his eye-opener. I told him some reporters came to interview me. I also told him that one of them was a medium and she expressed that I had guides following me while during my research. I told him of our conversation, and he ridiculed me for being so naïve in believing in spirits and mediums. He laughed at me and poked fun of me and my research. I felt belittled with his words. "You are nothing special. You're a piece of shit, and if it weren't for me, you would have nowhere to live, and your kids would have nothing to eat. You are worthless to society, and you should give up on that book you have been writing. You are never going to amount to anything, Corey. I am all you have. Stop this bullshit and come back to reality. There is no such thing as spirits guides or whoever she said guides you around town, telling you what to solve. This is bullshit, and I can't believe how naïve you are to believe them. When you die, you die. End of story." Negative basically.

Mrs. Delaney: So, what happened to Harley during this time?

Corey: It really started that evening when he went to bed. That night, when I lay in bed, I prayed that Harley would be made a believer by them.

Mrs. Delaney: Them, who? The poor farm people?

Corey: Yes. So, when Harley climbed into bed, I anticipated something happening. I welcomed it, and I invited it in! The kids were fast asleep down the hall. They slept in the older part of the house. In order to get to the kids, you had to walk through one bedroom, down four steps, across the foyer, and up four steps into their rooms. The steps going up to their rooms were clearly visible from our bedroom doorway.

During the middle of the night, we heard banging on our bedroom door. Three solid knocks. He asked who it was, but no one answered. The knocks continued. Three at a time. Still no one answered us. Nothing. We fell back to sleep only to be woken by three more knocks at the door. Harley again questioned who was knocking at the door. Still no answer, just three solid knocks, and they were getting louder. I then asked who was at the door. No response.

Harley jokingly looked at me and suggested it was my ghost friend. I sighed in frustration that he would even make a joke about it. Just then, there were three more very loud knocks at the door. Harley jumped out of bed, swung open the doors, and just stood there. He gradually backed up from the door, and his face turned white as a ghost.

Mrs. Delaney: *(Chuckling.)* I can imagine the look on his face. It must have been priceless.

Corey: It was actually frightening! I mean, I was afraid for my kids, but Harley, well, it was rather nice seeing him scared with no rationalization for the knocking.

Mrs. Delaney: Well, because you are a sensitive, there is a possibility that you opened more than just two portals. You may have opened several. Ms. Michaels, you are going to keep me very busy!

Corey: Is it that bad? I mean, do I really have the capability to open portals?

Mrs. Delaney: Within time, we are going to test your abilities as a sensitive to see what you are capable of. Before we get off the subject, tell me what happened next with Harley.

Corey: Harley backed up from the doorway, shocked. He looked over at me and then flew back into the wall against the dresser. Someone or something was lifting him off of the floor, and his head was touching the ceiling. Harley, a 180-pound, six-foot-two hunk of muscle, was no match for whatever was holding him up. I never saw Harley so frightened before. He had always shown an aggressive

"I'm on top of things" kind of attitude, and no one or nothing could harm him.

Harley grabbed for his neck to grab hold of whatever it was that was holding him up. But there was nothing there. I sprang from the bed and went to help him, but I was thrown back myself onto the bed.

Harley struggled to be released, but something held on to him long enough for him to wet himself. When he fell to the floor, grasping his neck, he blamed me for causing him to pee himself. Somehow, it was my entire fault. Although I was frightened, I still managed to laugh inside.

Dr. Raymond: So, you felt no anger toward the entity restraining Harley?

Corey: No. The damage he had caused to me and my kids was unforgiveable. I was too weak to defend us, but something else in the room was strong enough to step in when I could not defend my family. From that night on, Harley would never sleep in the bedroom. He found solace in drinking himself to sleep on the couch downstairs, and I was fine with that too. I felt a little uneasy, however, because the night terrors continued, and I felt vulnerable when I slept alone. I always slept with a night-light and the television on so I could see what was in the room. To this day, I follow the same routine.

Dr. Raymond: So, how was your relationship with your parents? Were you able to retreat to their house?

Corey: No, my relationship was nonexistent with the family during this time. All I had was my children. No one else. We were forced to stay with Harley until I could save up enough money to move out.

Dr. Raymond: How was his behavior during the time he removed himself from the bedroom?

Corey: He continued to ridicule me and my kids on a day-to-day basis. So, instead of going home after school and work, I always made arrangements for us to be out of the house until he passed out. Then, when he would become aggressive, we would pack our things and stay the night at a hotel until he sobered up. When he did, he would apologize and promise never to do it again, but he did. Every time, it got worse. We had nowhere to go and no one to turn to. My family didn't answer my phone calls or letters asking for help. Renee and his family were looking for reasons to take the kids away from me, and all I had was my research to keep me from going insane. My life was in a downward spiral, and I prayed to get it back one day.

Mrs. Delaney: So how did your interview end with Carol and her group?

Corey: It ended with a warning. She said that I needed help with channeling the dead. She told me that it was only the beginning. She explained that the dead are drawn to me because I am a sensitive and compassionate about my work. It's true; I enjoy researching histories of the people that once lived on the poor farm.

Dr. Raymond: We all have moments in our lives that we are ashamed of. I would like to suggest that you attend a support group for those that have also been sexually assaulted. Now, I know there is a lot going on right now, but within time, I would encourage you to look into getting some further support. Okay?

Corey: I have a feeling I am going to be your patient for longer than we both anticipated.

Dr. Raymond: It's okay, Corey. You can take all the time you need. You do have to quit blaming yourself for things that you had no control over. This Harley sounds like a bully. You will find much-needed support from the group. I hope to see you in it. We meet on Friday evenings at the hospital at seven o'clock. I am sorry our time is up. Corey, I want to see you again next week to continue our conversation. Is that all right with you?

Corey: Yes, that's fine. I would like to think about that support group if you don't mind. I have a lot on my plate, as you can see. But I will let you know when I am ready.

Dr. Raymond: Corey, I know this session was an eye-opener for you. I know how hard it must be to try to accept things that occurred that are hurtful, but you shouldn't try so hard to forget them. Therapy will make you stronger and help you accept and understand the tribulations in your life. I want you to know that we are here whenever you need us. Okay?

Corey: Thank you. Thank you both for talking with me. I feel a lot better having talked about it with someone.

Dr. Raymond: Okay. I would like to see you in a few days, okay?

Corey: Yes, I'll see Judy on my way out. Thank you.

March 17, 2010, Therapy Session

Dr. Raymond: Corey Michaels, March 17, 2010. Good afternoon, Corey. Good afternoon, Anne.

Corey: Hello, Dr. Raymond.

Mrs. Delaney: Hello. How was your week?

Corey: It was okay.

Dr. Raymond: Let's begin with a regression session. Is that ok?

Corey: Sure. I'm ready.

Dr. Raymond: Ok, I would like to jump right in where we left off last week. Why don't you lay back on the couch? Put your feet up and listen to my voice. Close your eyes. Take some deep breaths in and out. In and out. Deep breaths in and out. Your eyes are getting heavier and heavier. Falling deeper and deeper into sleep. Relaxing every muscle from your head to your feet. Deeper and deeper relaxing. Breathing in and out, relaxing further with every exhale. Further and further, deeper and deeper, slowly relaxing every muscle. At the count of three, you will be completely relaxed. One, two, three. Corey, can you hear me?

Corey: Yes.

Dr. Raymond: I want you to go back to 2006. Back when you were married to Renee. Can you do that?

Corey: Yes.

Dr. Raymond: Can you tell me where you are?

Corey: I'm at home. I'm eating dinner and talking about my research.

Dr. Raymond: The poor farm research?

Corey: Yes.

Dr. Raymond: What was it like the first time you visited the cemetery grounds?

Corey: Peaceful.

Dr. Raymond: How does your family feel about your research?

Corey: I don't know. When I talk about it, I don't even think they are listening.

Dr. Raymond: Did your husband listen?

Corey: Yes. He helped me. He was very supportive.

Dr. Raymond: You were with Renee for a long time. Did anything negative ever happen to him while you were with him that you can recall?

Corey: No.

Dr. Raymond: You were married to him for a long time. Surely, there must have been something. For all of these things to happen to you over the years, not once was he the source of this negativity?

Corey: I don't know. I want to forget. I want to forget all of them. They will be safe if I forget them.

Dr. Raymond: Corey, no one can hurt you or anyone you are associated with here. You have to trust me. Was Renee ever a source of the negativity?

Corey: Yes! But he didn't know. He still doesn't know.

Mrs. Delaney: Why do you say that?

Corey: He has an addiction.

Dr. Raymond: What kind of an addiction?

Corey: He likes to drink.

Dr. Raymond: Has he been doing this long?

Corey: Yes, well, no. Never this bad.

Dr. Raymond: Did you try to get him help?

Corey: Yes, but he didn't think he had a problem. He still doesn't think it's a problem. He doesn't know what's coming for him.

Mrs. Delaney: What do you mean?

Corey: I see him swerving off the road. He has my children with him. The car is cut in half. They won't survive the crash.

Dr. Raymond: This is the dream you continue to have?

Corey: *(Sobbing.)* Yes! He has to stop, but he won't let me help him. He does not trust me anymore. He must listen to me. He has to listen before something terrible happens that neither one of us can repair.

Dr. Raymond: Take a deep breath in and out. In and out. Okay. Corey, what other things happened while you were with Renee?

Corey: Little things happened over the years that Renee would always pass off as a coincidence.

Mrs. Delaney: What kind of little things?

Corey: He knew of my journal, and he witnessed some of the premonitions as they occurred.

Mrs. Delaney: Tell us about the little things.

Corey: I knew something had to change after the vacation. It was a warning.

Mrs. Delaney: What vacation?

Corey: We had planned our family trip to the East Coast. We were all excited about going, but nothing went right the whole time we were there.

Dr. Raymond: What do you mean?

Corey: Renee was injured when one of our tires blew out. He burnt his arm really bad, and my daughter nearly drowned while swimming in the pool. That was just a few things but big ones that told me I needed to leave in order to save them.

Dr. Raymond: But you never left your children, just Renee?

Corey: Yes, but I couldn't stay with him without jeopardizing their well-being. My children would always be protected by others.

Mrs. Delaney: Others?

Corey: George and the children.

Dr. Raymond: George and what children?

Corey: The children of the poor farm. They protect them. They have always protected them.

Dr. Raymond: How do you know this?

Corey: George told me.

Dr. Raymond: When did George tell you this?

Corey: A long time ago. He told me that he would always protect me and my children. But someday I would be tested. My happiness would be jeopardized to save them all. He told me not to be afraid.

Dr. Raymond: Did you always see or feel George in your life? Your dreams?

Corey: No. George goes away when I take medication for anxiety attacks.

Dr. Raymond: Corey, how long were you on medication for anxiety?

Corey: Three months maybe. I did not want to take medication.

Dr. Raymond: Did you find that you were having more nightmares or night terrors when you were on the medication?

Corey: I was on the medication the first time I had the experience with the mist. But I haven't taken them in years. And the nightmares have returned.

Dr. Raymond: Okay, let's shift the subject and talk about your research. In your book, you talk about the discovery of unmarked burials, separate from the poor farm. How did you know where and how to find them?

Corey: I would feel funny when I drove past certain sites. I felt different, as if I had been there before but in a different time. It was as if I had been drawn to these places just like the cemeteries. No one was supposed to find them again.

Mrs. Delaney: What did you just say?

Corey: No one was supposed to find them.

Mrs. Delaney: What did you mean by that?

Corey: They built a school, houses, parking lots, and town halls on top of them. They moved headstones but left the bodies. Not everyone was moved to the new cemeteries.

Mrs. Delaney: You are talking about other potters' fields?

Corey: Yes. They are everywhere. In every town.

Mrs. Delaney: Corey, do you have records to support this?

Corey: I have some documents and some photographs in my files. I could not put everything in the book that I found.

Dr. Raymond: Why could you only mention some and not others?

Corey: They wouldn't allow me to release the locations in the book. And I could not find evidence on all of the properties I visited.

Mrs. Delaney: Corey, who would not allow you to release the locations of the unmarked cemeteries?

Corey: County officials. They worried it would frighten citizens knowing that there were bodies under their homes.

Mrs. Delaney: So, you know of other sites with unmarked graves?

Corey: Yes.

Mrs. Delaney: Can you tell me where they are?

Corey: Yes.

Dr. Raymond: Where are they, Corey?

Corey: Along the canal, near Hickory Creek, near Oakwood, and near Squire's Mill. That's just in the city limits. There are more in unincorporated towns too.

Mrs. Delaney: How many people are we talking about that are buried in these unmarked graves?

Corey: Thousands. Hundreds of thousands.

Mrs. Delaney: Omg! Those poor lost souls. You mentioned that you have some records on these grave sites. Can you tell me where you have these records?

Corey: At home. I have a list of names of people buried.

Mrs. Delaney: You mentioned that you researched these areas for evidence.

Corey: Yes, but some of the property owners were not willing to listen to me.

Mrs. Delaney: So you approached property owners of these sites?

Corey: Yes. I walked up their sidewalks and knocked on their doors.

Mrs. Delaney: You mean these are residential homes on these gravesites?

Corey: Yes.

Dr. Raymond: Okay, at the count of three, you will awaken fully. One, two, three. Corey, are you awake?

Corey: Yes.

Mrs. Delaney: How do you feel?

Corey: Okay, I guess. A bit tired. But pretty good.

Dr. Raymond: Our session will be short today, but we can pick up again this Friday. I would like to look into a few things to help with your therapy. Can you make it here by four?

Corey: I have a meeting with the museum that night.

Dr. Raymond: How about on Monday then?

Corey: Okay. I'll be here at four?

Dr. Raymond: Yes, four o'clock. See you then, Corey.

Corey: Okay. Goodbye, Dr. Raymond. Goodbye, Anne.

Mrs. Delaney: Corey, before you go, I would like you to join me at one of my spiritual groups. Would you be able to attend it this evening? There is much you need to learn about your gift, and until you know your capabilities, you will continue to be a source of attacks. I think it would be a good idea for you to come and meet some of the others that share your gift.

Corey: Sure. I don't get my kids back until Wednesday morning. Is this some sort of a séance or something?

Mrs. Delaney: No. It's a spiritual class on meditation and channeling. I really think it's time you start learning your gift. Here is my address. The class starts at seven.

Corey: Okay. I will be there.

March 17, 2010, Journal Entry

I am not sure if I am ready to open up my life to a bunch of strangers. I know that Anne wanted me to go to the class this evening, but I just couldn't find the courage to attend. This is still very overwhelming for me.

I came home from seeing Dr. Raymond and Anne to an empty house. It will be a productive few days, working on putting things in order at the house. I know I am alone, but I don't feel alone. I know something is in the house. I can feel it.

I prepared a nice dinner for one this evening—my favorite, homemade spaghetti with cheesy garlic bread. I sat at the table eating when I heard what appeared to be pacing upstairs in the attic. Surely it must be an animal, probably a squirrel that managed to find his way into the broken windowpane that was on my to-do list this weekend. But then something ran from the living room under the dining table where I sat. Still chewing my last bite, my heart skipped a beat as my plate and glass began to vibrate so violently until they came crashing down on the floor. A small piece of glass managed to bounce off of the floor and cut into my leg. I felt the blood stream down onto my ankle, but I was motionless from fright as I remained still for whatever would make an entrance next.

Upstairs, I could hear the squeak of the attic door slowly begin to open and then suddenly slam shut. Then, one by one, beginning at the nearest door from the attic, the doors began to open then slam shut. Bam, bam, bam! I had a feeling it was not an intruder that I needed to be fearful of. Something was coming. That was for sure.

I sat patiently at the dining room table waiting for something to peek its head out from the stairwell. But the house was silent and still. The ringing in my ears reminded me of the damage to my eardrums from listening to Duran Duran a bit too loudly as an adolescent. And yet I could still hear and feel my heartbeat pounding in my chest as if it were amplified throughout the house.

When nothing happened, I quietly got up from my seat, careful not to step on the broken glass that was scattered across the floor. I crept around the doorway until I had a full view of the stairwell going up to the bedrooms. I grabbed my Bible from the bookshelf then I walked up the first set of stairs. I noticed that the door to my daughter's room was closed. I was always having to remind her to keep her door open so that Bear could sleep in her room during the day. She enjoyed the morning sunlight shining in her room through the windows. But it wasn't her who had shut it. I knew better.

I continued down the hall to my son's room; again, the door was shut. I passed the bathroom and my room, and again, all shut. Was I hearing things? The logic part of my brain wanted to rationalize that there was a reason for the doors slamming, but I just couldn't think of one. Perhaps Anne was right. Perhaps I needed to learn how to relax more and meditate and all that weird stuff.

I shrugged my shoulders and turned around to head back downstairs. Unexpectedly, my daughter's door slowly opened, followed by my son's, then mine, and finally the bathroom. I was in the middle of the hallway, between all the doorways. Something was coming for me. I heard the thumping of the stairs as I peered over the railing. It was Bear! Bear was back, and she was racing up the stairs toward me. Was she mad? Where did she come from? I pondered. She ran up to the second landing and stopped. She began to bark ferociously, and she snarled and lunged toward the ceiling. Out from the doorways came black mists in the shape of what appeared to be people. They appeared to know the house. They walked into the hallway toward me, but Bear didn't react to them. She was transfixed on the ceiling. Who were these people? I wondered. Two, three, and four at a time would come out of the bedrooms and walk down the hallway and then disappear. What did they want? I questioned.

I started to run for the stairwell. I could feel the hair on my neck stand up. A heaviness filled the hallway and Bear began to howl. I quickly grabbed for her collar, but she wouldn't budge. With my back to the stairwell, I tried to drag her behind me but she would not leave the hallway.

I slowly turned around, and there it was looking back at me at the landing on the stairs. That sinister smile and blackness filled the landing all around me. The mist was everywhere—in the hallway, the stairwell, and in my daughter's room. I was cornered. I tried to run down the stairs, but I stumbled to the ground. It took hold of my arms and carried me to the ceiling. My Bible fell down at my side and then slid across the foyer. My feet were dangling fifteen feet off of the ground. I knew I was in trouble, and when Bear tried to pull at my pant leg, the mist threw her against the wall. Bear lay there motionless.

I yelled and screamed at it to leave me alone. Then the beatings began. My face was slapped repeatedly, my legs spread apart and whipped with unseen hands. Blood streamed down my face as the entity pulled out chunks of my hair. The lights flickered, doors opened and closed, and the house seemed to come alive. I continued to hang from the ceiling as my body was being beaten. I lost consciousness soon after that.

It's two in the morning. I spent the last few hours in the emergency room getting my leg x-rayed and a brace put on. When I woke, I was lying in the foyer next to the phone. Bear was injured too. Bear received twenty-one stitches to the abdomen and suffered seven broken ribs.

I don't remember phoning Anne, but she summoned an ambulance. I had severe bruising on my legs, thighs, face, and arms, a concussion, and torn ligaments in my leg from when it got entangled in the stair rail on the way down.

My kids will surely question why I am wearing a leg brace when they return. I don't know what I am going to tell them. Mason has basketball practice at the high school tomorrow. I can't hide the brace, let alone all of the bruising. I am sure I will think of something. I usually do.

March 19, 2010, Journal Entry

Anne picked me up and drove me to her house today. I met several
people who claim to be sensitives to the spirit world. By the looks of
them, they look like normal people. Several claim to see spirits, a few
others claim they can hear them, and others claim they can touch
objects and tell you a history about it since creation. I feel as though
I have walked into a scene from *One Flew over the Coo Coo's Nest*.

I think Chrissie and Alessandra were the first to approach me.
Chrissie was an older woman in her sixties. She reminded me of an
old neighbor from my childhood. She wore her hair long and didn't
wear makeup. I guess she was more like a plain Jane, but she was
pretty smart. She talked of crystal healing, moon phases, and how
everything was relative to your zodiac sign. Chrissie used crystals to
help map out her life path. She showed me natural ways to heal the
body, mind, and spirit. Her approach with the elements was quite
peaceful. She was fearless, and I hoped that I would someday feel
that peace too.

Alessandra appeared to be a younger version of me. Twenty-one,
maybe twenty-two. She was a dainty brunette with a passion for life.
She was high spirited and reminded me of a superball that could
bounce up and down for hours. Yes, Alessandra was hyperactive for
sure, and by the looks of her premature crow's feet, she hadn't slept
much because of it. "I see dead people," she said. "I talk to them too."
Alessandra claimed to have been awoken when she was in a fatal
car accident when she was four. She lost both parents and an infant
brother to a drunk driver. Alessandra was the sole survivor outside
of the drunk driver that hit them.

But the one thing we all had in common was the dreams of the
dead. They all expressed how they began reading, seeing, and feeling
spirits in their lives, and they claimed it started with their dreams.

All of them claimed to have had premonitions at a young age.
Most of them even sought physicians. All of them were eventually

medicated with psychotropic drugs, and all admitted to being tormented or visited by evil spirits. This was my story too.

I listened to their stories one after another, as their awakenings were similar to mine. Each had had traumatic experiences that lead to suppressing their memories. One by one, they told me their stories, and each ended with needing the help of Anne and Dr. Raymond.

March 20, 2010, Journal Entry

Another book review hit the press today, and I was swamped with phone calls for book signings and lectures. I am enjoying the enthusiasm the public shares about the research. But I dread the repercussions when I discuss an individual's story. I still dream of them. I am still afraid of how to respond to them. I can see them in their death state or what they looked like when they passed in my dreams. It's hard to look sometimes as the glimpse of someone coming through appears. I am still learning how to handle it all at once. It's all still quite frightening and strange to me. I feel it is still a curse, for I did not wish for this to happen to me.

March 21, 2010, Journal Entry

I was awakened this morning by the sound of pacing footsteps outside my bedroom door. I yelled at them to stop. I wanted to sleep, but apparently they had other plans for me today. I could hear children crying out for their mothers, men groaning in pain from injuries in battle. I hated the feeling, but I knew I had to help them. I just didn't know how to help them all. I had to prepare for the lecture tonight, and the constant pacing and sobbing left me sleepless and unable to focus.

I learned that I glorify them by sharing their life stories. In a sense, I feed them energy when I speak of them to others as if I were speaking of a loved one that I once held dear to my heart. Good stories, bad stories, it doesn't matter to the audience. It matters to me to express the injustice of how we took care of them. Someone needs to tell the community that there may be gravestones under their back porch or under their swing sets. How much further do I push to preserve the cemetery grounds? How much more energy can I spare to protect it? I can't lose my creditability as a researcher. If people find out about what is happening to me, how do I explain it to the public? This is my life, but who is ever going to take my story seriously? Harley was right. I am nothing special. What I am is different.

March 22, 2010, Journal Entry

I headed to the grocery store after work today and experienced something I cannot quite explain. Nothing like this has ever happened before. When I was approaching the checkout, I heard someone call my name. As I looked around to see who was calling for me, I saw no one. I proceeded to place my items on the conveyor belt, and again, my name was called. I looked around—and nothing. Then I heard a whisper in my right ear. "Save him. Don't let him die this way." I quickly spun around to see who was playing a joke on me, but there was no one there. "Save him. Don't let my Theodore die." *Theodore?* I wondered. *Who is Theodore?* Just then, I fell against the cart. It was another premonition of a young man riding a motorcycle. He was in a hurry to get home, and he forgot to put his helmet on. When he was exiting the parking lot, he turned the corner too sharp and lost control of the motorcycle. He hit a fire hydrant and was thrown from the bike about ten feet. He landed on the sidewalk headfirst. There was nothing anyone could do to save him.

When I came to, the clerk and the bagger were fanning my face and asking if I needed an ambulance. I told them that I was fine and inquired if there was a Theodore working in the store. The clerk looked puzzled but stated that there was a stocker in the back room who was named Teddy. "Yeah, that would be him," I said. I asked the clerk to call him to the front. When Teddy arrived at the customer service desk, I asked him if he rode a motorcycle. He stated that he did and that he had just gotten his driver's license. "It's Aunt Jennie," I heard.

I asked Teddy who Aunt Jennie was, and he replied, "That's my aunt. Did you know her?" I responded by noting that he spoke of her in the past tense. He informed me that she had passed away recently. I explained to him that I did not know her, but I needed to tell him that I received a warning from her. Teddy and the clerk looked rather puzzled, and I felt as if I were the center of the freak show. I told Teddy to wear his helmet no matter how late he was going to be getting home. I warned him to drive slowly and to make sure he always wore his helmet no matter what. Jennie was continuing to put visions in my head of Teddy on a ventilator, practically brain-dead from a motorcycle accident. It was more graphic than I could express to him. I did not want to scare him, and I was so shaken up by it all I did not know how to express it. So, instead of sticking around with an ever-growing audience, I quickly abandoned my groceries and ran out the door.

Teddy came running out of the store, yelling for me to talk to him. I continued to walk toward my car. I did not want to do this any longer. This is a small town, and people will begin to talk. I don't need this right now.

Teddy stopped me as I was putting the key in my door. He pleaded with me as to how I knew the things I knew. I explained that I didn't know what just happened and that I was sorry for his loss. He was persistent and wanted to know if his aunt Jennie was trying to speak to him. Jennie forced her way into the conversation by relaying messages through me. Jennie told me that Teddy was a troubled youth, and he was searching for something that his parents could not provide at this moment in his life. She told me to tell him that what he was doing was wrong and that he needed to stop it at once. He then got defensive and inquired as to what I knew. I was beginning to feel his aggressiveness, and I became frightened by his facial expressions.

Jennie continued to show me visions of Teddy's reckless behaviors—heroin use and stealing money from the grocery store to support his habit. Teddy slowly walked backward toward the store, then quickly turned around and ran inside. I quickly got in my vehicle and headed home but not before I saw the headlines in the newspaper stand that was next to my parked car: "Two almost perish in Tanner City freak fire."

March 24, 2010, Therapy Session

Dr. Raymond: Corey Michaels, March 24. Good afternoon, Corey. How are you doing this morning?

Corey: Really? You know how I am doing. You saw the papers! They almost died in there. I told you this would happen. I told you!

Dr. Raymond: Corey, I am sure there is a logical explanation for what transpired. The incident is under investigation by authorities.

Corey: Where's Anne? Why isn't she here?

Dr. Raymond: Mrs. Delaney will be here shortly.

Corey: I need to talk to Anne.

Dr. Raymond: Anne is on her way here. I would like you to take some deep breaths in and out.

Corey: No, I want to speak with Anne.

Mrs. Delaney: Sorry I am late. There was some traffic in Tanner City. Corey, are you all right?

Corey: No! Did you read the papers? It happened. Just like I said it would.

Mrs. Delaney: Yes, I read them. I know how you must feel. Let's talk about this.

Corey: Anne, I should have warned them. They could have died in that house! I know that if I told them what I saw, they would have thought I was nuts. And if I warned them and then nothing happened? Either way, they would take my kids away.

Anne: I understand, Corey. I do. Do not second-guess yourself. You must believe that these premonitions are a gift to help others. And if you can help others by warning them of bad things, then you must find peace that you helped avoid the negativity when it does not happen. But only other believers will take stock in what you tell them. You have to have faith in yourself and your guides that are helping you.

Dr. Raymond: Corey, at our last session, several things came to light. I want to talk about that for a bit. When I read your diaries, I discovered something quite interesting, and we didn't get a chance to discuss it previously. On several occasions, you describe the small child falling from a bridge and drowning in the river below.

Corey: Yes, I remember. I have it often still. But I was never able to find out who it pertained to. It was just a random dream that made no sense.

Dr. Raymond: What I found was quite interesting. All of the entries in your diaries indicate situations when a life was jeopardized. Usually it involved those that were close to you. However, the dream of the little girl was different. You didn't know how she was connected to you, and so you continued to dream about her over and over again. What I discovered was really remarkable. Shortly after the first mention of premonitions in your diaries, you would later validate it with actual newspaper articles or notations on the occurrences. I was able to verify several on my own. Corey, the young girl you dreamt about was a real person. Her name was Ingrid, Ingrid Cooper, and she was born in Germany. She died on her ninth birthday while she was with her mother and brother. They had been sitting on the edge of a bridge when Ingrid lost her balance and fell. She broke her neck from the fall. The newspaper reported that she died from drowning. It also mentioned something else.

Corey: So, I am not just creating this character in my dreams or regressions? This really happened? What did the article say?

Dr. Raymond: Here, the article stated that Ingrid had an older brother names Charles. Your Charles Cooper was the brother of Ingrid.

Corey: Are you kidding me? Let me see that.

Mrs. Delaney: Corey, we believe that you have lived past lives. One as Ingrid, Charles's sister, and another as Lulu, Charles's daughter. Somewhere there is a connection to George as well. We are going to find out, and when we do, perhaps it will help shed some light on what this is all about.

Dr. Raymond: We will both be asking you questions pertaining to several events that have occurred in today's session. Some may be hard to comprehend. When it is all done, we can discuss options. Okay?

Mrs. Delaney: This is not an easy process. Do you understand?

Corey: Options? What options? I can't believe this. How is this even possible? There has to be a connection somewhere though. I mean, Ingrid and Charles were related. Charles worked at my poor farm. Then Lulu worked there too, but what about George? Where does he fit into all of this?

Mrs. Delaney: It is evident that you have a spirit guide. The first thing we want to do is put you under and ask you a series of trigger questions. You must believe in God and a higher purpose in your life. You must trust in him. You were given a gift to help the lost. The spirit world knows your good qualities, which is why they are drawn to you for help, but there are also very, very bad ones that don't want you to craft your gift. You need to be firm in your heart and strong-willed, or havoc will continue to come to you and your family. You are dealing with lost souls that have reason to meddle in your life. You hold keys to unlock many unanswered questions. Those keys when turned will set their souls free so they can move on. But for some, it will deliver them to hell.

Until you know how to use your gift, when you step foot on a property or site that has had spiritual activity, the doors open. When I speak of doors, it means you originally opened that door with your craft. You create portals in these locations. You are an old soul, Corey, but you hide the true scale of your capabilities within. Your enemies already know this. It's important you develop your craft first before you meddle any more in your research. For everything that you uncover, discover, or unearth, if there are lost souls associated with the sites, they can attach themselves to you. Do you understand?

Corey: Yes, I understand.

Dr. Raymond: Okay, are you ready to begin?

Corey: Yes, I am.

Dr. Raymond: Okay, let's begin. I want you to close your eyes and relax. I want you to imagine you are lying in your bed with your husband on the night the terrors began. I want you to feel the heaviness in your eyes, counting back with me, ten, nine, eight, your body is getting relaxed, seven, six, five, your eyes are getting heavy, four, three, two, heavier still, and one. Are you relaxed?

Corey: I am.

Dr. Raymond: I want you to go back to when you were writing the book. When was that again?

Corey: Two thousand six.

Dr. Raymond: Okay, let's go back to the fall of 2006. Remember when you were discussing your research with your husband. Where were you?

Corey: I am lying in bed.

Dr. Raymond: What are you doing?

Corey: Talking to Renee about the cleanup crew coming that weekend to the farm.

Dr. Raymond: Is he aware of your night terrors?

Corey: Yes.

Dr. Raymond: What does he say about them?

Corey: Nothing. He thinks I just have bad dreams.

Dr. Raymond: Let's talk about the night when the terrors began.

Corey: I don't want to. I'm afraid.

Dr. Raymond: Why are you afraid?

Corey: I have no control. It will hurt me. It will hurt the others.

Dr. Raymond: What will hurt you? Does it have a name?

Corey: I don't know. It's like a thing. A short, dark, troll-looking thing. It's going to hurt me. It thinks I know something. It's trying to protect something.

Dr. Raymond: What is it that you know?

Corey: I don't know.

Dr. Raymond: Does this thing have a name?

Corey: I don't know.

Dr. Raymond: Think, Corey. What is its name?

Corey: I don't know.

Dr. Raymond: How does it communicate with you?

Corey: I can hear what it says through its thoughts.

Dr. Raymond: It must have a name. Tell me its name. Corey, it's okay. It can't hurt you. You are safe here.

Mrs. Delaney: No, wait! Don't speak its name! Don't say it! Don't tell me its name! Corey, do you understand me?

Corey: Yes, I understand, but I'm afraid. *(Sobbing.)*

Dr. Raymond: It's okay, Corey. There is no need to be afraid. I want you to relax. Imagine there is a long hallway and a door at the end of that hallway. I want you to walk towards it slowly. Noting that there are several doors on either side of you that hold memories of times you have had in your life. As you walk closer to the door at the end of the hallway, I want you to think about what it is behind the door. When you open the door, the year will be 1877. Can you tell me what you see when you open the door?

Corey: Yes.

Mrs. Delaney: Do you remember when you first opened the doors at the poor farm?

Corey: Yes. *(Sobbing.)*

Dr. Raymond: What do you remember?

Corey: The children. They were so innocent.

Dr. Raymond: How many are there?

Corey: Twenty-seven. They are all different ages.

Mrs. Delaney: What is it that you do on the poor farm?

Corey: I tend to the children.

Dr. Raymond: What year did you arrive at the farm?

Corey: Eighteen seventy-four.

Dr. Raymond: Eighteen seventy-four?

Corey: Yes.

Dr. Raymond: Can you tell me your name?

Corey: Lulu.

Dr. Raymond: Hello, Lulu. Do you remember working on the poor farm?

Corey: Yes.

Dr. Raymond: I am sorry, Lulu. Can you tell me what your father's name is?

Corey: Charles. My father is the caretaker.

Dr. Raymond: Can you tell me what the poor farm looks like?

Corey: It's dirty. Father has no clean water for us. They said the water is making everyone sick. I help out as I am able.

Dr. Raymond: How do you help out?

Corey: My brothers and I gather water from the spring and bring it back to the house. I wash clothes in the river by the Spurgeon farm.

Dr. Raymond: What are your brothers' names?

Corey: Charlie and Louis.

Dr. Raymond: How old are Charlie and Louis?

Corey: Ten and seven.

Dr. Raymond: Do they go to school with you?

Corey: No. Charlie has to help Father tend to the farm. He works with them in the fields, and he washes the horses for travel. He accompanies Father when a new charge comes to the farm. Louis must stay with Papa in Wisconsin in the winter months to help with his farm.

Dr. Raymond: I want you to fast-forward to the day when the officials came to clean house. Can you do that?

Corey: Yes. *(Sobbing.)*

Dr. Raymond: Lulu, do you know who took your journals?

Corey: I'm not supposed to talk about this.

Dr. Raymond: It's okay to talk about this now. That was a long time ago. Your journals, where are they now?

Corey: *(Sobbing.)* He took them. He took them when they took over.

Dr. Raymond: Why did he take them?

Corey: I can't talk about this anymore.

Dr. Raymond: Lulu, it's okay. No one will harm you. Why did someone take your journals?

Corey: He's the one responsible for all of this. He's responsible for the death of my family.

Mrs. Delaney: What do you mean he is responsible?

Corey: He was the farm's doctor, and they had the flu. I tried to take care of them. Disease was spreading. I couldn't help them. *(Sobbing.)*

Dr. Raymond: What happened to your family?

Corey: He took them.

Mrs. Delaney: Where did he take them?

Corey: Father said they were being taken to the hospital, but I know they were turning people away. They would not allow anyone else in the hospital. They were sending them all here.

Mrs. Delaney: How many of them did he take with him?

Corey: I don't know.

Mrs. Delaney: Why was he taking them from the poor farm?

Corey: He was our doctor. He was some special doctor that helped on the battlefields of the Civil War. We trusted him.

Mrs. Delaney: Then why did he take people from the poor farm if he had no connection to it?

Corey: He was in charge. He called it his house.

Mrs. Delaney: What do you mean his house?

Corey: The county supplied the farm with a doctor. They appointed him before we arrived on the farm. I found out he was a butcher in Pennsylvania prior to the Civil War.

Dr. Raymond: How did you find this out?

Corey: One of the charges said they saw him treating the wounded during the battle in Gettysburg. He was fearful of him.

Dr. Raymond: Did the charge tell you anything more about the doctor?

Corey: That he was evil for what he did in battle.

Dr. Raymond: What did he do while in battle?

Corey: He experimented on those that were wounded. He took several of the men to his home in Gettysburg. He held them there against their will and performed experiments on them. No one knew. No one knew what he was doing.

Dr. Raymond: Did you find any proof to back up his claim?

Corey: No. I never tried, but I could look into the eyes of those he tended to that were in battle, and they knew something, but they said nothing to anyone about it.

Dr. Raymond: The charges he took with him, did any of those people ever return to the farm?

Corey: No, no one ever came back. Father said they were going to another place to get better. That's all I know. But I know Father knew otherwise, and it frightened him to talk about it.

Mrs. Delaney: When the doctor took your ledgers, did he say anything to you? Do you know where he took the journals?

Corey: *(Sobbing.)* I don't know where or what he did with the journals.

Mrs. Delaney: What did he do to them, Lulu? It's okay. You can tell me.

Corey: *(Sobbing.)* He took them from the farm. Then some of us he took to the timbers by wagon. I thought we were going to the hospital. We ended up in the grove just past the Spurgeon farm. No one ever traveled there. Father was told it was used to confine the contagious. There was a small cabin back in the grove, but no one could see it from the road. No one was ever allowed to go there. Only the doctor.

Mrs. Delaney: What happened when you arrived there?

Corey: They had another wagon waiting there, and several of us got into it and left. As we left, I heard screaming coming from the road leading to the cabin in the woods. I couldn't see anyone, but the screams made us all uneasy.

Mrs. Delaney: What happened to the others? The other charges that got out?

Corey: (Sobbing.) The wagon was emptied, and the charges were escorted to walk to the edge of a slope. I lost sight of them when we drove around the bend.

Mrs. Delaney: Where did you go?

Corey: They escorted us to a farmhouse. They tied us up by our wrists and ankles then separated us from the children. I can still hear them crying out. They are so lonely! Oh, God, please save them. Save us all!

Mrs. Delaney: Someone tied you up?

Corey: Yes, he tortured us!

Mrs. Delaney: What happened once you were inside?

Corey: (Sobbing.) They forced us into the attic. They tied us up and told us not to scream. They told us that they would try to cure us. We pleaded with them to let us go and that we would never tell anyone. He told us we had to be separated from the rest of the poor farm so he could find a cure for the disease. If we tried to escape, he would cut out our tongues and punish us.

Mrs. Delaney: Lulu, what did they treat you with?

Corey: We were given injections by the doctor, but it sickened us all. It put me into labor.

Mrs. Delaney: How long were you subject to the injections?

Corey: I don't know. I don't know how long I was there. Two maybe three weeks.

Mrs. Delaney: Lulu, what happened to your baby?

Corey: *(Sobbing.)*

Mrs. Delaney: Lulu, can you tell me if you were still with child when you arrived at the farmhouse?

Corey: I'm not supposed to talk about it. They will hurt me!

Mrs. Delaney: It's okay, Corey. You can tell me. It's okay. Tell me what happened.

Corey: *(Sobbing.)* They took my baby! They took my baby!

Mrs. Delaney: What happened to your baby, Lulu?

Corey: I began to bleed. They came for me and took me to the cabin in the grove. There were others there waiting.

Mrs. Delaney: What happened in the grove?

Corey: They bound my legs and gave me another injection. It sped up my contractions. It hurts! It hurts so badly.

Mrs. Delaney: It's okay. Try to relax and tell me what happened when you got to the cabin.

Corey: The doctor is here and three others I saw on the farm.

Mrs. Delaney: What are they doing to you?

Corey: They won't let me have the baby. Oh, God, please don't let them kill my baby. Please, God, don't let them kill my baby! *(Sobbing.)* No, God, it hurts, it hurts!

Mrs. Delaney: Try to relax. It's okay.

Dr. Raymond: Note: Patient is beginning to bleed in lower extremities. We have to keep going. We cannot stop now.

Corey: *(Sobbing.)*

Mrs. Delaney: Can you tell me what happened to you and your baby?

Corey: He wouldn't let me deliver the baby. I tried to push, but the baby wouldn't come out. He bound my legs and arms so I could not move. He wouldn't let me. I tried to scream, but they covered my mouth. *(Sobbing.)* Please, God! No!

Dr. Raymond: Okay, I need you to relax and take some deep breaths. In and out, in and out. Okay, at the count of four, I want you to fast-forward to that first night with Renee when the night terrors began. One, two, three, and four. Do you remember having the night terrors?

Corey: Yes.

Dr. Raymond: Do you remember looking in the mirror?

Corey: Yes.

Dr. Raymond: Can you tell me what you saw in the reflection?

Corey: I'm afraid to look.

Dr. Raymond: It's okay to be fearful, but you are safe here and in your home.

Corey: No, I am not safe anymore.

Dr. Raymond: Nothing can harm you. You can trust me. Nothing can happen to you here.

Mrs. Delaney: Corey, tell me, what did you see when you looked in the mirror that night while lying in bed with Renee?

Corey: I'm afraid. It knows I'm afraid. It wants to hurt me.

Mrs. Delaney: I want you to look in the mirror and confront this thing—now!

Corey: It's coming for me, it's coming for me! Help me please! God, help me! Look at me, look at me, look at me! *(Voice changes.)*

Dr. Raymond: Corey? Corey? Oh my God! Anne, look at her face.

Mrs. Delaney: Oh, dear Lord, no!

Corey: Look at me, look at me! *(Deep growling.)*

Dr. Raymond: Note: It's 5:45 p.m. Mrs. Michaels's facial appearance has changed drastically. Her complexion has turned pale, and her lip creases are extending to her eyelids. The creases in her lips have torn, exposing gum lines and muscle tissue near the cheekbones. Patient is arching back and crawling backwards on the floor. Judy, please call for an ambulance!

Mrs. Delaney: Dr. Raymond, look at her neckline. There seems to be a discoloration and red markings around her neck.

Dr. Raymond: Look at the position of her arms. It is as if someone is holding her down. Notice the bruising on her wrists?

Mrs. Delaney: Dr. Raymond, this is not good. Wake her up, Dr. Raymond. Hurry! We have to get her to a hospital. Judy, call 911 quickly. Dr. Raymond, this is not Corey we are dealing with here. It's something else now.

(Note: Power goes off in office as bookshelves are emptied one by one with some unknown force. Books are being thrown across the room, nearly missing Judy's head upon entry into office. Anne begins to site St. Michaels' prayer as picture frames on wall begin to shatter as they hang.)

Corey: Ring around the rosy, pocket full of posy, ashes, ashes, they *all* fall down! *(Sinister laugh.)*

Dr. Raymond: Corey, this is Dr. Raymond. I need you to take a deep breath in and out, in and out. At the count of three, I want you to awaken completely relaxed. One, two, three.

Corey: *(Screaming.)* No! Corey is mine! Ring around the rosy, pocket full of posy … You can't have her, she's *mine*!

Dr. Raymond: Corey, this is Dr. Raymond. At the count of three, you will awaken completely relaxed. One, two, three. Corey?

Judy: Oh, my God, what is happening to her?

Corey: You can't save her! Ring around the rosy, pocket full of posy, ashes, ashes, they *all* will fall down! *(Sinister laugh.)* Hey, Doc, you like what you see? You like this little bitch's smile? I can do a lot more than this. You seen her kids lately? You know what I've got planned for them? You can't stop me! Ashes, ashes, they're *all falling down!*

Dr. Raymond: Judy, is the ambulance on their way?

Judy: Yes! They are parking in the rear of the building.

Mrs. Delaney: Corey, this is Anne. You have to be strong. I know you can hear me. Think about your children. Think about George and all the lost souls this entity is trying to hurt. You have to have faith! I know you can hear me. Corey, be strong! Stand up to him! Tell him you know who he is! Tell him you won't let him get away with it anymore! Be strong, Corey! You need to fight this!

Corey: *(Sobbing.)*

Dr. Raymond: Corey, you are going to be okay. Just relax and lay still please.

Corey: *(Sobbing.)* It hurts! What is happening to me?

Mrs. Delaney: Corey, sit still. We are going to get you some help. We need you to lay perfectly still.

Dr. Raymond: Just listen to my voice and try to relax with your breathing. Everything is going to be okay. I will ride along with you in the ambulance. Anne, I need you to call her parents. Please tell them to meet me at the hospital.

Mrs. Delaney: Okay, I will.

March 25, 2010, Hospital Visit

Dr. Raymond: Hello, Corey. How are you feeling?

Corey: Something is wrong with me, isn't there?

Dr. Raymond: Corey, I have asked Anne to accompany me today. Have you been able to eat much? I need to know how you are doing.

Corey: Okay, I guess. It still hurts when I chew. They have me on some meds for the pain. I had twenty-two stitches in my mouth. Eleven on each side.

Dr. Raymond: There is something we need to talk about.

Corey: Okay?

Dr. Raymond: I read your medical record, and I am requesting they take you off of the sedatives. I need your consent to remove the meds from your chart.

Corey: Okay. Can I get the IV taken out too?

Dr. Raymond: Yes, I will request they remove it all, but I will advise you take over-the-counter meds for pain. I also spoke with the attending about the evening you arrived. He agreed to sign a statement regarding your reason for being in here, and under the circumstances, you will not have to worry about this making any papers.

Corey: So, how did you manage to keep his mouth shut about what happened to me?

Dr. Raymond: You don't need to worry about that. Just know that no one will ever find out about what happened. Okay?

Mrs. Delaney: Dr. Raymond, do you think I can talk to Corey about her experiences while in your office?

Dr. Raymond: We definitely need to talk about the other evening, yes. This is not the appropriate time, however. Corey, would you like it if we asked you a few questions? Are you okay with that?

Corey: I guess. I mean, I am not going to be released for another four hours, according to the nurse. Go ahead.

Mrs. Delaney: Corey, do you remember what you saw in the mirror on the night the terrors started?

Corey: I don't know what it was. Its skin was gray. It had stringy hair. Its hair was moving, like Medusa in *Clash of the Titans*. I wanted to look away, but it would not let me.

Mrs. Delaney: Corey, tell me, what else do you remember?

Corey: It was laughing at me. Its lips, they were moving. They were thin and pointed at the end. It was smiling at me but not an ordinary smile. It wouldn't stop laughing at me. Its lips, they were growing thinner. Its face was getting all distorted. Then its lips were stretching upward to the corners of its eyes. I wanted to look away! It's the same thing I see in my dreams hurting people, like the fire in Tanner City. *(Sobbing.)*

Dr. Raymond: Corey, I know this is difficult and painful. We are here to help you.

Corey: *(Sobbing.)* I don't understand what happened. What is happening to me? Who did these things to me?

Mrs. Delaney: Corey, you were regressing to a previous life. These are not random dreams; they are memories. I believe that your regressions have unlocked two traumatizing events—your gall bladder surgery and when you had the abortion. I also believe that what you are experiencing now in this life is because of what you have experienced in your past lives. There is one more thing too.

Corey: What? What is it?

Mrs. Delaney: Something wicked has indeed attached itself to you. I believe it definitely has something to do with that poor farm.

Corey: What are you talking about? How do you know these things?

Mrs. Delaney: The first time you were regressed, you traveled back to when you were a small child but not as Corey Michael, rather as Ingrid. You noted that you have several fears upon your first visit with Dr. Raymond. You mentioned a fear of heights and a fear of drowning. Your therapy unlocked a memory of what you thought was a dream; however, I believe it was of you reliving a past life. I believe you were drawn to the research at the poor farm by your guide and those that have passed on. However, your interest in the operation and the lack of records acknowledging the residents opened up these previous life memories. The memory of an injustice was regressed through Lulu's inability to give birth. You also experienced that yourself. What the others experienced is regressed in your dreams. These are ways that your guides communicate with you. They show you memories of those on your poor farm. They are speaking to you in your dreams, and you are living some of them too. Painful, painful realities.

We also have to find out the name of the doctor during the time Lulu spent on the farm. And it's obvious Lulu was a child of Charles.

Corey: No, I looked in his records. He only had boys. I could not find a Lulu in any of the censuses.

Mrs. Delaney: That's because Lulu was traveling during the censuses and died before the next one was taken. Your premonitions are totally different. The premonitions are when your guides are trying to warn you. That is why you feel an anxious feeling when you have them. You can change the outcome of your premonitions, but you have to trust God and your guides when they occur. Rely on them to change the outcome. Have faith in them, and things will turn around.

If you reflect back on your life now, the déjà vu that you have experienced may awaken a memory of your past or someone else's. This is how they communicate with you. Let me give you an example. Lulu was unable to deliver her baby because someone would not allow it to be born. The child was purposely aborted. I know this is difficult, but you also lost a child under similar circumstances.

Corey: Are you kidding me?

Mrs. Delaney: No. These are not just coincidences. These instances of past lives all play an important role in your life path now. Lulu's death was indeed unjust. She relayed that memory to you in your dreams, but you also experienced it when you were with Harley. You experienced her pain with the loss of your own child. And I feel she also tried to communicate it with you during your own pregnancies. I know this is difficult to understand, but for those that have lived past lives, there are instances that occur in their current life that remind them of what they have already lived. To simplify it, you are living one of Lulu's experiences back in 1877. It is also what drew you to the research. Lulu knew there was an injustice going on, and in your research, you unearthed her memory of the injustice. That is why you found such interest in writing about it. Because you remembered a fraction of her life. It is no doubt related to your work at the orphanage. You are again reliving Lulu's life spent with children that were either handicapped or poor. You have an opportunity to pick up the pieces and put things back together. You wanted to protect it, just as she did during her life. Do you understand it more clearly now?

Corey: You have got to be kidding me. You expect me to believe this? I mean, really, this is stretching it.

Mrs. Delaney: Corey, your own children will be subject to terrible things if you don't resolve this. That thing told us in your regression. Your children's lives are at stake now. Do you understand me?

Corey: But my kids have not been subjected to the things I have.

Mrs. Delaney: Do you know for sure? Do either one of them have reoccurring nightmares? Do either one of them talk to you about what they see or hear or even dream about?

Corey: Well, sure, on occasion they have nightmares but nothing like me. And as far as my son sleepwalking, well, he never did it again.

Mrs. Delaney: Are you sure about that?

Corey: Come on! I don't want to frighten my children with this stuff. I have done everything I can to hide this crap from them, and now you want me to ask them if they are dreaming about demons and monsters?

Mrs. Delaney: What I am saying is that you have the ability to do something about it. We need to do it quickly before your children get pulled further into this mess and become targets for something very evil.

Corey: This is way too much for me to comprehend. I don't understand. Why me? Why now? I had a life. I was happy with that life, and then this book comes along and rips everything apart.

Mrs. Delaney: You have to fix this. You have to find out what this thing wants.

Corey: So you mean to tell me that my whole life purpose is to fix something that happened over a hundred years ago? Is that what you are saying? Are you kidding me? Why did it take so long for all of this stuff to come out if you say I am the one to help fix it? Why did I not see these things more often as a child? Why now?

Mrs. Delaney: I know that you have a lot of questions still unanswered. You lost your faith, and because of that, you are an invitation to the negative spirits associated with your research. The time has come, Corey. You are ready to fulfill what you were intended to do all along. It's all a part of God's plan.

Corey: Why am I only seeing terrible things around those that have already passed on? How can I save them when they are already dead?

Mrs. Delaney: I know this is difficult. But there is something that you need to find in order to resolve something that is affecting so many people. Find what this entity is hiding, and perhaps you may help hundreds of lost souls find their way to the light.

Corey: Why am I supposed to help the dead? What about the living? What about my family? Who is going to protect them from this?

Mrs. Delaney: You need to know how to do both with the help of your guides. You have to have faith in God and your guides to protect those around you. Often, people look for their purpose in life. I am sure you had conversations with yourself and others as far as what your purpose is in life. But, Corey, you don't have to seek a purpose for why you are here, and this is happening to you now. Focusing on your purpose will not give you answers to these questions. God has a purpose for you. When you are purpose driven on yourself, you lose sight of God's plan for you. Let him be your copilot and lead your heart to what is right and just. It all begins with your relationship with God.

Corey: So, I shouldn't seek what I am to do in life?

Mrs. Delaney: You won't find happiness, fame, or fortune by thinking that way. Stop thinking about you and let God guide your way. Everything will fall into place when you take down the blockades that have kept you from your faith. Believe, Corey. You must believe he has a much brighter plan for you. Now tell me, what else do you know about Charles Cooper?

Corey: He and his family resided there on the poor farm. He served in the Twentieth Mass. during the Civil War. He was injured at the Battle of Gettysburg. That's why I visited there. To find more information on him.

Dr. Raymond: Do you know who his family is?

Corey: I know he had a wife and two children. That's all I know. They all lived with him on the poor farm. His children's names were Louis and Charlie. But there was no Lulu—that is, until now.

Dr. Raymond: Can you tell me what happened to his family?

Corey: They all appeared in the five-year census, something that only a few communities did, but by 1885, they were all gone. I did manage to find where Charles is buried, but his family? I have no idea where they ended up.

Dr. Raymond: Where did you find Charles buried?

Corey: At Mount Vernon in a double plot, but by himself. He died in 1881 from heart disease. I have a copy of his death certificate.

Mrs. Delaney: Their deaths were public, correct?

Corey: I believe they were waked in town. I inquired with the caretaker for the cemetery, but he told me that Charles was there with five blank headstones, but his was the only body in the plot.

Mrs. Delaney: Corey, I need you to think about Charles and why his family's burial is not known. Can you tell me what you feel?

Corey: I don't know. They could be anywhere.

Mrs. Delaney: Close your eyes and tell me what you see. Go on … Relax, close your eyes, and picture Charles. Picture him grieving over his family. You do not need to be regressed to feel and see these things. You have already made a connection with his family through Lulu. Where do you see Charles?

Corey: I don't know. I just don't think I can do this. You are making me out to be someone I am not.

Mrs. Delaney: Corey, stop this nonsense and listen to me. You have the ability to channel them! Use your gift and make things right for her, all of them! You can do this. Try to think. Tell me, where do you picture Charles when he is grieving for his family?

Corey: I don't know. I just don't see anything. I am trying. I am. I just can't concentrate.

Mrs. Delaney: Close your eyes, Corey, and picture Charles. Picture yourself grieving over your child. I know you know what it feels like. Corey, tell me what you felt when you lost your child. Tell me how Charles felt. Show me you can feel his sorrow. Tell me!

Corey: (Sobbing.)

Dr. Raymond: Anne, I am not sure this is something we want to get into right here and now.

Mrs. Delaney: No! We must continue this. She knows where they are. Don't you see? And this mist or thing knows what she is capable of. It knows this, and it will use her family as pawns to punish her. We need to press harder with her. She holds the key! You have to push her harder! Make her remember. She is holding back, Dr. Raymond, and when she suppresses these memories, all hell breaks loose, and that's when the mist takes over her. Please put her under again. We have to press further.

Dr. Raymond: Anne, you know I cannot do this in her current condition and especially while she is in here. There are consequences if someone comes in. I cannot do it here, Anne. I just cannot! We will have to continue in another session.

Corey: (Sobbing.) No! I can do this. Put me under again. I want to know what happened to them. I want to know why I am being terrorized. Please, Dr. Raymond, help me before something else happens to someone.

Dr. Raymond: We cannot do this here. I will have the attending physician contact my office upon your release. Anne will pick you up from the hospital and bring you to my office. Okay?

Corey: Yes, please.

Dr. Raymond: I don't think we should continue further until you have been released. Okay?

Mrs. Delaney: Yes, I will come and get you once you are released. Okay?

Corey: Okay.

March 25, 2010, Journal Entry, St. John's Medical Center

These past few days have been anything but relaxing. My mind is racing with thoughts, and I cannot help but get angry at society for its many mistakes throughout time. Ending up here was the last place I wanted to spend my day, but it has given me time to reflect on a few things other than the uncomfortable linens that are scratchy and the ridiculous gowns we have to wear. I mean, I have an injury to my face, so why the hell does my ass have to stick out?

I can't wait to get out of here, but then again, like a painful visit to the dentist, I have things that I need to fix. Sitting here, I cannot help but think about what the country has done to protect our history. I know there were unthinkable acts back in the day. And don't think for one minute it's not still happening. As I lay here, I realize I have lived in a state with two governors who were sent to prison for criminal acts. It's part of our history, and it happened once before, long, long ago, but no one talks about it. But because some things are removed from the media or swept under the rug, the next generation will never know the acts of those crimes and the families that were destroyed in the process.

For God's sake, we are tearing down monuments, bulldozing historic sites, and knocking down the very foundation that our founding fathers built because our history is offensive to some. We're putting veterans on the streets and disabled children on a list of services for years, yet they call it the PUNS list or Prioritization of Urgency of Needs for Services. What the hell is that? What people don't realize is history will repeat itself if we don't have reminders of our past present for the next generations after us.

Our children can't even read cursive writing or tell time on a clock. How will our children read historical documents if they no longer teach cursive in our schools? How will our children learn to tell time by reading a clock or how to read a calendar? What are we really teaching our children to protect, preserve, or cherish? Surely someone is putting thoughts in my head and putting them in this journal. It won't be the last I speak of the injustices I have witnessed. There are indeed secrets buried in the ground in this community, and I intend to unbury them all, one by one, until true patriots start protecting and preserving our past. Our founding fathers at least deserve that.

In all my years as a historian, I have met some rather interesting and influential individuals. I have traveled across the country, lecturing on the historic sites I research. I am proud of my research. And I am proud to have the ability to captivate audiences of genealogists, historians, and preservationists on my subjects. But I lose the audience when it comes to those who really could make a difference— that being our leadership in government. I am so frustrated with our politicians, for not much has changed over the past 150 years. They would prefer to tear down the buildings and move headstones rather than landmark the sites for historical reference. I am ashamed of our community leaders.

I am furious at the lack of responsibility and accountability of our political figures. Perhaps when they read about their ancestors being inmates on the poor farm, then will they open their eyes? Perhaps that is the approach I need to take with the media. Perhaps I should talk about how their ancestors dropped their pregnant, unwed daughters at the doorsteps. Perhaps I should tell the story of how the unwanted children were disposed of. And it happened under the watchful eyes of those in government. I wonder if they will listen and protect the grounds then. Anne and Dr. Raymond will help me. I know they will be supportive of me.

March 25, 2010, 6:00 p.m.
Therapy Session

Dr. Raymond: March 25 therapy session. Hello, Corey. Did you have any issues with your release?

Corey: No. But one of the nurses was whispering to the attending physician upon my release. I think she suspects something.

Dr. Raymond: Don't worry. I have a statement from the attending releasing you into my care. He is not able to discuss your hospital stay with anyone; nor is the hospital for that matter. They would be facing a lawsuit if they go against it. I don't think they want that.

Corey: I hope you are right. Some of those people may recognize me from the media. I have been in the paper a lot lately. I'm just worried someone will find out before I have had a chance to figure it all out myself.

Dr. Raymond: Well, we had better get started then. Corey Michaels post hospital, March 25, 6:04 p.m. Mrs. Delaney is present to assist with the regression therapy. Are you ready to begin?

Corey: Yes. I'm ready.

Dr. Raymond: Corey, I need you to lay down and relax. Put your feet up on the chaise and close your eyes. Concentrate on your breathing, taking nice, long, deep breaths in and exhaling out. Deep breath in and exhaling out. Relax your shoulders and arms, moving down to your stomach, hips, thighs, and knees. Imagine a gentle, warm spray of water moving its way down your body. Beginning at your head, shoulders, arms, and stomach. Slowly working its way down your hips, thighs, legs, and feet. At the count of four, you will be relaxed, and you will answer to my voice. One ... two ... three ... four. Corey, can you hear me?

Corey: Yes.

Dr. Raymond: I want you to go back in time. Back when you were working on the poor farm. Do you remember working on the poor farm?

Corey: Yes.

Dr. Raymond: Can you tell me what year it is?

Corey: Two thousand four.

Dr. Raymond: Two thousand four?

Corey: Yes.

Dr. Raymond: What is it you are doing on the farm?

Corey: We are cleaning it up. It's a mess.

Dr. Raymond: Okay, I want you to imagine a long hallway. At the end of the hallway is a door. As you walk down the hallway you see other doors on each side of you. Still walking to the end of the hallway you reach for the handle of the door. Turn the door knob to the left and open it. Can you tell me where you are?

Corey: Yes. I am on the farm.

Dr. Raymond: Can you tell me what year it is?

Corey: Eighteen seventy-six.

Dr. Raymond: Can you tell me your name?

Corey: Lulu.

Mrs. Delaney: Can you tell me your full name?

Corey: Lulu Cooper.

Dr. Raymond: Your father, he is Charles Cooper?

Corey: Yes. He is the caretaker.

Dr. Raymond: Lulu, I happen to know someone that is very interested in trying to write the history of your poor farm. She is as dedicated as you. She is quite the researcher and historian. However, she is having a hard time trying to validate certain individuals on the poor farm. Do you think you can help her?

Corey: Poor farm?

Mrs. Delaney: Dr. Raymond means an almshouse.

Corey: Oh, yes, the farm. What would you like to know about our farm?

Dr. Raymond: Let's start with you.

Corey: Okay. What do you want to know about me?

Dr. Raymond: This friend of mine, she knows the poor farm, I mean almshouse, families quite well—except for one thing, your name.

Corey: I told you, my name is Lulu, Lulu Cooper.

Dr. Raymond: This friend of mine, she knows your father and siblings. She knows that Charles did not have a daughter named Lulu. So tell me, who exactly are you?

Corey: Lulu Cooper. I am the daughter of Charles and Mary Cooper. I was born Alice Cooper on June 18, 1858.

Dr. Raymond: Alice?

Corey: Yes, Alice, but everyone calls me Lulu.

Dr. Raymond: That's interesting, because our friend knows a lot about your father and the farm but does not have any record that Charles had a daughter.

Corey: What records are they looking for?

Dr. Raymond: Oh, perhaps a birth certificate or immigration papers?

Corey: I have my immigration papers, but I am not a citizen of the States. My father has everything on our family.

Dr. Raymond: What about a census of the poor farm? Are you listed as a resident of the poor farm in 1870?

Corey: No. We did not arrive until 1874.

Dr. Raymond: What about the 1880 census?

Corey: I was not listed in that year.

Dr. Raymond: Why is that?

Corey: I don't know.

Dr. Raymond: Alice, I mean, Lulu, what is going on at the poor farm in 1876?

Corey: *(Sobbing.)*

Dr. Raymond: Why are you upset?

Corey: Mother and Charlie are dying. Louie must come home. He is the youngest. He cannot stay with Papa anymore. They are sick, and I need to take care of them.

Dr. Raymond: What are they dying from?

Corey: Typhoid fever.

Dr. Raymond: I know this is difficult for you, but can you tell me what happens when they pass?

Corey: Father must help carry their bodies to the root cellar.

Dr. Raymond: Why the cellar?

Corey: The doctor cannot come for them until the morning. There is a terrible storm. We nearly lost half of our crops.

Dr. Raymond: Okay. So what happens when the doctor comes to get them?

Corey: He will take them, and they will be waked in town.

Dr. Raymond: Okay, I want you to fast-forward to the wake. Can you tell me where your father is?

Corey: Father is in a study, looking over documents. He is holding my hand. *(Sobbing.)*

Mrs. Delaney: Can you tell me where they are being waked?

Corey: I don't know! I don't know!

Dr. Raymond: Lulu, thank you for talking with us today. At the count of three, I want you to fast-forward to 2006 when you were cleaning up the poor farm. One, two, three. Corey, are you with me?

Corey: Yes.

Mrs. Delaney: I need you to reach out to George. Ask George to help you.

Corey: Help me with what?

Mrs. Delaney: I need George to show you where the Cooper family was waked. Can you ask him to help you?

Corey: Yes. George is here.

Dr. Raymond: Note: Lights in office flickering on and off. Mrs. Delaney is checking the cords to the outlets for malfunctions.

Mrs. Delaney: Dr. Raymond, the lights … they are unplugged.

Dr. Raymond: Corey, is George there with you?

Corey: Yes, he is here.

Mrs. Delaney: Is George in the room with us?

Corey: Yes. He is standing by the window.

Mrs. Delaney: George, I know that you can hear me, and I know that you are trying to help Corey. We need you to help her find where the doctor took the Cooper family. Can you help us?

Corey: He will help, but he wants you to answer a question first.

Dr. Raymond: George has a question for Anne?

Corey: Yes.

Mrs. Delaney: What is your question, George?

Corey: He wants to know where Logan is.

Mrs. Delaney: Logan?

Corey: Yes, he wants you to bring him here.

Dr. Raymond: How can she possibly know about Logan?

Corey: Where is Logan? Where is he? George wants you to bring Logan. Bring him here!

Dr. Raymond: Corey, I need George to first show you where the Coopers were waked. Then I will talk about Logan.

Corey: George must like you, Dr. Raymond.

Dr. Raymond: Why do you say that?

Corey: Because you are helping me find my way home.

Dr. Raymond: Home?

Corey: He is guiding me to a farmhouse in the country. I recognize the house.

Mrs. Delaney: Can you get closer to the house?

Corey: Yes.

Mrs. Delaney: Please describe what you see.

Corey: I am walking up the porch stairs. I can see the foyer through the drapes that are slightly parted. I am opening the front door and walking in. The inside looks familiar, but the décor is quite different. I know I have been here before. I know this house. There is a tall slender man standing in the door way. He looks familiar. Like the man in my dreams, at the cabin.

Mrs. Delaney: The poor farm doctor?

Corey: Yes, he is taking care of the arrangements. I can see him in the parlor. He is standing alone watching us.

Mrs. Delaney: What arrangements?

Corey: Funeral arrangements for the town's people.

Mrs. Delaney: Whose house is it?

Corey: I don't know. I think it's the doctors.

Mrs. Delaney: Can you tell me what the doctor is doing?

Corey: He is in the parlor, prepping the bodies.

Mrs. Delaney: What bodies?

Corey: Those that died during the storm. Disease was spreading through the county. Many of our friends and families died.

Mrs. Delaney: Can you tell me who he is waking on this day?

Corey: A mother and son.

Mrs. Delaney: What happens after everyone leaves? Where were the bodies buried?

Corey: I don't know.

Mrs. Delaney: Concentrate. Where did the mother and son end up?

Corey: George is pointing to the hill with the others. There are many others just standing on the hill staring at me.

Mrs. Delaney: Others? What others?

Corey: Those I saw in the bright light. When I had my gallbladder surgery. They are all there waiting for me.

Mrs. Delaney: Do you know where this location is?

Corey: I don't know. I just know it looks familiar. George is pointing at the hill. I can see coffins coming out of the ground. Oh my God!

Mrs. Delaney: Where?

Corey: Oh my God! There are hundreds of them buried there. Their caskets are being washed out from the storm. He is afraid that someone will see the bodies coming out of the ground.

Mrs. Delaney: Who? Who is afraid?

Corey: The doctor.

Dr. Raymond: Is the doctor there?

Corey: I don't know. Something bad is going to happen. I can feel it.

Dr. Raymond: Can you describe what you are seeing?

Corey: It is dark. A midnight rain seems to add a mist in the cold air. I can see their breaths rising between the trees. There is a lantern swaying back and forth near a small clearing.

Dr. Raymond: What else do you see?

Corey: There are men removing sacks from a wagon. They are wheeling them over to the clearing. There is a man in the earth. He is spitting out the ground from below. He is digging. He is digging a hole in the ground.

Mrs. Delaney: What kind of a hole is he digging?

Corey: A mass grave! There are bodies under the blanket on the wagon. They are placing them in the hole. They are panicking. The rain has washed many to the surface. The bodies, they are becoming exposed as he digs for another burial.

Mrs. Delaney: Look for him. Look for the doctor. He has to be around.

Corey: I can't see him. I don't know.

Mrs. Delaney: Ask George to find him for you.

Corey: George is pointing across the street. It's a pest house! George is pointing at the pest house. There is a man standing in the doorway watching the men bury the bodies. It's him! It's the doctor.

Mrs. Delaney: Okay, where is the pest house?

Corey: Oh my God! It's there.

Mrs. Delaney: Where? Where is the pest house?

Corey: It's hidden in the grove.

Mrs. Delaney: Explain to me what the purpose is of this pest house.

Corey: It's where they took terminally ill people to die.

Dr. Raymond: Are there people in this house?

Corey: Yes, there are at least thirty women and children. Not all of them are incurable. There are children crying out for their mothers. I can feel their loneliness. They know they are going to die. They don't want to be without their mothers. *(Sobbing.)*

Mrs. Delaney: It's very important that the doctor does not see you. Do you understand me?

Corey: Yes. He is just standing there watching them dig holes and reburying the bodies. I can smell the decay. It's terrible. I think I am going to be sick. *(Retching.)*

Mrs. Delaney: Dr. Raymond, grab the basket. Corey, are you sure it is the same doctor that came and took people off of the poor farm?

Corey: Yes, I think so. It's raining out, and it's dark. I know it's him. It has to be him. I want to be sure.

Mrs. Delaney: Do not let him see you. If he sees you, he will know that you have the ability to relive his memories. If he figures it out, there is no stopping him in your dreams or in your wakened state. It's very important you look away if he should look in your direction. Do you understand me?

Corey: Yes. It is him. I am sure of it.

Mrs. Delaney: Okay, thank George and quickly walk away from the grove. *(Couch suddenly moves on its own.)*

Corey: He is coming. George, help me!

Mrs. Delaney: Who? Who is coming?

Corey: The doctor. He is coming for me. I have to hide. He knows I am here.

Mrs. Delaney: Did he see you? Did he see you, Corey? Corey, it is very important that you do not look at him. Look away! Walk away!

Corey: It's too late! *(Screaming.)*

Dr. Raymond: Anne, we can't let anything happen to her. Please restrain her arms so she will not hurt herself.

Mrs. Delaney: It's too late, Dr. Raymond. There is not much time left. We have to do something quick, or this girl is going to end up right back in the hospital or even worse.

Corey: *(Screaming.)* No! Leave me alone! Leave me alone!

Mrs. Delaney: Dr. Raymond, quickly, wake her up! Wake her up now!

Dr. Raymond: Okay, at the count of three, I want you to open your eyes. One ... two ... three.

Corey: *(Screaming.)* It hurts! It hurts! God, please help me.

Dr. Raymond: Anne, look at her eyes!

Mrs. Delaney: Dr. Raymond, please bring her out of this now before it kills her!

Dr. Raymond: I am trying, Anne! Corey, at the count of three, I want you to open your eyes. One, two, three. Corey, are you still with me?

Corey: *(Laughing. Back arches, and arms extend outward.)*

Mrs. Delaney: Oh, Lord, please help her! Corey, I need you to wake up now.

Dr. Raymond: Anne, her arms! Look at her arms. They are bruising again. Corey, at the count of three, I demand that you awaken! One, two, three!

Corey: *(Screaming.)* Leave me alone! Leave me alone! Leave me alone! God, please help me!

Dr. Raymond: Please grab my camera. I want to take some pictures of her arms.

Mrs. Delaney: Corey?

Corey: What? Oh, my God! It happened again! Look at my arms! He saw me! I tried to hide, but it was too late! He saw me!

Dr. Raymond: Anne, I need to take her vitals. Can you please snap a few shots of her arms?

Mrs. Delaney: Yes. Okay, Corey, I need you to just lay still while Dr. Raymond and I document a few things, okay? What you did was channel memories through your spirit guide, George. You have the capability to channel memories of those negative entities too. Do you understand what I am saying?

Corey: Yes, that's why he doesn't want me to talk or write about them. It makes sense. But how do I prove it? How do I prove that he tortured then buried a bunch of people on the slope of a hill?

Mrs. Delaney: That's where your background comes in. You need to look in old newspapers and old records. There has to be evidence somewhere; you just have to find it! You can start with the pest host location.

Corey: What do I do in the meantime? How do I protect myself?

Mrs. Delaney: It's not going to be easy. But you have to trust me and Dr. Raymond on this. We have to find something on this doctor and quick. I have this friend that is a great researcher. He grew up in this area. Perhaps I can reach out to him, and he can help.

Corey: I don't know if that is a good idea. I know this town, and I know everyone in it, as they do me. I don't want any negative publicity.

Dr. Raymond: Corey, I think Anne has a good point here. I think you should take her advice and contact this researcher to help you.

Corey: What if he comes after me? Like in my dreams. What do I do? I mean, Anne, I'm afraid something bad is going to happen now that he has seen me.

Mrs. Delaney: I think this would also be a good time to consult with the church.

Dr. Raymond: I don't want to get them involved just yet. We have to be absolutely sure first.

Corey: Sure about what? What? *(Sobbing.)* I knew it would boil down to this! I just knew it!

Dr. Raymond: Corey, I need you to calm down. We are not going to let anything happen to you. Try to relax.

Corey: I told you this stuff terrifies me! How can I relax?

Mrs. Delaney: There is much we need to prepare for, Corey. You have to trust your instincts on this, and we will work quickly. When the time is right, we will make this entity aware of what we know about him. Do not provoke him or speak his name. We are going to do this together, remember? We are not going to let anything harm you. Do you understand?

Corey: Yes, but you know how this stuff still frightens me. I still have to go home tonight alone. Who is going to protect me from him? I'm scared, Anne!

Mrs. Delaney: I'll assemble the group tonight. I'll call you in the morning. Just try to get some rest tonight. Tomorrow is going to be a busy day.

Corey: Are you serious? How in the hell am I going to get any sleep tonight? What if this thing comes after me? What do I do?

Mrs. Delaney: I will stay with you if you wish. Perhaps I can have a few words with the house while I am there.

Corey: Yes, I would feel better. I don't want to go home alone.

Mrs. Delaney: Well, I am going to gather the group tonight, and I will see you later on this evening, okay?

Corey: Okay. Goodbye, Dr. Raymond. Goodbye, Anne.

Mrs. Delaney: I will call you when I am on my way to your house, okay?

Corey: Okay.

March 25, 2010

I arrived home tonight to another mess after therapy. The furniture was scattered all over the house. The doctor was indeed aware of my presence. I am so afraid of what will come of me once this is all over with. I will pray to God that this never gets out. The public would surely ridicule me if they heard these things. I just want my life back the way it was. I want my life to be peaceful and predictable again, as it once was. I want the night terrors to stop! I want to be happy again. I miss those days when I awoke from a peaceful sleep, made breakfast for my kids, got them off to school before I headed off to work. Then I would rush home to greet their little faces as they jumped off the school bus. They would tell me their stories about their day at school, and Renee would tell me how miserable it was driving in traffic on his way to and from work. I miss those days. I wish I could have it all back again, no matter how stressful it seemed at the time. When I come home from work now, I don't see the little smiling faces coming off of the school bus. They do everything they can to keep from coming home nowadays. They don't like this house. They know that I am not telling them everything about what is going on with me. I don't want to frighten them any more than they already are. I have tried so hard to protect them from Harley, and now this? How do I protect them from this? I am so drained from all the restless nights.

Anne arrived about a quarter to ten. I made some tea for us. She shared some protection prayers with me and shared stories of those she and Dr. Raymond have helped over the years. Anne can sense something here too. She has agreed to stay with me for the next few days, and she is determined to get answers from the house.

We must have stayed up well into the midnight hour when we both caught each other hiding a yawn. Anne and I both laughed and agreed it was time to retire for the evening. Bear, still nurturing the wounds she received slept quietly near my bed. Anne slept in my daughter's bedroom, down the hallway and nearest the stairwell. It wasn't as drafty in her room, and the lights from the church didn't pierce through the window blinds like the other rooms. My son and I were used to the spotlights, but I didn't want my guest to toss and turn from the bright lights shining through my expensive light-blocking blinds. But it would not be the lights keeping us up tonight. We weren't asleep too long when both of us were awoken by the constant pacing outside our bedroom doors. Slowly opening our doors, we peered down the hallway to find each other looking for the same cause of the noise. But there was nothing there.

I shrugged my shoulders and started to turn back toward my room when Anne motioned for me to wait. She pointed upstairs, as if the noise had somehow traveled above us. We waited and listened. Slow, dragging footsteps across the attic floor caught my breath as Anne began to quietly tiptoe down the hallway to my doorway. "Do you have access to the attic?" Anne questioned.

"Yes, through my son's room," I said. I quietly opened the door to my son's room and opened the door to the attic. Slowly I leaned over the threshold and peered up the staircase. It was dark, but the spotlights from the church shined through the vents of the attic, allowing me to catch a glimpse of swaying shadows against the ceiling.

Anne motioned for me to follow behind her. I grabbed a hold of the railing and allowed Anne to proceed before me. Slowly, we climbed up the stairs. When we had climbed halfway up the stairwell, that's when we saw them. There hanging from the joists was a woman, a man, and what appeared to be a young boy. They were just hanging there motionless. Hung up by butcher hooks that had been nailed to the ceiling joists. I began to scream when Anne quickly placed her hand over my mouth. "This is a memory from the acts of this home," she whispered. Anne motioned for me to be quiet and still. I was terrified at the sight of them. *What happened to them? Who did this?* I wondered. Deep welts covered the young boy's body. I shut my eyes and grabbed Anne's arm for comfort.

We continued to slowly walk up the stairs, finally getting a full view of the attic as it must have appeared a long, long time ago. I looked around the room as if it were the first time I was seeing it. Off to the left of me was a long, metal table on wheels and another body lying motionless on top of it. There were several burning candles around the room, illuminating what appeared to be several work stations. A half dozen medical books were spread about the room, and medicine bottles were toppled over as if someone had ransacked the place. I did everything I could to keep from looking at the hanging bodies, especially the young boy. He couldn't have been much older than my own son.

Anne was brave enough to make it to the top of the stairs, but I remained at the middle of the stairwell. It was difficult not to notice the blood dripping from their mouths, eyes, and deep welts on their flesh. Their bodies were twisted and contorted into mangled pieces of filleted meat. It was disgusting! There were tubes coming out of their arms, and blood was pouring out of them into a bucket. There was a machine nearby that was turning like an old-fashioned tape recorder. The blood was flowing into it. Their blood was being completely drained from their bodies! "Oh my God!" I screamed. Anne sped around to where I was standing on the stairs and again motioned for me to be quiet and still. But it was too late. My scream had caught the attention of the shadow figure in the far northwest corner of the attic. It was hunched over, and we hadn't seen it until I screamed. When I did, it quickly jolted its body upright and turned around.

It stood tall, a grossly slender man writing something down. We watched it grow larger and larger, until the mass consumed the space from the floor to the ceiling. It was all of ten feet tall with long, branchlike limbs extending out toward us as if to welcome us into his den of horrors. The room filled with a horrendous smell and made us both retch in disgust. Never in my life had I ever been sick from a smell as appalling as this. And there was more to come.

The three hanging from the ceiling projected the sense of fear of him, as I could hear them warning us to leave at once. But I was curious, just as Anne was, and she began to speak to it. "What have you done to them? And why are hurting this family?" she asked it. Its mouth opened, exposing hundreds of tiny, sharp teeth. It laughed. It laughed that hideous laugh I'd heard in numerous dreams. That laugh—that terrible, terrible laugh. I felt weak, dizzy, and barely held myself up without the support of the handrail of the stairwell.

"Anne we have to leave here!" I yelled. Anne stood there waiting for an answer. "Anne, please, we need to leave!" I pleaded with her, but she ignored me. Frustrated, I ran down the stairs and into my bedroom to grab my Bible.

11:03 a.m.

We have lost six hours. I remember grabbing my Bible, and I know that Anne was right behind me on the stairs. When I awoke, I was in the kitchen and had more welts on my legs and arms. My kitchen windows had been blown out from the inside. Something came through there, and something was very, very mad. I screamed for Anne. Then suddenly I felt a sharp pain at my heel. There was a piece of the window glass protruding out of my heel. I quickly grabbed a dishrag and pulled the glass out. I tied the dishrag around my foot and began to walk from room to room, looking at the damage. Anne came running out from the upstairs bedroom and saw the blood all over the kitchen floor. She quickly grabbed another towel and began to apply pressure to my wound. It was dead silent in the house. We were both confused at the missing time.

In the distance, I could hear something outside—a jingling sound that I would often hear as the dogs raced up the stairs toward the children each night. I looked at Anne, and she looked at me, wondering what the noise could be. I realized that I had not seen Bear since before we went to sleep. It would be unlike her not to bark when strange things happened in the house.

We slowly made our way to the screened-in porch and noticed where the sound was coming from. The noise we heard was the IDs on Bear's collar. Bear was hanging in the backyard from the willow tree. I raced outside to pull her down, but the rope was burned into her neck. Anne tried her best to help bring her down. When we were able to cut the rope, I sobbed as I held her lifeless limbs. Bear had made it home, only to die from something we could not quite explain.

I phoned Beth that moment. Beth took Bear's remains, and I had her buried at the clinic's cemetery that evening.

Anne told me that it is time to tell my children what was going on. It is time to tell them the truth. When they arrive home, I will sit them down and tell them what is going on with all the strange things happening in the house and with me. I will tell them what I have become and the responsibility I have to the people of the poor farm. I will do my best not to frighten them. Anne will be there too. I will pray that my guides will protect them. I will remain hopeful they will not be too frightened by it all.

March 29, 2010, Therapy Session

Dr. Raymond: March 29 therapy session. Hello, Corey, Anne.

Mrs. Delaney: Well, there is definitely something in her house. We had an experience together, and I am sure that it is the doctor.

Corey: Anne agreed to stay with me for a few days. I feel safer with her there. Anne was also with me when I told my children about what has been going on.

Dr. Raymond: I can understand how your life has become overwhelmed with this new outlook on why you were drawn to your research. But how did your children take the information?

Corey: It's hard to say. My daughter seemed to be the most frightened by it. She claimed to have had nightmares but had a hard time explaining them to me. I have asked her to try to draw pictures of what she remembers in her dreams, and perhaps that will help.

Mrs. Delaney: One thing that troubled me was when I approached her daughter, I noted the nursery rhyme that we have heard many times before—that being "Ring around the Rosy." When I asked her why she continued to sing it, she claimed that she heard her mom signing it at night. Yet Corey claims she would never sing that song to the children because of its meaning.

Dr. Raymond: That is very interesting. Corey, have you considered having your daughter regressed?

Corey: Hell, no! I do not want to frighten her. The nightmares are one thing, but then subjecting her to regression therapy. No. I will not allow that. She is too young.

Mrs. Delaney: You may not have a choice if things get worse. Corey, earlier in your sessions, you mentioned that you prayed to God that he remove this ability to see things. What happened that made you feel this way?

Corey: When I was in high school, I had a premonition that a close friend of mine would be involved in an accident. It was fatal, but luckily he survived. I was able to see the highway, the truck involved, and the license plate of that truck as it played like a slow-motion picture in front of me. It all happened three hours before the accident occurred. I prayed for God to rid me of the curse. For many years after that, I only suffered from night terrors. I no longer had premonitions. Only terrible, terrible, dark dreams about the afterlife and about people that had passed.

Mrs. Delaney: Perhaps it would be a good idea to discuss Logan now?

Corey: Logan who?

Dr. Raymond: I believe Anne can tell you a little about Logan first and why it is important that you reach out to him with this research.

Corey: Are you talking about Logan that survived? Is this the person you want me to talk to? My Logan?

Mrs. Delaney: Yes. It is the same Logan.

Corey: Why? I haven't spoken to him in over twenty years. What does he have to do with my research and therapy?

Mrs. Delaney: You may be quite surprised. I really think you should meet with him.

Corey: Are we talking about the same Logan? It seems awful coincidental, don't ya think?

Mrs. Delaney: You should know better than that by now. Haven't we taught you anything about coincidences?

Corey: Hmmm, yeah, that's true. Okay, so what does he have to do with what's going on in my life?

Dr. Raymond: Within time, Corey. I think within time, all of the pieces will be put together. Have you thought much more about going to the victims' group at the hospital?

Corey: Well, yes. But not just yet. I have been pretty busy reading up on the paranormal.

Dr. Raymond: So how did the meeting with Anne's group go?

Corey: I think pretty well.

Dr. Raymond: Well, I have to apologize we will not be able to have a full session today. I have to tend to another patient. I hope you don't mind.

Corey: No, that's okay. Really. I have to get back to the library before they close anyway. I was hoping that we could conclude early today. In fact, I was thinking about canceling so I could get a head start before my kids got home from school.

Dr. Raymond: Well, that is perfect for both of us then. Why don't you make an appointment with Judy for next week then? Okay?

Corey: Okay. Goodbye, Dr. Raymond.

Mrs. Delaney: Perhaps I may join you at the library?

Corey: Sure. That would be great.

Dr. Raymond: Goodbye, ladies.

March 30, 2010, Journal Entry

I am so saddened today. Today's paper had the following article: "Theodore, age 16, remains hospitalized after a motorcycle incident Monday evening. Employees stated Theodore had had an argument with a customer late afternoon in the parking lot, before the end of his shift. Witnesses claim Theodore sped off on his motorcycle in anger and then lost control. He was not wearing a helmet. Police arriving at the scene found a large sum of money on Theodore and are waiting for his health to improve."

This is all I need right now—for someone to identify me as the arguing customer in the parking lot. I knew something like this would happen. Instead of this being a positive thing and saving this kid's life, I almost ended it. Why would his aunt send me messages if she knew he would end up like this anyway? Why did he not listen to me?

I had another dream this morning. I am at my new house looking inside from the front porch. I can see the house changing over time. I can see people, celebrations, and sadness. So much sadness comes out of the house. People are coming and going and wandering the house as if they are lost. I can see walls inside the house being torn down and built back up. It's like a snapshot of various chapters in the house's history. I don't understand what it means.

April 1, 2010, Journal Entry

When I arrived home from work today, all of the cabinets in my kitchen were opened. Feeling overwhelmed again, and I wish this would all just stop. I watched TV tonight for about an hour and saw an interesting program called the *Tony McMaster Show*. It was pretty interesting that he is able to communicate with the dead as he does. It frightens me too. I don't want to be like him.

I placed a chalkboard on my kitchen table with some chalk alongside it. Before I head for bed, I will ask George to write down two things about himself. I want him to communicate to me something I know and something that I don't know about him. I want to know if he is in fact real or just some childhood imaginary friend I made up to deal with the dreams. And if he is real, I want to know why he is in my life. If this is really happening to me, I have to make a choice. I either have to accept it and learn how to use it or deal with the consequences if I don't.

I will pray to God tonight too. I will ask that I be forgiven for the wrongdoings that have led me to this moment. I pray that he will guide me if this is the road he wishes for me to follow. I will ask him to protect me against the negativity. I will plead with him to show me by leading me to where to begin in helping those who were forgotten about.

April 4, 2010, Journal Entry

Last night I dreamt that I was visiting one of my friends, Charlotte, at an unveiling for her artwork at a historic landmark. Charlotte had passed away in 2001 after a long battle with a rare lung disease. The dream didn't really make sense at first. But she is hosting the event, and it is filled with familiar faces—senators, mayors, business representatives, and local humanitarians all wanting to help. It was not like Charlotte to have such an event, for when she was alive, she was studying to be a nurse. In the dream, she played an entirely different role in our community. It just didn't make any sense. I wondered why she was there now when she had been distant from my life for so long. I wondered why this was the first time she was contacting me through my dreams. Where had she been all this time? In fact, I wondered why none of my ancestors or close family members that had passed on came through in my dreams. Where were they all?

Regardless, Charlotte had something to say to me in the dream. She guided me throughout the course. I was in a parlor room with some acquaintances from the museum. Everyone was shaking hands and sipping champagne and enjoying themselves and the beauty of one famous artist. In the corner of the dining room stood several murals for the guests to admire. I don't recall what the mural depicted, but it was an important event due to the people in attendance. Whatever Charlotte was trying to relay to me was important.

Bankers, historians, park service staff, and politicians were all in attendance too. They all congratulated the organization, and as they walked out of the exhibit, their pocketbooks were opened for donations to Charlotte.

Charlotte pointed to one of the murals in the dining room. It was of brick construction and looked like a barrier or wall. The design had a Civil War soldier standing against a tree near an old building. A small child was in the background of the mural, pumping water. The little girl looked familiar, but I could not place where I had seen her before. Charlotte then whispered, "Forgotten over time, remembered in stone. You'll find more if you listen to them."

When I awoke, I remembered what the mural looked like, the construction of the brick wall, and all of the politicians that were in attendance. I knew God had indeed chosen me to do a task. Charlotte helped me identify that task. I quickly got dressed and headed to the kitchen. When I glanced at the kitchen table, my jaw dropped in awe. "Agrue23" was drawn on the chalkboard.

It was George. I am sure of it. Agru was one of the common reasons for death back in the day. I didn't know what the twenty-three meant though. It was a positive feeling, and I know I am on to something. There was indeed an injustice, and this is happening to me because of it. But there was something else too. Something so terrible has been interfering with my life. It's trying to keep me from telling the truth and exposing something. I have to be careful.

April 5, 2010, Journal Entry

When I got to work this morning, I placed a call to Anne. I told her what I had done and what had happened. She met me at a local pub in town, and that's when I told her what I needed to do. Anne agreed to help me make things right. No matter what the public would think about my story, she would be there to support me. She would bring others as well.

The next few days will be spent scheduling appointments with the local organization that threw the mural reception in my dream. I knew exactly who they were from the community, and to my surprise, they already knew who I was as well. They knew me as the Cemetery Lady.

April 10, 2010, Journal Entry

The artists met with Anne and me several times over the past couple of days to discuss putting a mural up on the grounds of the poor farm. Two design teams were assigned to the project. I told them what I thought it should include. I should have an artist rendering by the end of the week. I know I have to communicate with the property owners of the poor farm and the museum to help me raise awareness and funds to build it. This is not going to be easy. My hope is that my passion for preserving their history will show in my sales pitch. I know I can do this. I just know this is what they want from me.

April 11, 2010

I arrived home from work this evening to the flashing of police cars and fire trucks in my neighborhood. My heart skipped a beat when I pulled into my subdivision to discover that the audience was at my home. The police were in the process of breaking the door down when I emerged from the car screaming for them to stop.

It was Officer Ryan Ogle, a longtime police officer and a fellow classmate from high school. I told him that I was just returning from work and that no one was in the house. Ryan then asked me to open the door and to wait outside for him. Four officers would accompany him inside my home. They would search the house top to bottom as I waited patiently to find out why they were there. When Ryan emerged, he claimed that they had received a 911 call from the house. He claimed that a woman was in distress and requested a patrolman to come to the house. I told him that I didn't know why the call would have come from the house since no one was home.

Ryan continued to question me when the four other policemen emerged from the house. "There's no one inside, but we found something I think you may want to take a look at," one of the officers advised. Ryan turned around, and I followed as the other officer led us upstairs to my son's bedroom. There on the attic door was a message written in feces, and only I knew who it was meant for. "Ring around the rosy, pocket full of posey ... ashes, ashes, you'll all fall down!"

Ryan looked at me as if I was hiding something. How would I answer this? I wondered. And what about the 911 call to dispatch? Did someone seriously call in to 911 from my house?

It was obvious, my evening was not over, and Ryan advised me to come to the police station to review the 911 call once I had locked up the house.

On the ride down to the police station, I phoned my kids and asked if they had been in the house. Both replied their dad had picked them up from school rather than the usual bus stop near the house. They were never even in the neighborhood. When we arrived at the police station, the officer continued to question me. He wondered if I had ever been broken into or had something like this happen before. I told him that I had not.

We entered the police station, and he motioned for me to have a seat near his desk. He asked the dispatcher to forward the 911 call to his computer. When he played it back for me, I was dumbfounded. It wasn't a woman's voice at all! But I knew that voice. It was threatening, and I knew if I told Ryan, he would never believe me.

I told the officer I did not recognize the voice and that I could not explain how it happened. He looked puzzled, and I went along with it. I was amazed when he told me to forget about it. He suggested it was lines being crossed and a bad connection since the voice was distorted. I knew differently though. I shook his hand and thanked him for his kindness and walked out the door.

When I returned home, I could hear the jingling of Bear's tags again. Something was still in the house, and it was trying to taunt me. I was leery about entering the house alone, but I was reminded of what Anne had told me in therapy. I needed to be strong in my faith. This was my house, and this was my life. I had to be strong, and I needed to reclaim it.

I entered the house through the kitchen door, and I could sense the heaviness from the moment I planted my foot on the tile. Something was there. I headed to my room to change out of my clothes and prepare for bed. The closer I got to the bedroom, the more uneasy I felt. I was not going to let this thing take over my life anymore. I needed to be strong. I needed to fight.

My daughter's door was open, and I glanced momentarily inside. There was no disturbance. Everything seemed to be in place, so I continued down the hallway to my son's room, peering in at the feces still spread out across the attic door. The smell was overwhelming. I turned to face my bedroom door. It was closed. There was a commotion inside as shadows ran past the space below the door. I slowly reached for the doorknob and slightly turned it. I opened the bedroom door with caution.

I stood in amazement at the display before me. Contorted on my bed lay the dolls my grandmother had given me over the years. They were positioned in various poses on my bed. It was unnatural, and as I went to approach them, the heads on all of them turned to look at me. Their little legs and arms stretched out to reach me as their jaws dropped at the sight of me. I jumped back and turned to run out of the room. The dolls leapt off the bed and into the air. One by one, they flew at me, tangling my hair with their tiny hands. The sinister laugh amplified throughout the house. They pulled at my cheek and neck, leaving blood-filled welts across my face and arms as I tried to pull them off. Then the beatings began.

When I awoke, I grabbed for my phone and dialed Anne. I told her what had happened earlier in the evening and regarding the 911 call. She told me to stay at a hotel for the night.

I took her advice and gathered an overnight bag and left immediately for the next town over. It didn't matter where I slept though. It seemed this terror would follow me everywhere. The nightmare of little trolls looking back at me in the mirror happened everywhere there was a mirror.

I checked into a small hotel in downtown Tanner City for the night. It was the nearest place to lay my head for the night. Probably a dozen or so rooms on the ground level. The usual truckers would find loving here during their long journeys across the country. They were good men and women, just lonely on the road was all.

I must have drifted asleep shortly after one in the morning, but I knew I wouldn't get much sleep. Shortly after three, I woke up to the sound of someone weeping. It was coming from the room next door. I didn't want to pry, so for the first thirty minutes or so, I kept to myself. But the crying just got louder and louder, as if she was actually in my room with me. Without warning, there was a knock at the door. I sat up and watched the door handle move as if someone was trying to get in. I called out several times, but no one answered. The doorknob continued to turn from left to right and then violently, as if someone on the other side was ready to bust down the door.

I quickly grabbed the phone and dialed the front desk. I stated that someone was trying to break into my room. The receptionist as the front desk stated that he was looking at the camera positioned in my room's hallway and no one was outside my door trying to get in. Yet he heard the doorknob being violently turned in the background. They sent a security guard up to my room while I remained on the line with the front desk. Once the guard reached my doorway, the activity stopped.

April 13, 2010, Journal Entry

The kids came home today. It was nice to have them home with me again. I miss them dearly when they leave for their dad's house. I worry too. I worry about his demons and his actions while under his care. I pray they will be safe. They need to have a night full of rest.

My daughter woke up quite some time after we had all gone to bed. She had had a terrible dream—one of many that would leave me questioning her sensitivity as well. Around two, she awoke, screaming from her bed that someone was in her room yelling at her. She was crying and demanded that she sleep in my room. I shrugged it off as the typical nightmare and sent her back to her room sobbing.

It wasn't long after I fell back to sleep that I heard the footsteps, followed by her dreadful scream. I jumped out of bed and ran to her room, and the bedroom door slammed shut. I yelled for her to open the door, but she didn't respond. She just keep screaming for me to help her. I did everything I could to pry the door open to get to her. I could not imagine what she was witnessing on the other side of the door. I was terrified as to what was in there with her. Still, I continued to push on her door as she continued to cry out. Hearing us both scream, my son rushed to the hallway to see me pulling on the doorknob.

Suddenly, the house began to moan. The lights dimmed, and the floors began to buckle underneath me. This was no nightmare she was screaming from. I felt helpless. I begged for God to help us.

My son tried ramming the door, but it would not open. Inside, she was screaming for me, and I couldn't get in there fast enough. A terrible feeling came over me, and I prayed to God nothing would harm her. She pleaded with me to open the door. And then, silence. The door swung open, and on the floor lay my daughter, her nightgown tattered and torn. A black mist shot out across the room and into the hallway. It was gone.

My daughter had been beaten just as I had numerous times before. I ran to her and picked her up. She cried out in agony. There were welts across her legs, arms, and face. "You bastard!" I screamed. "I know who you are! You're going to rot in hell when I'm done with you! Do you hear me?" I threatened.

I remembered what Anne had taught me. I took two very deep breaths and began to pray. I asked God to make me strong. I asked George to protect Sara and Mason. I escorted them both back to my bedroom, locked the door, and held them close to me with my Bible right next to us. I reached in my jewelry box and removed two necklaces with crosses on them. I placed them on my son and daughter and told them to never take them off.

The next morning, after they left for school, I hung a crucifix in every doorway of the house. When the kids came home from school, I took my daughter aside and asked her what had happened early this morning. Her response sent chills down my spine. She claimed to see a black smoke in the corner of her room grow larger and larger until it seemed as if it were right on top of her. She said when it got close to her, she was unable to cry out to me. She was paralyzed and could not move from her bed. She didn't remember anything else. She didn't even remember me coming into her room. All she remembered this morning was waking up in my bed with cuts and bruises on her.

April 15, 2010, Journal Entry

I arrived at Anne's house a little before six tonight. I brought along some of my research for her to look at in hopes of her helping me with the deceased. We continued to unearth many negative things about the people who ran the poor farm over the years. I was ashamed of my county for hiding the information, but I understood why it was so difficult to find documents in the beginning. When I first started this project, I wondered how an operation that existed for over a hundred years could leave nothing behind about the operation or the

people who lived there. I was beginning to understand the reasons.
It was all coming to the surface.

April 16, 2010, Journal Entry

Today I took the day off to meet with Anne. She was persistent that
I talk with Logan. I don't understand how he can help with this. He
doesn't believe in this stuff. At least he didn't when we were in high
school. I'm nervous to meet with him.

April 18, 2010, Journal Entry

Today, I lost my job at the orphanage. They claimed they needed to
make some cuts in the budget. I am devastated. I can't believe that
I was there for over fifteen years. I am not sure what I will do now,
but I hear "when one door closes, another door opens" in my head.

I am bothered this evening about the time spent with Harley. I
remember when I began to save up for a place of our own. I would
wait for Harley to leave for work before I began looking at houses in
town. I had little time to view houses while he was away at work. I
even managed to save up ten grand to move out.

I remember one night when I came home from a meeting as if it
were yesterday. I was pulling into the driveway when a sense of déjà
vu came over me. It was overwhelming, and a heaviness came over
me. I felt as though I had lost my best friend in an accident. My eyes
filled with tears before I was even able to pull into the garage. Just
then it hit me. *I have been here before.* Out of the corner of my eye, I
saw a shadow moving around near the back of the car and heading
for the driver's side. *I have dreamt this before. Oh God, please help me!*
I gently closed my eyes and began to pray.

Harley was anxiously waiting for me to arrive home. As the

garage door closed, the kitchen door swung open, and there he was. Full of piss and vinegar and ready to come out swinging. He grabbed my arm and dragged me up the stairs to the bedroom. When he opened the door to the bedroom, I froze in my tracks. The bedroom was in disarray. The mattress was leaning against the wall, the television was on the floor, all of our clothes were out of their drawers, the nightstands were thrown against the closet, and the lights were all strung together in a knot.

"What the hell did you do, Corey? What are you and your kids doing to my house? Clean this shit up and get the hell out. I am tired of this bullshit. When your kids get here, they are going hear about this shit!" he barked out. I didn't know what had happened to the bedroom, but my kids were not capable of doing such things. They knew to stay away from Harley. They were living on pins and needles as it was. Why would they try to make him angrier than he already was? I thought.

When the kids arrived home, Harley grabbed my son by his arm and threw him against the wall. "What the hell did you do to my bedroom, kid?"

Mason was caught off guard and began to cry out to me. "Mom, what did I do? What did I do?" he cried.

"You know what you did, and you and your sister are going to help your mother clean it up!" he screamed. My daughter walked in from outside and pleaded with him to let him go. I stood there motionless. I felt helpless. I tried to get him to release him, but he threw me to the ground. I yelled for Sara to go next store and call the police, but Harley jumped up and stopped her. "Get your shit and get the hell out of my house, now!" he yelled.

We packed a few things and headed to the Dixon hotel. There we would talk about getting rid of Harley for good. We all had high hopes that we could do it. It meant me placing a call to my family for assistance and saving up enough money to put a down payment on a home.

The following morning, I phoned my mother and told her we

had to move out. "You made your bed, Corey. Now lie in it," she said. I hung up the phone and began to sob. There was no way anyone was going to help us. I had to do this on my own.

The following night, I received a call at the hotel. It was Harley, and he was pleading for us to return home. After talking for over an hour, he had me convinced that I could not raise two kids alone. They needed a place to sleep, and they needed food in their bellies. I gave in once again.

"Things are going to be different, Corey. I want you to stop writing that book, and I want you to start being a real woman," he argued. "You are wasting your time with that book, and it is getting you nowhere." I didn't believe him though. I knew there were things going on, and he was too frightened to accept that I was into something bigger than he could handle. It scared him what I was doing. He told me things would get better if I stopped living in a fantasy world filled with angels and demons, lollypops and sprinkles.

I never did put my research down. I hid it from him. When the book was published in the winter of 2007, I felt a sense of completion. I was getting interviewed all the time about my research and became quite the celebrity in the community. Little did anyone know, I was guided by the deceased when I wrote it.

One night after a book signing at a local bookstore, I came home to find Harley had been drinking. I went straight upstairs to avoid any confrontation, but he followed me. He grabbed my arms and began to strip my clothes off and rape me on my bed. I cried out for him to stop, but he wouldn't listen. It was not him who was doing it. I felt it. He said things to me only I knew about researching the deceased, and he tortured me with stories of how they pleaded for mercy for their life. "Go ahead, bitch, let me hear you plead for yours!" he screamed.

Harley's eyes had turned black. His hair began to move, and his lips began to thin. I knew this face.

I pleaded with Harley to stop, but it answered with, "Harley who? There is no Harley here. Perhaps you would like to leave a message, and Harley will call you back later. Hahahahahaha!" It said. I was terrified. Harley was strong, but this thing was even stronger. It stretched out my arms, and two curtain pullbacks flew across the room and weaved my hands up into the bedpost. My legs were spread across the bed. I couldn't stop it. "Ring around the rosey, pocket full of posy, ashes, ashes, you'll all fall down! Come on. You know the words. Sing it with me, Corey.

"You cannot save them. You have no control. Your little ones are next!" he threatened. I struggled and fought as hard as I could, and when I was about to give up, I heard the voices calling out.

"Our father, who art in heaven, hallowed be thy name." I began to recite the Lord's Prayer as loud as I could. It fought me by forcing Harley's hands around my throat. "God help me" I prayed. "Help me!"

"Remember, Corey, you welcomed me in, and no God can save a soul that is damaged goods. They want you to help the lost to cleanse your soul from wrongdoings? Hahhhhha! You don't have it in you to save them or yourself. You did this to yourself. Weak, weak little bitch. How's your happy little home now?" he asked.

I continued to pray to God for help. But I was losing consciousness. Harley was growling, and something had a hold on him. Inside, Harley fought it. He even cried out in agony. I remained on the bed, witnessing what looked like a battle between good and evil. He looked helpless, for whatever was inside of him was taking its toll on him. Harley was losing.

"Get out of here! Quickly, go now," I heard. I struggled to break free. I grabbed for his hands that were still wrapped around my throat, but his grip was too tight. I could not loosen the grip. I managed to move my legs to where I could knee him in the balls—a brief moment that allowed me to break free from his grip. I jumped off of the bed and ran next door for help. Beth drove me to the hospital that night. The attending physician took photographs of my neck, legs, and arms. A restraining order was filed, and the following day, we were moving our possessions out of Harley's home and into a storage unit across town.

I contemplated what could have happened if we had stayed with Harley. I knew he would kill me, and from that night on, I knew if he had a chance, he would kill Renee too. Harley always told me that as long as I stayed with him, no harm would come to Renee. So I made a bad choice to stay with him as long as I did.

April 20, 2010, Regression Session

Dr. Raymond: Corey Michaels, April 20 regression session. Good evening, Corey.

Mrs. Delaney: Good evening Corey.

Corey: Good evening.

Dr. Raymond: How are you doing today?

Corey: Not good. Not good at all. This thing is beginning to go after my children.

Dr. Raymond: Why do you say that?

Corey: Something tried to get to my daughter the other night. It was frightening.

Dr. Raymond: Would you like to talk about it?

Corey: Yes. I thought it was a bad dream. I think she is being attacked like me.

Dr. Raymond: Tell me what happened.

Corey: Well, she woke up screaming the other night from what I thought was a bad dream. I sent her back to bed. A few minutes later, she awoke screaming again. I ran to her room, and the door slammed shut clear in my face. When I finally got into her room, she was scratched from head to toe. Her nightgown was torn, and she was trembling with terror.

Dr. Raymond: Did you try to discuss it with your daughter?

Corey: I did later in the day, when she came home from school. She remembered smoke filling her room and not being able to cry out or breathe. She didn't remember anything else. In fact, when she awoke in my bedroom later that morning, she couldn't remember how she got there. But I know something was in that room with her. I know it wasn't smoke; it was the doctor. I know it.

Dr. Raymond: Perhaps the door was locked on the other side?

Corey: Dr. Raymond, this is an old house. The door locks were never installed in the interior doors. They don't stick. They don't rub against the doorjamb. I am telling you he was keeping me from getting into her room.

Mrs. Delaney: Have you been practicing your faith more frequently?

Corey: I have been attending church with my children, yes. I am practicing my channeling and protection prayers too. A lot of good it's doing, huh?

Mrs. Delaney: Corey, remember you are only beginning to learn how to use your gift.

Corey: So why can't I protect my kids? Why must we continue to be tormented like this?

Mrs. Delaney: You have to have faith, Corey. You have to remain strong. Don't give up on yourself or your children. Dr. Raymond, Corey and the group have been meeting twice a week as well. She is still learning, but I think she has become a much stronger person now that she has been enlightened.

Corey: I think the power of prayer has helped my situation. I do feel stronger, but I am not sure I am ready to face this thing.

Dr. Raymond: Have you had any negative dreams lately?

Corey: Yes. I still have dreams about Renee and the boy on the hill.

Dr. Raymond: Have you had any more recollections?

Corey: Yes, well, I remember one night after work, when I was with Harley. I found him drunk and on the couch. I quietly walked upstairs to change, but he heard the squeak of the floorboards and quickly awoke. He sprang from the couch and grabbed me. He pulled up his shirt, and his back was covered with deep scratches, and blood trailed from each wound. He blamed me for making the scratches. I laughed and then continued to walk upstairs. He followed quickly behind me and grabbed me around the neck. He said that something was in the house and that it was my fault.

Mrs. Delaney: Did you sense that there was something in the house?

Corey: I don't know. I don't remember. Things happened while we were there, but they were subtle things. Lights turning on and off, the radio changing stations randomly, TVs turning on and off. I didn't think anything of it back then. But I think it was while I was living there I started hearing more voices. Maybe I shouldn't say voices, but they were like random whispers. I don't know.

Mrs. Delaney: What do you mean?

Corey: Well, sometimes a word or thought just pops into my head, and I guess I just follow what I hear, or what I think I hear.

Mrs. Delaney: So even then you listened to the voices or thoughts that were playing out in your head?

Corey: Yes. I pushed my way past him and ran out the door. When I reached the end of the driveway, I looked back to see that something was up in the bedroom window. The face, that face that I had now seen over a hundred times. It was there waiting for me. I had to get out, and it had to be soon before anyone else got hurt. A few weeks later, I appeared in Dr. Raymond's office.

Dr. Raymond: Did Harley attempt to contact you after you moved out?

Corey: Yes, before I came to your office in January of this year, he found us.

Dr. Raymond: Is Harley a local here in Winchester Grove?

Corey: No. But he owns the Hillcrest General Store in town. But he never comes to Winchester Grove unless he has a score to settle. He's lived in Tanner City nearly 15 years now. Everyone knows him. When the kids and I moved here, we never thought he would find us. He hated this town, especially because of the feud between the Hillcrest and Dixon families. When he showed up at my door and dragged me down the street, something was different about him.

Mrs. Delaney: What do you mean?

Corey: He was scared of something. I mean, really scared. He forced me out of my home and nearly killed us both when he lost control of his car. If it wasn't for James Dixon, Harley would be dead. We were both nearly killed by a train.

Dr. Raymond: That was you, Corey? I remember reading about it in the paper.

Corey: Yes. Well, after that happened, I told him that it was over and we never wanted to see him again.

Dr. Raymond: Was he upset that you left him? Is that why he went looking for you?

Corey: I am sure that was the reason for some of it. He claimed that I had plastered pictures of the Dixon family in his house. Surely you've heard about the Hillcrest and Dixon feud? It's been a subject of talk for over a hundred years. Harley kept every article written about the two families. And he accused me of hanging Dixon photographs all over his house. I never did though. I have no idea how they ended up on his walls. Regardless, I took care of the issue.

Dr. Raymond: What do you mean, you took care of the issue?

Corey: Well, I think he may have witnessed what the mist is capable of, and it frightened him off that cold day in January.

Dr. Raymond: I have a feeling you know more than what you are telling us.

Corey: Well, I don't think he will be bothering us anymore. That's all I want to say about Harley.

Dr. Raymond: Okay. Then let's talk about the children's reaction to the move. Would you like to talk about that?

Corey: They were very excited to be out of Harley's house. The first few days in our new house were peaceful. I think all three of us sleep all the way through the night. We weren't used to that.

Mrs. Delaney: How did you react to the house? Was it a pleasant feeling moving in?

Corey: Well, I did sense things in the house at first. However, a lot of it was anxiety due to the unknown—whether or not I could truly afford the mortgage and responsibilities that came with it. I was scared in that sense.

Mrs. Delaney: Did you experience anything paranormal in the house when you first moved in?

Corey: You could say that. The lights flicker on an off. The appliances malfunction and turn on by themselves. The usual things that I was used to. I always brushed it off as coincidences. Something interesting occurred to me early on. I had a sense of déjà vu when I first walked through the house. It felt familiar. I mean, like as if I had been in it before. The rooms were slightly different though. The wallpapered rather than painted, and the light fixtures seemed familiar.

Dr. Raymond: What about your sleeping patterns? Did they change at all?

Corey: The night terrors of little trolls continued. To ease my mind, I had all of the mirrors removed from the house before we even moved in. The kids are still frustrated with this and didn't understand why I would not allow a single mirror to hang.

Dr. Raymond: But they were able to relax and settle in well?

Corey: Yes, in fact, I received a phone call from one of my friends one morning that helped us all settle in. They had a fairly young dog that needed a home and offered to give him to us. I thought it was a great idea, and the dog would help the kids keep their minds off of the negative things that were happening around them. It would also keep Bear occupied during the day.

We named him River. The first night we had him, he howled like any other dog would do while confined to a crate. After a few sleepless nights, River adjusted to his surroundings and soon would find comfort in his cage. He got along great with Bear too. Within a few weeks after living in the new house, River's behavior began to change. Eventually I ended up having to put him down. He became aggressive and often would follow me around the house, growling. Once I sat down, he would bark and growl at me. Sometimes lunging at me as to bite. Bear always protected me though. She sensed his aggressiveness too. I had the feeling that no matter where we lived, Bear would always be on alert and let me know when things were about to get ugly.

Bear would run off into another room and start barking at a corner. It didn't matter where we were in the house. I would sense it the moment she started howling. Bear would bark and howl for minutes on end and then go running into River's crate as if she were afraid. Other times, Bear would growl and tug at my pant leg. The kids always wanted Bear to sleep in their rooms, but Bear always found her way into my room. She protected us all, but she knew I was the one who was in the most danger. We both sensed it.

We had been in our new house for nearly a month when I realized something odd about it. A sense of déjà vu once again filled my days as I went about my daily chores. I found items stashed away in various concealed places that the previous owner had never shared with me. I found old bottles hidden in the rafters when I was feeling the need to unwind with a glass of wine. I pulled a draft of the original construction of the house from the insulation when I was looking for the floor plans of the garage for the electrician. It was odd how these places were in my memory.

Mrs. Delaney: This is quite interesting. Why did you not share this with us sooner?

Corey: I don't know. I guess it's because it happens wherever we live.

Judy: Excuse me, Dr. Raymond. You have an emergency call on line 3.

Dr. Raymond: Please excuse me for a moment.

Mrs. Delaney: Sure.

Corey: Certainly.

Dr. Raymond: I am sorry, but I have a medical emergency to attend to. I will have to reschedule our session. I am sincerely sorry, Corey. Can you come by tomorrow?

Corey: Sure. Same time?

Dr. Raymond: Yes. Judy will set it up for you.

Mrs. Delaney: Okay. Well, Corey, how about we go grab a bite to eat, yes?

Corey: Sure. How about the pub on Main Street?

Mrs. Delaney: Okay. I will meet you there. Is it okay if I bring a friend with me?

Corey: Sure. Someone from the group?

Mrs. Delaney: No. Actually, it's Logan.

Corey: Ya know, I have been thinking about it, and I don't know if that is such a good idea.

Mrs. Delaney: Corey, Logan is a part of your past. You also both were a witness to something very unfortunate. You need to talk about it. You may find him very resourceful.

Corey: Okay, okay.

April 20, 2010, Journal Entry

Anne and I arrived at the Main Street Pub about eight o'clock. Logan was already there waiting at the bar. I approached rather slowly, not knowing if he would recognize me after all of these years. Age had treated him well. He looked up at Anne and then me and smiled. He looked amazing, and I could not help but drift back to my high school years when we were together.

Logan was about five nine, with curly blond hair and a medium build. He was wearing blue jeans, a button-up T-shirt, and a pair of Converse. He hadn't really changed much at all. His eyes were still a brilliant blue. It was if he had barely aged. I, on the other hand, had streaks of gray and had put on a few pounds since the high school days. Nonetheless, his smile told me he didn't care about my appearance. I loved that about him.

I smiled back at him as I drew closer to him. There was no denying that he hadn't forgotten about me. We were both amazed that our paths had again crossed. Instead of the casual handshake, Logan greeted me with a tender hug and kiss on the cheek. Instantly, I felt the butterflies swirl in my stomach. Here was a man that I had fallen in love with as a teenager. Oh how I missed him over the years. I was thrilled to see him, but a part of me was still angry at him for ignoring my calls and letters so long ago. It felt good to hold him again. I had missed him so much. There were so many thoughts running around in my head. *Where do I begin? What should I say?*

We talked for about an hour as Anne sat there listening to stories of our high school romance. She laughed along with us even when she really didn't understand why we were laughing so much. It felt as if we hadn't skipped a beat.

Anne asked about the incident that occurred the summer of 1986. I allowed Logan to tell the story. Logan sat back in the stool and began to tell his version of the incident but with much more detail than I had written in my journal.

"Corey and I met after I graduated high school in May of '86. We spent the entire summer together, going to the movies, the beach, dining out, or just hanging out together. We loved the river, and oftentimes we'd just grab a blanket and curl up on the shoreline of the Kankakee and stare up at the stars," Logan said.

"Just before I left for college, Corey confided in me about her dreams and premonitions. At first, I was skeptical about the stories she was telling. Believing in her would have gone against all that I was taught as a Catholic. I knew she was troubled, and I encouraged her to seek guidance from her church. She never did though.

"One Saturday morning, I had been invited by some classmates to join them on a trip to the Illinois River for some waterskiing. It was a bit of a drive, but it was not out of the ordinary that I accepted the invitation. I spent a lot of my Saturdays hanging out with the guys. I grabbed my keys and a six-pack of Jolt and head for the door, and then the phone rang. It was Corey, and she seemed quite upset. She was crying and pleading with me not to leave the house. At that point, I hadn't even told her where I was going. Somehow she knew I was leaving though. When I questioned why she was so upset, she told me what she had envisioned. Corey said that my friend's car would be stalled on the highway, and while they were trying to repair it from the roadside, a semi would lose control and hit the vehicle from behind, killing all of us.

"I assured her that it was only a dream and for her not to worry, that I would be fine. Corey was so upset, and I couldn't get her to calm down. I cared a lot for Corey, but I didn't want her to project her fear into me. We were so young, and there was so much more yet to experience. I didn't want to stay home worrying about whether or not something was going to happen. I wanted to live my life, and listening to Corey at the time, honestly it frightened me. But in order to get her to calm down, I lied and told her that I would stay home.

"When I got off the phone with Corey, I geared up my Jeep, slipped in my Violent Femmes tape, and headed to meet up with the guys. I arrived at Ken's house around nine thirty. Ken was working on his car—a '69 Dodge Charger that he and his dad had restored. It was a sweet car with a glossy Ferrari-red finish, white interior, and a complete rotisserie restoration. Under the hood was a 383ci V8 mated to a Torque flite three-speed automatic transmission. It was a hell of a Mopar.

"Anyway, I arrived at the house to find Ken and his dad working under the hood of the car. I inquired as to what was the hold up, and Ken stated that the carburetor intake was pouring out gas and would not close properly. I remembered my conversation earlier with Corey. A red flag was being waved in my face, but I ignored it and continued to load Ken's car.

"John and Tommy pulled in shortly after me. Ken closed the hood, and we headed off to the river. We must've made it about fifteen miles into the trip when the car began to backfire. The engine chugged, and a strange smell came through the vents from under the hood. It was a terrible smell. Ken quickly pulled off onto the side of the road, popped the hood, and got out to see what the problem was. Again, a red flag went up. I thought it was just some coincidence that Corey had predicted. Immediately, I felt an adrenaline rush throughout my entire body. My body was shaking with such an excitability that to this day I haven't again experienced or can begin to explain the feeling. All I knew was that something was coming. I felt it. And I needed to get out of the car and now.

"John and Tommy remained in the car, laughing at me as I ran up the embankment. I saw their faces, poking fun of me for running away from them. 'Logan, get back in the car!' Ken yelled. But I couldn't. I just couldn't go back. I yelled and screamed for the others to join me up under the viaduct. They were safe there, but they continued to laugh. I felt dizzy and for a brief moment, their laughs became all distorted. Like a demented clown at a freak show. It was terrifying. Do you want to hear the strangest thing about this whole thing? John and Tommy were signing as they laughed. Ring around the Rosy, you know that nursery rhyme?

"Ken continued tinkering under the hood. *Come on. Hurry*, I thought. Over and over, I kept remembering what Corey said earlier. I should have listened to her. I should have stayed home. I didn't notice the truck until it was too late. I heard the squeal of the tires on the pavement to the left of me. I turned, and there it was. Barreling down the highway was a freighter full of fuel, and the driver was losing control. The semi weaved in and out of the lanes, plowing into two vehicles and wedging them into the guardrail. Still the semi continued on, weaving in and out of the lanes and heading straight for Ken's car with the guys inside it.

"I kept screaming for them to get out of the car, but all they would do is sign and laugh at me. I waved and screamed for them to get out. They had no clue, and at this point, no time either. The semi plowed into the car, pushing it into the median, splitting the car in half. Ken was thrown twenty feet into the air. He landed on the pavement and in the line of oncoming traffic. Ken died instantly when a second semi ran him over. The tanker ignited upon impact, engulfing both vehicles in flames. They all died, three of my best friends that I had known since childhood.

"The following week, a memorial service was held for all three, two of whom would have joined me in college. After the service, I packed my bags and headed to college. I never said goodbye to anyone. It was easiest that way," Logan shared.

Anne took our hands and reminded us that this was not a coincidence of us reuniting. There was something that we both needed to do, to fix, and it involved both of us.

Logan explained that he came back home because of nightmares that he had been having. He said that with my permission, he would document the events that were taking place in the house and with me. I accepted but explained that I did not want my children involved in any of the video recordings. Logan agreed and stated that he would only be documenting the events on paper. He would not be videotaping anything.

Logan then told me that he had wanted to look me up but heard that I had married. He didn't want to complicate things. He had many questions about the incident back in 1986. He said he had a lot of questions about my research on the poor farm too. I told him to read the book then ask questions, and I said it in a humorous fashion. He didn't laugh though.

Anne said that we could learn a lot from each other despite the gap in years. I had a feeling that she knew more than what she was telling us. For some reason, I think he is here for more than just his own personal issues. I think he is here for me too.

He was happy that I had moved on, but he wondered how I was doing or if I continued to have premonitions. He said that he had returned to the area to do some research and perhaps resolve some issues of his own. He had contacted Dr. Raymond months earlier due to some disturbing dreams that he was having. I was curious but afraid to pry. I didn't ask any questions. I believed within time, perhaps he would tell me what drew him back to the area.

It was about midnight when we finally paid our bill and headed for the door. I was anxious to see him again. I didn't want to be pushy though. A lot of time had passed, and surely we have both changed and matured since the old days. I'm not looking for love, but Logan really has a way of stirring up the butterflies in me. That is one thing that hasn't changed at all.

When Anne and I returned from dinner, all I could think about was seeing Logan again. I missed him. We walked up the stairs to the front porch. It took me a while to grab my keys, for the thoughts of Logan consumed me. Anne knew something was wrong. I fiddled with the keys, but none of them would open the front door. I was confused and wondered why they looked so different to me. Anne then took the keys and advised me to stay outside for a minute.

Anne inserted the key, slowly turned the doorknob, and walked in. She flicked on the foyer light and began to look around the parlor and living room. She knew something was out of place. I slowly opened the porch door and began to walk in. When I crossed the threshold, anxiety came over me. I fell to my knees.

I saw Harley pulling into the driveway, and he held a gun in his lap. But it wasn't my driveway. It was Renee's driveway. Harley was waiting anxiously for Renee to arrive home. When Renee pulled into his garage, Harley quickly ran up to Renee's car and then pulled the pistol out of his back pocket. Harley raised the gun to Renee's window, and then everything faded to black.

I knew what I had seen was soon to happen to Renee, but I had no idea of knowing when so I could intervene. I tried calling Renee, but he wouldn't return my calls. I prayed to God Harley was not going to do anything stupid. That night, I dreamt the same dream, and I found myself pleading for Renee's life. I pleaded with God and my guides to help Renee.

April 21, 2010, Therapy Session

Dr. Raymond: Corey Michaels, April 21 therapy session.

Mrs. Delaney: Hello, Corey.

Dr. Raymond: I am again sorry about yesterday. I hope that was okay with you.

Corey: Yes, that's fine. Mrs. Delaney and I went out for a bite to eat, and we kind of talked about a few more things. Logan was there too.

Dr. Raymond: Very interesting that your paths have crossed again. How does that make you feel?

Corey: Well, when I first saw him in the pub, I got butterflies in my stomach. It was as if I was a teenager again.

Dr. Raymond: So you had a romantic relationship with him in high school?

Corey: Well, sort of. I mean, we hung out a lot but nothing really serious. He moved away to college, so nothing really happened between us romantically.

Mrs. Delaney: Well, I seem to get a different sense.

Corey: Ok, well, I liked him a lot. Call it my first real crush.

Dr. Raymond: How long were you with him?

Corey: The entire summer back in '86.

Dr. Raymond: Logan was one of the individuals that was in the car accident years ago, which you spoke about?

Corey: Yes.

Dr. Raymond: This is the incident resulting in the three deaths?

Corey: Yeah, and shortly after it happened, Logan left for college.

Dr. Raymond: Did you keep in contact with him after their deaths?

Corey: I tried. I wrote him letters, but they were all returned.

Dr. Raymond: So, after all of these years, were you able to talk about the accident with Logan?

Corey: Last night was the first time we talked about it since it happened. He told the story to Anne last night.

Mrs. Delaney: Yes, he told me about their days together and the things he witnessed. It was very interesting.

Dr. Raymond: Did he talk to you about why he was here?

Corey: He did a little. Something about seeing you because he was having bad dreams.

Dr. Raymond: This is good. So do you plan to reach back out to him? Now that he is in town?

Mrs. Delaney: That is actually a great idea, Dr. Raymond.

Corey: Oh, I don't know. I don't want him to get the wrong idea or anything.

Mrs. Delaney: I think what Dr. Raymond is trying to say is that you should invite him out for coffee. You can start with that.

Corey: I don't know.

Judy: I am so sorry, Dr. Raymond, but you have an emergency call that you need to take.

Dr. Raymond: Excuse me, ladies. I won't be but a minute.

Mrs. Delaney: Well, I guess we know where this is going.

Corey: Yup!

Dr. Raymond: Corey, I am so sorry, but we are going to have to reschedule again. I really apologize.

Corey: It's okay. I understand. Anne, would you like to come over tonight?

Mrs. Delaney: I have a few things I need to take care of tonight. Perhaps I will stop by later on this evening. Will that work?

Corey: Sure.

Dr. Raymond: Let's reschedule for tomorrow, shall we?

Corey: Sure. Bye, Anne. I will see you later. Bye, Dr. Raymond.

Dr. Raymond: See you tomorrow.

April 21, 2010, Journal Entry

I decided to call Logan when I got home. I invited him out for coffee, as Dr. Raymond and Anne suggested. Logan agreed to meet me at the Wild Bean for a cappuccino. The Wild Bean was a quiet little café on the east side of the river. It was the hub for gossip, as the many local old-timers would often assemble there spewing their stories of assumptions across town. I was subject to that too when I first arrived here. I got the stares each and every time I would shop the stores on Water Street. The snares, giggles, and finger pointing made me uncomfortable at first, but then again, Winchester Grove is a small town, and the townsfolk were dying to find out the story that brought me and my family here. I wanted to keep them guessing. Everyone loved to talk, and the local paper had ways of feeding ideas into the minds of its readers with or without evidence to back it up. It sold papers and especially if the Hillcrests and Dixons were involved.

I was labeled by the townsfolk as the "writer that bought the old butcher's house." I was never told the story though about my house. I just knew I had to have it when I saw the For Sale sign in the yard. It had character and charm like the other homes in the historic district. And one day, I plan on researching the history of it too. It's just too busy right now.

I arrived first, shortly after nine, ordered my cappuccino, and sat anxiously waiting for Logan to arrive. The chimes above the café door jingled every time the door opened, and the butterflies, they were there too, twirling in my stomach. At one point, I thought I was going to throw up. How embarrassing would that be? And so I began to second-guess myself. *What if he still thinks I'm a quack? What if he doesn't show up? Perhaps this wasn't a good idea after all,* I thought. It was nearly nine thirty, and he obviously wasn't coming. I decided that I wasn't going to wait anymore. I finished the last few sips, paid my bill, and headed for the door.

The bells on the door chimed once again as I reached for my purse to exit. I looked up, and there he was. Logan had arrived. A bit late, but he was here. "I'm sorry that I am so late," he said. "Where should we begin?"

"It's okay. Would you like to postpone and maybe do this another day?" I asked. Logan wasn't going anywhere. He had something on his mind. He motioned for the waitress to find us a table. Logan took my hand, and with the most sincere look of tenderness, he said we needed to talk. He then escorted me to the back of the café away from curious onlookers that had already started to observe us. We wanted our story to be left out of the papers. It's like the old saying, "misery loves company," and for that moment, we were their number one fans.

We must have talked for hours about our lives and where they had taken us. It must have been about three in the afternoon when we decided to head to the Irish Inn for a drink. I couldn't help but feel as though this afternoon's coffee had turned into an actual date. It felt good to be with him again. He made me laugh. He made me smile. I couldn't think of any place I wanted to be other than with him right at that moment. I felt safe. I didn't want the day to end.

Logan walked me to my car, and as we said our good nights, I leaned over and gently kissed his cheek. Graciously placing his hands on the sides of my face, Logan looked into my brown eyes and drew me in for a long-awaited kiss. I was seventeen again! My heart skipped a beat, and the feelings I felt from high school came pouring in.

I was so excited with emotion that I could not let him go. Not now and not again. I held him as long as I could. I didn't want him to leave me again. Logan took my hand and told me that he was here for more than just nightmares. Sensing his urgency, I invited him back to my home.

Again, I had trouble getting the front door open. I was anxious, but it was a different kind of anxiety. When I finally got the front door open, I head toward the kitchen to start up a pot of coffee. I phoned Anne and politely told her that I had taken her advice and invited Logan out for coffee. I told her that I would call her in the morning. Anne was smiling on the other end as I hung up the phone and turned my attention to the house.

Logan's eyes panned across the rooms with the look of restlessness. Logan looked weary and distraught. I asked him if he preferred we go somewhere else, but he declined. Logan claimed that the house felt familiar to him, but he could not recall ever stepping foot in my home. It was quite frightening to me. I knew deep down the house knew him too, and tonight would be anything but normal. I prayed that the house would behave at least for this night while Logan was there. I worried that something would happen to him. I prayed that we could have a peaceful night alone and he would feel comfortable talking to me about whatever it was that had brought him home again.

Logan explained that he had been seeing Dr. Raymond under the advisement of Anne. He explained that for several years he had had dreams about the accident. He also had dreams about a young man. He didn't understand them, so he decided to contact Anne for help through a mutual friend. Three months ago, Dr. Raymond began counseling him. I could not believe they did not tell me that during my sessions with them. Why would they hold that from me?

Logan was strong in his faith, always had been. He explained that he never really dreamt much until he left for Michigan. He said he began dreaming about a young man when he graduated college. The dream was of a young man that was sick and dying. He went on to explain that he would have the same dream over and over again, and he didn't understand why. It was only a few years ago that the dreams changed. The dreams, he explained, included visions of me, and he decided to return home to find out why. I have to admit that was rather exciting to hear that he was dreaming about me after all of these years. It was quite flattering.

When I asked him about what happens in the dreams, he leaned forward as if to prepare me for some deep, dark secret he had held on to. He said that he sees me standing in a cornfield staring into a grove of trees. He is there, and he is standing in front of a grave marker. He went on to explain that near the grave markers were several people, and they were all trying to get my attention. He said that he remembered the cornfield as a child, yet he was never actually on the property. He was unaware of a cemetery on the grounds, and when he returned home, he was anxious to visit the property to see if it was true.

When Logan returned home, he decided to stop and walk through the cornfield. That's when he discovered the graves. Tucked away deep in the timbers and away from society stood the grave markers. He claimed to have never been there, but he felt a sense of déjà vu while he was there. He didn't know what to make of it, but then he remembered the tombstones in the dreams. There was one tombstone that was different from the others in the cemetery. He stated that this tombstone had a name on it. He just couldn't make out the name on the tombstone.

I told him that the cemetery sounded like my poor farm cemetery I had written about. When I asked him when the dreams started, I just about passed out. He claimed the dreams began shortly after he went to college. It frightened us both that he had been dreaming about what was yet to be written. My book hadn't been published when the dreams began. It would be another fifteen years before I took my research to the publisher. It was indeed eerie, and we wondered how his dreams were connected to my book.

It was too late to call Anne with questions about our connection to the poor farm. We were both anxious to find a connection, and only Anne and Dr. Raymond could help us figure it all out.

I invited Logan to stay the night since it was so late and we still had so much to talk about. In conversation, I warned him that my house might be haunted. Logan didn't care though. He wanted to stay with me, and sharing with him what Anne and I had encountered didn't scare him off. He agreed to stay, so I prepared my son's bedroom.

It was nearly two in the morning when Logan and I awoke to the sound of footsteps coming from the attic. Hearing the heavy steps drew Logan and me from our rooms and into the hallway. "It's just an old house, Logan. Let's just go back to bed," I whispered. I didn't want anything to happen and played it off as much as I could. But then I shined the light of the flashlight down the hallway at the ceiling, and Logan refused to go back to bed. In the hallway near the stairwell stood a blackness—a smoky mist that hovered over the corner leading to the stairwell. It was thick, tall, and endless, and it was swaying back and forth as if it was agitated. It grew bigger and bigger and was slowly moving toward us.

Logan grabbed my arm and drew me into my son's room and slammed the door. "What the hell was that?" he questioned. I wasn't really sure myself. Suddenly, the shuffling of footsteps directed us to the ceiling. Logan quickly grabbed my son's bat and began to slowly open the attic door. Knowing of Logan's dreams and the possible connection it might have to me, I worried what he might witness. I did not want to scare him away. He had just returned to my life. This was the last thing I wanted to happen, for him to pack up and leave again.

The attic door quietly squeaked as the bottom of the door rubbed against the threshold. Logan took the flashlight out of my hand and began to shine the light on the joists. There hanging were the three individuals Anne and I had seen previously. Logan fell to his knees and began to weep. "We need to go!" I screamed. I grabbed his arm and helped him out of the attic doorway and quickly closed the door behind us.

I led him down the stairwell to the main level, but the mist was still there hovering in the stairwell. The thick darkness filled the foyer with a horrible smell of sulfur, and Logan began to gag with disgust. Retching, he managed to get to the second landing, but we were trapped. There was no other exit. The punishment would now begin for disturbing whatever was in the attic. We should've never opened that door.

The mist grew larger until it was surrounding Logan entirely. Logan was lifted off of the stairwell and slammed against the wall. Something was holding him up by his throat, and Logan was choking. I tried to help him as he grabbed for his throat to pull at the hands that held him. But the darkness was far stronger than the two of us. Logan was in so much pain, and it looked like he was losing the fight. I had to do something quickly.

I ran for my Bible in my bedroom, but when I arrived at the doorway, the door slammed shut. I would have to rely on what Anne had taught me. I began reciting prayers that I had learned and pleaded with God and my guides to protect Logan. But as I asked for the protection of white light to save Logan, I violently received my first lashing. One after another, something was tearing into me. I felt the claw marks cut deep into my skin, leaving blood spewing from my back, chest, face, arms, and legs. We were both repeatedly beaten as I began to pray.

Logan continued to fight back. He struggled to be released, and I continued to recite prayers. Suddenly, the mist grew to cover the entire stairwell. I felt as though my prayers were useless. I fell to my knees and begged God to help me. "Lord, help us fight this evil entity that has plagued our lives. Give me strength to fight what is unseen, so that I may help him. Please, God, help me!"

Suddenly, Logan fell to the ground, still holding his neck in pain. I ran to his side and hugged him. I told him that I was sorry that something had hurt him. I pleaded with him not to leave me. I thanked God for giving me strength to help him. I prayed again that Logan would be safe. Logan and I packed a few of my things, I dropped Logan off at home, and I found myself checking into another hotel. Later that morning, I made an appointment to see Dr. Raymond.

April 22, 2010, Therapy Session

Dr. Raymond: Good afternoon, Corey. So, how are you today?

Corey: Not at all good! But we will get to that. Logan and I went out last night, and he told me that he is a patient of yours?

Dr. Raymond: Well, yes, he is, but due to client confidentiality, I am not able to discuss his case with you.

Corey: I already know about Logan. He told me about his dreams and my poor farm. We experienced something together too, at my house earlier this morning. Logan is involved with it somehow too. We both know it. You have to help us.

Dr. Raymond: As your regressions began to unfold some interesting stories pertaining to your research, Logan's dreams, and those associated with your research, it became evident that the two of you had encountered something together. However, this is a very unique case. The two of you, I mean. Anne should be here shortly, and I have also invited, with your permission, Logan to sit in. I will explain more when everyone arrives. Okay?

Judy: Excuse me, Dr. Raymond. Shall I send Logan in?

Dr. Raymond: Yes, please. Thank you.

Logan: Hello, Dr. Raymond. Do you mind telling me what this is all about?

Corey: Yeah, what is going on here?

Mrs. Delaney: Sorry I am late.

Dr. Raymond: Okay, well, I have asked you both here for a reason. However, due to the privacy of your therapy individually, I need you both to sign a waiver stating that you agree to participate in each other's therapy.

Corey: I don't understand. Why are we doing this together?

Logan: What's going on here?

Mrs. Delaney: Corey, Logan, you both will be quite amazed at what Dr. Raymond and I have discovered pertaining to your regression sessions. Logan, do we have your permission to allow Corey to listen to your therapy sessions?

Logan: Dr. Raymond, Anne, Corey, I am here so I can make sense of all of this. Corey and I had something really nasty attack us last night, and there are so many coincidences—

Mrs. Delaney: No, they are not coincidences. Things happen for a reason. The reason is you and Corey.

Logan: Okay, well similar things have come to light between what I dream about and what she wrote about. I cannot explain why I was dreaming about her research before she even wrote the book. I mean, we all need resolution here. And then what happened last night to us.

Well, we have to resolve this now before anyone else gets hurt. Did you know that Corey has kids and they live in the house with her?

Dr. Raymond: Yes, I know. Believe me. Anne and I are working on what needs to be done.

Corey: Logan, I know that many years have passed, but there are things that happened to me that no one knows about. I am not sure that I am ready to talk about everything. I am ashamed, afraid, and overwhelmed. I just don't know if this is a good approach. I mean, I felt so close to you back in high school until the car accident, but then you left, and we never spoke about it again until the other day. There are some things that I just can't talk to you about yet. Please don't take it personally. I'm still having a hard time dealing with everything that happened in my previous relationship.

Logan: I know, Corey, but you and I experienced something quite extraordinary last night. I think we are indeed connected, and we need to be honest with each other. I am not going to judge you for what you have or have not done. Right now, there is something really wrong and something meddling in our lives. I care about you, and I don't want to see anything happen to you. I know a lot of time has passed, but I never stopped feeling those butterflies either. Yes, I remember the butterflies we often talked about. Please understand that when I left for college, I was not ready for what was going on with you. I was afraid. It went against everything that I was taught. I cared about you then, and I care about you now. But this time, I am not going to run away from what I do not understand. I want to know. I want to understand how you knew those things back in high school. I am here now, and I am not going anywhere until we find out what it is we need to resolve.

Corey: I am sorry to bring you into this, Logan. I really am. I just don't want you to get hurt. I know what this thing can do. I have to do this on my own.

Logan: I know what it can do too! Remember what happened last night? You are no longer alone in this. This thing wants me too, Corey. I am part of it. This has followed me too. I've experienced beatings in the middle of the night no matter where I go. We have to figure things out together. And I am not leaving until we do.

Dr. Raymond: Okay, Corey, what I want to do is begin by sharing something with you, now that I have Logan's permission. I want you to listen to one of Logan's regressions recorded during therapy. What you may find interesting is what happens to him during these sessions.

Mrs. Delaney: The best way for you to understand is for us to just play the recordings, and then we can start putting the pieces together. Okay? Are you ready?

Corey: Yes. Logan, are you? I mean, are you ready for all of this?

Logan: Corey, I don't know what this thing is or what it wants, but obviously we are tied to it. I don't know how or why, but there is a reason for all of this, and I am not going to leave until we find out what that is.

Dr. Raymond: Okay, here we go. Logan Anthony, January 4, 2010, regression therapy.

(Start tape.)

Logan: Good afternoon, Dr. Raymond.

Dr. Raymond: Good afternoon, Logan. How have you been sleeping?

Logan: Still not well. I keep having the dream about an old friend from high school and the cemetery.

Dr. Raymond: Have you tried to contact this friend since you have been back?

Logan: No. I believe she is married. I don't want to stir anything up in her life.

Dr. Raymond: What harm will it do reaching out to her?

Logan: I am not sure if she is still the same person that I remember her as.

Dr. Raymond: What makes you feel that?

Logan: Well, she had visions when we were in high school. We had an experience together, and I am not comfortable talking about it.

Dr. Raymond: What kind of an experience?

Logan: She had a dream or a vision of me and my friends dying. I can't explain how she knew that. But then it happened. I have had dreams about it ever since. I just never told anyone. I couldn't make sense of it. How did she know? How did she know that they were going to die?

Dr. Raymond: Have you ever tried to reach out and talk to her about it?

Logan: I can't. It's just too painful. I don't know why they perished and I didn't. I couldn't do anything to save them. They would not listen to me. They would not get out! *(Sobbing.)*

Dr. Raymond: Do you feel as though you should have died with them?

Logan: I should have done something. I should have tried to save them. I just couldn't move. My legs were paralyzed. I couldn't run to save them.

Dr. Raymond: Since you have been back, have you visited the cemetery where your friends are buried?

Logan: No. I can't. I just can't face it. I still question why it happened. Why I couldn't save them. Why she knew it was going to happen. Why was I the only one that survived? Why?

Dr. Raymond: Survivors guilt carries a heavy burden on many. You have to understand that it was not your fault they would not get out of the car when you told them to. It is not your fault. You cannot make decisions for anyone other than yourself. You have to believe that you did everything that you could to save them.

Logan: I just don't understand why.

Dr. Raymond: And you may never know why it happened.

Logan: And how did she know that it was going to happen?

Dr. Raymond: That is a very good question. Perhaps while you are here, you should reconnect with her and ask her.

Logan: I don't know. I don't know if I am ready to see her.

Dr. Raymond: Do you blame her for what happened?

Logan: I don't know. It's just not possible. How could she know? She told me things that happened throughout her life since she was a kid. She couldn't explain it. Nor could I. I kind of felt sorry for her.

Dr. Raymond: What would you say to her now if you ran into her? This is a small town. I am sure she may even know that you returned.

Logan: I don't know what I would say. I have so many questions to ask her. There is so much uncertainty in my life. The dreams, coming home, and facing their deaths again. This is a lot to take in. It has been so long since I have been back home.

Dr. Raymond: Okay, let's go ahead and talk about the dreams and what brought you back home.

Logan: Okay.

Dr. Raymond: Please lie down on the couch. Put your feet up. You can lay your arms down at your side. I want you to close your eyes and take a few deep breaths in and out. In and out. Your eyes are getting heavier and heavier as your body becomes more relaxed at the sound of my voice. Deeper and deeper into sleep, breathing in and out. Your arms are feeling heavy at your side as they slowly fall to the side of the couch. Falling deeper and deeper asleep. At the count of three, you will be fast asleep but fully aware of what transpired. One, two, three ... Logan, can you hear me?

Logan: Yes.

Dr. Raymond: Logan, can you tell me why you are here today?

Logan: I have bad dreams.

Dr. Raymond: Can you tell me about your one of your bad dreams?

Logan: Yes.

Dr. Raymond: Okay, where are you in this bad dream?

Logan: I am standing next to a tombstone looking out into a cornfield.

Dr. Raymond: Are you in a cemetery?

Logan: I don't know what it is. There are blocks lined in rows. They have numbers on them. I have to help her. I have to help her find them.

Dr. Raymond: Who? Who do you have to help?

Logan: Corey.

Dr. Raymond: Corey who? And why do you have to help Corey?

Logan: Corey Michaels, someone from my past. I need to help her because she saved me. We are connected.

Dr. Raymond: What do you have to help her with?

Logan: The farm people.

Dr. Raymond: Tell me, what is she doing in your dream?

Logan: She is walking the rows of corn on the farm. She is lost. She needs help. She needs to find her way back home.

Dr. Raymond: Okay. Logan, I want you to go back. Back to the first time you were on this farm. Can you do that?

Logan: Yes. It was in '83.

Dr. Raymond: Can you tell me what month?

Logan: September.

Dr. Raymond: What are you doing on the farm?

Logan: I was sent here. I am not well.

Dr. Raymond: What do you mean you were sent there? What is wrong?

Logan: I was returning from the Klondike. I got sick.

Dr. Raymond: The Klondike? Can you tell me what year it is again?

Logan: Eighty-three.

Dr. Raymond: Nineteen eighty-three?

Logan: Ha-ha. No, 1883.

Dr. Raymond: Ahh. Can you tell me your name?

Logan: George, George Miller.

Dr. Raymond: George, can you tell me what year you were born?

Logan: Eighteen sixty-five.

Dr. Raymond: Can you tell me where you were born?

Logan: Gettysburg, Pennsylvania.

Dr. Raymond: George, what were you doing in the Klondike?

Logan: Looking for gold. My family is poor. I am the eldest. I have to support my family.

Dr. Raymond: George, what happened when you arrived at the farm?

Logan: They took me to the ward with the others.

Dr. Raymond: Do you remember what they treated you with?

Logan: I don't know. I remember a doctor coming to see me. They took me to another building for treatment.

Dr. Raymond: Do you recall where? What city were you in?

Logan: Winchester. They did terrible things there.

Dr. Raymond: What terrible things?

Logan: They cut out my tongue.

Dr. Raymond: Why was your tongue cut out?

Logan: Because I argued with him to allow us to die gracefully.

Dr. Raymond: Who did you argue with?

Logan: The doctor. He did terrible things to us. He held us against our will. Most of us were too ill to escape. I was so weak, but I managed to gather enough strength to escape.

Dr. Raymond: What happened when you escaped?

Logan: I made it to the farmhouse, and the caretaker took me to the sheriff. I was barely clothed, malnourished, and my feet were turning gangrene. It's by the grace of God that I made it to the farmhouse.

Dr. Raymond: What happened when you met the sheriff?

Logan: He questioned me, but I was not able to talk very well.

Dr. Raymond: Were you able to tell what you witnessed?

Logan: Yes, but then I died.

Dr. Raymond: What do you mean?

Logan: I fell asleep and never woke up.

Dr. Raymond: Do you know where you are buried?

Logan: Yes, I am buried on the farm with the others.

Dr. Raymond: Where exactly is this farm?

Logan: Down the road by the Spurgeon farm.

Dr. Raymond: Thank you, George. At the count of three, I want you to fully awaken, remembering everything that transpired. One, two, three. Logan, can you hear me?

Logan: Yes. I don't understand why I have these thoughts or memories or whatever they are.

Dr. Raymond: This is not the first time that I have witnessed regression of past lives. You are one of hundreds of cases that I have worked on.

Logan: So, what does it mean? What do I do with the information?

Dr. Raymond: Within time, Logan. But until then, I really think you need to connect with that friend of yours from school. I think it would be very therapeutic for you to try and reach out to her. You have to understand that she is probably experiencing guilt herself regarding the death of your friends.

Logan: How would she feel any guilt? She wasn't there. She wasn't there trying to get them to listen.

Dr. Raymond: Surely, she may suffer from guilt because she told you what would transpire. She may feel guilty for how it may have affected your life.

Logan: I am going to talk to Anne about it when I see her next week. I want to get her feeling on all of this too. Not saying that I doubt anything here. I just want her to give some spiritual advice.

Dr. Raymond: Okay. I understand.

(End tape.)

Corey: Why didn't you tell me about this earlier?

Dr. Raymond: Patient confidentiality is definitely a priority in all of my cases. I hope you understand that I am not able to share client content with just anyone.

Mrs. Delaney: Corey, Logan, we had to be sure that there was a connection, and we believe that the two of you are connected to the poor farm.

Corey: But why didn't you tell me this months ago?

Dr. Raymond: It wasn't until recently that we discovered the connection ourselves. We had to be sure.

Corey: So, do you think there is a connection with Logan's George and my George?

Dr. Raymond: It's very possible.

Logan: So what do we do now?

Mrs. Delaney: Well, first we have to start by blessing the house that Corey resides in.

Dr. Raymond: Logan, has Corey shared with you much about her research on the poor farm?

Logan: Not much. I read some articles in the newspapers, but I haven't had a chance to read her book entirely. I was rather disturbed by what I read in the newspapers already.

Dr. Raymond: Why did it bother you?

Logan: It was kind of scary.

Corey: So what happens now? What do we do?

Dr. Raymond: Corey, have you had any more night terrors?

Corey: You are getting off of the subject. What are we supposed to do now?

Dr. Raymond: I think I will let Anne answer that question.

Mrs. Delaney: It is possible that Renee has a connection to the poor farm as well.

Corey: And how in the heck am I supposed to find that one out? Do you want me to call and ask him if he is visited by black mists and shadows? Or no, how about nightmares of little trolls setting things on fire?

Dr. Raymond: I can sense you are upset, but Anne may have a point here. Have you talked to Renee recently?

Corey: No, we really don't speak a whole lot. Even with me leaving Harley, Renee just doesn't like to talk to me unless it pertains to the kids.

Dr. Raymond: Have you tried to sit down with him and talk? Perhaps at one of the children's school events?

Corey: That's if he shows up, but yes. I try. He has his own issues that he is dealing with right now. I can't exactly talk about this stuff in front of my kids either. I've tried to talk to him, but it usually ends in an argument about who is the better parent for the children. I know he is dealing with his addiction as well.

Dr. Raymond: Have you tried to contact Renee about your premonitions?

Corey: No. I have enough dealing with whether or not my children are safe with him.

Mrs. Delaney: You said he believes you though when it comes to premonitions, correct? Do you think he will still believe you?

Corey: I don't know. I am afraid he will try to take the kids away from me if I tell them what is going on. He has no idea what I have been through. I don't know if he will still believe me. If he doesn't, he may try to take them away from me. Then I have to worry about what harm he could do to them. I know something terrible is going to happen to him. I don't want my children there when it happens.

Dr. Raymond: I still believe it would be in the best interest to speak with Renee about what has transpired at least for this past year.

Corey: I don't think that is a good idea. I don't want to hurt him anymore, and I don't think this will make things better for him. I just don't want him to know yet. I will tell him in good time but not now. Not while Renee and I still have things to resolve.

Mrs. Delaney: It may actually help things. There is strength in numbers, you know. I think the best thing you can do is reestablish your relationship with Renee. The negative entities associated with the poor farm do not want to see this happen. They will do everything they can to destroy your family. In fact, you mentioned earlier that you see what is to become of him, no?

Corey: I know. I know. But I tried to warn him. I tried talking to him about what could happen if he didn't stop drinking. It is out of my hands. I cannot make him change.

Mrs. Delaney: Yes, you can! You have to have faith in God and your guides to protect him. If you lose faith, your premonitions will become a reality to him. It will destroy him. It will destroy you and your children.

Corey: Yes, I know. Anne, please don't remind me what I need to do. I just know he is not going to believe a word of this. Talking about spooks, spirits, and bumps in the night will not convince him. I know something is still in that house. I can feel it. I just know he won't listen to me.

Mrs. Delaney: You must both work together to find out what this thing wants.

Logan: Well, I am not going anywhere. So, let's get on with it. Where do we start?

Dr. Raymond: Okay, then perhaps we should talk about where we left off yesterday. Corey, are you willing to allow Logan to remain for the duration of your session?

Corey: Yeah, that's fine. Where did we leave off?

Dr. Raymond: We were talking about when you left Harley.

Corey: Well, when I left Harley, we began moving into the new house. The Realtor told me a little about the previous owners. She did tell me that the house was built in 1875. It was also rumored to house a butcher, but she could not find the original deed of when he took possession of it. It had only three families other than the original owner.

When I walked through it the first time with the Realtor, I had a sense of déjà vu. I walked the house very slowly to see if anything would jump out at me, and all I got was a warm feeling in every room. Well, except the attic. I really didn't like the attic, but who does, right? Anyway, it had a beautiful garden in the back with a pond. It was everything that I wanted. I felt it was meant for me and my children. It was perfect, so I got it.

Mrs. Delaney: Do you still feel the same about the house?

Corey: No. Things are different now. I can picture things, but there is no way that I can truly validate if the events transpired there. I mean, I have visions of people dining there on special occasions, holidays, but I can see people being mourned there as well. I don't recognize them though.

Dr. Raymond: Were you able to do this in other houses?

Corey: No. I never had feelings like this before in any of the houses that I owned. I remember when I first looked at the house. The first time I walked in the doorway, I felt as if I had been there before. I kept seeing the house change over time. I saw the trees grow taller, the porches being added on, the parlor fireplace being removed. It was odd. I brushed it off as a vivid imagination.

Dr. Raymond: Tell me what the first week was like when you moved in. Did you experience anything out of the normal?

Corey: Yes. Ever since the first night with Renee and the mirror, I have never been able to put mirrors up. Then, when I bought the house, there were mirrors everywhere. As a precaution, I removed them all and placed them in the attic, but when I awake in the morning, some of the mirrors are back on the walls. I just don't understand how they end up on the walls. My kids think I am losing my mind by hanging them up then taking them down. They don't understand, and I don't want to frighten them. I just want this to be done and over with.

Mrs. Delaney: I know this is taking longer than you had anticipated. But we know what it wants. And that is for you to stop doing what you are doing. You understand that? You have to remember that you welcomed these poor souls in. Remember, they are drawn to you. They accepted your invitation. Good and bad. Now, you have an obligation. You must help find resolution for them, or this will never end. And remember, at some point in time, you must tell Renee what you did. His life is at stake here too.

Corey: I know. You keep saying that I have to find resolution for them. But what am I really looking for? Could the missing ledgers hold something? Where do I even begin to search for them? Everything that happened on that poor farm was shady, just like in the other institutions. But I have no proof.

Logan: There must be something that you overlooked. Perhaps it's in the ledgers you speak of.

Corey: Possibly. I did manage to find the name of the doctor serving as the physician of the poor farm during the years Charles Cooper was there. Many records are still missing, and if there was an injustice, they would not have written about it, would they have? It would have exposed their sins.

Mrs. Delaney: So you were able to find out about the doctor?

Corey: I believe so, unless they had more than one doctor serving the poor farm during the years that Charles was there.

Dr. Raymond: Let's start by regressing you again. Would that be okay?

Corey: Yes. Logan, will you stay with me?

Logan: Yeah. I am not going anywhere.

Dr. Raymond: Okay. Lie back and listen to my voice. Relax and imagine you are drifting on a boat. Drifting farther and farther from shore. The waves are calming, and a gentle mist is spraying your body as you drift farther and farther, further and further. The sun is beaming its warm rays over your entire body. Your head and shoulders, cascading down your chest and stomach, your hips, your knees, and your calves. The mist is spraying your body, first your face, your shoulders and chest, while the sun rays follow. Drifting farther and farther away from shore until you see land again. At the count of three, I want you to tell me where you are. One, two, three. Where are you Corey?

Corey: I am at home.

Dr. Raymond: I would like to talk to you about your new home. Can you tell me about it?

Corey: Yes. It's a beautiful home.

Dr. Raymond: You mentioned that you had several mirrors removed from the walls. Can you tell me why you chose not to hang them?

Corey: It's where the mist comes.

Dr. Raymond: The mist that has troubled you?

Corey: Yes.

Dr. Raymond: Do you know where the mist came from?

Corey: Yes. The poor farm. I opened the door, and it came in with them.

Dr. Raymond: So how did the mist form in Renee's home?

Corey: It comes in through the bedroom mirrors.

Dr. Raymond: Does Renee know about this?

Corey: No.

Dr. Raymond: Do you think it would be a good idea to share this with him?

Corey: No. He won't believe me. I have to protect him. I am afraid he won't listen. He won't see what is coming. Something is coming for him.

Mrs. Delaney: Tell me what is coming.

Corey: The mist.

Mrs. Delaney: What does it want?

Corey: For us to die.

Mrs. Delaney: Corey, the dreams that you often talk about, are the poor farm people in your dreams as well?

Corey: Yes. They are all there. I don't know who they are. I can hear them. I hear them whispering, and he doesn't like that. It's like the hot and cold game. I ask a question, and sometimes I get an answer, and other times, I get clues.

Mrs. Delaney: What do you mean?

Corey: I know what he did to them. I know how he tortured and beat them.

Mrs. Delaney: How do you know all of this?

Corey: They are telling me this. They are showing me pictures of a registry.

Dr. Raymond: The poor farm ledgers?

Corey: Yes. It has their names in it.

Dr. Raymond: Do you know where these ledgers are?

Corey: George says they are in the house.

Dr. Raymond: What house?

Corey: The doctor's house in Winchester.

Mrs. Delaney: Do you know where this house is?

Corey: Yes.

Dr. Raymond: Where? Where is this house?

Corey: I'm living in it.

Mrs. Delaney: Your house? The ledgers are in your house?

Logan: Oh my God! You have got to be kidding me.

Dr. Raymond: Please, Logan. Do not interrupt. Corey, I want you to imagine yourself walking from room to room in your house. I want to you play the hot and cold game with George. Can you do that?

Corey: Yes.

Dr. Raymond: Tell me what you see as you go from room to room. Okay?

Corey: The parlor is colored in dark maroon wallpaper. There is a dark print on the walls halfway up. It feels cold. In the corner are three lights hanging from the wall. They are shining down on three coffins.

Mrs. Delaney: Who do the coffins belong to?

Corey: Charles's family. They are being waked here. The doctor is preparing their bodies.

Mrs. Delaney: Can you walk around the room and see if there are any documents or ledgers?

Corey: There is nothing here. Just their bodies for the service. Many beautiful flowers. They smell so sweet.

Dr. Raymond: Continue to walk into other rooms and describe what you see.

Corey: I am heading to the back bedroom. There is a hospital bed and several cases full of medicine in them.

Dr. Raymond: Can you read some of the medications for me?

Corey: Strychnine. There are several bottles with skeletons and cross-bones on them. I don't recognize any of the bottles in the cabinets.

Dr. Raymond: What else do you see?

Corey: Instruments. There are instruments all over the room and on trays. It looks like an operating room. There are no books in this room either.

Dr. Raymond: I want you to keep walking throughout the house.

Mrs. Delaney: Tell me when you feel hot like when you play the game with George.

Corey: Okay. I feel warmer when I near the stairwell. George is there. George is at the top of the stairs. He wants me to come upstairs.

Mrs. Delaney: I want you to follow him upstairs. Can you do that?

Corey: Yes. He is pointing to my son's room. I think I need to go in the attic.

Mrs. Delaney: Go ahead. Open the door to your son's room and open the attic door.

Corey: I don't want to. I'm afraid.

Mrs. Delaney: It's okay, Corey, you can do this. Open the door to the attic and tell me what you see.

Corey: Okay. I am opening the door. I see the stairs going up.

Mrs. Delaney: Go ahead and climb up the stairs.

Corey: I can't. I'm afraid. It's here! It's in the corner! It's here!

Mrs. Delaney: What's there, Corey?

Corey: The mist! It's in the attic! I'm afraid. I don't want to go. Please help me! I don't want to go! It's coming straight for me. It is smiling at me with those teeth. I hate that face. I have to get out. I have to run. *(Voice changes, sobbing.)* He knows I am here!

Logan: What is happening?

Corey: No! Let me go, let me go!

Logan: What is happening to her?

Dr. Raymond: Logan, please, let us continue.

Logan: What is happening? What is it doing to her?

Dr. Raymond: Anne, look at her arms. Quick, grab my camera.

Corey: God, please help me! Make it stop! *(Rising from the couch.)*

Mrs. Delaney: Oh, Jesus, Dr. Raymond. Look at her cuts! You have to wake her now.

Logan: Wake her, Dr. Raymond! Wake her up!

Dr. Raymond: Please, Logan, you must refrain. Corey, can you go back downstairs?

Corey: No. It won't let me go. God, please make it stop!

Mrs. Delaney: Tell it you are in control, Corey. Tell it to go away! Corey?

Corey: *(Sobbing.)*

Dr. Raymond: Corey, where are you?

Mrs. Delaney: Corey, can you hear me?

Corey: Yes. *(Sobbing.)*

Dr. Raymond: What is happening to you?

Corey: I am hanging in the attic. The mist … it's beating me. It just keeps beating me. I want this to stop. It hurts, and I'm so tired. I feel nauseous. I think I'm going to be sick.

Mrs. Delaney: Dr. Raymond, please grab the garbage can. Quick.

Corey: *(Retching.)*

Logan: Please do something!

Dr. Raymond: Okay, at the count of four, you will awaken relaxed, and you will remember everything from this conversation. One … two … three … four.

Corey: Oh my God! Did I just throw up on myself? What happened? Look at me! Look at my wrists!

Dr. Raymond: Corey, here, have a few tissues while I get you a glass of water and some gauze for your wrists.

Mrs. Delaney: Corey, you have been working with our group for several weeks now. I would like to bring the group to your home for a cleansing. Would five o'clock this evening be okay with you?

Corey: *(Sobbing.)* When is this all going to end?

Mrs. Delaney: It ends tonight! Is there someone that can watch your children tonight?

Corey: Yes, I think my sister can watch them. I can give her a call when I leave. Can we have group at my house then?

Mrs. Delaney: Corey, I think we have to handle this immediately. If we don't act now, it could jeopardize the safety of you and your family.

Corey: So what do we do?

Mrs. Delaney: Get rid of it for good! Corey, I believe you know the name of the man that tortured these people and who is doing this to you and your family. I felt it when I was at your house. It is him, Corey. It is the doctor that is causing you harm. And there is one more thing that we must do too. We must seal the portal in the mirrors to keep anything from ever coming back through. You have to tell Renee what is going on or he will hurt himself or others. I have seen what these entities can do to families. You must reach out to him soon. If you don't convince him, the portal may never be sealed, and his life will be in jeopardy.

Corey: That's easier said than done. He still doesn't trust me as far as he can throw me. How am I going to explain this to him? He is going to think I am crazy if I tell him what could still be in his home.

Mrs. Delaney: You have to, Corey, or else your kids' lives could be in danger. I think you know where I am going with this. And if we don't stop this now, you won't be the only one suffering.

Corey: I know! I know! I'm just afraid he will think I am crazy.

Mrs. Delaney: I will call the group this evening, and we will schedule it at your house for five o'clock. Logan, I need you to be present as well. Can you make it?

Logan: Absolutely. I will be there.

Mrs. Delaney: You both have to be strong. Just like what we talked about. Okay?

Corey: I know. I know I can do this.

Mrs. Delaney: Corey, the Catholic Church has been notified about what is happening to you. However, they have to have proof. We will need to provide them with your regression tapes as well as the photographs we took during your therapy sessions. Do you give Dr. Raymond permission to forward your tapes and photographs?

Corey: Yeah, that's fine. So, what happens when they review it all? What can they do to help me?

Mrs. Delaney: They would have to perform an exorcism.

Corey: A what? An exorcism on me? Are you kidding me? Oh my God, no! This isn't happening to me! But you said that I didn't need an exorcism. That's what you said when I first started coming here. *(Sobbing.)*

Dr. Raymond: Corey, I know this is a lot to consume. But this is the best option you have for the safety of you and your loved ones.

Corey: I am scared! Don't you get it? What if this thing takes over me? What then?

Mrs. Delaney: Corey, it already has. It has been attached to you for a long time. It's time to perform an exorcism. It's time to get rid of the doctor and his mist.

Corey: *(Sobbing.)* Oh my God! I can't believe this is really happening to me.

Logan: Corey, listen. Get a hold on yourself. You can do this. All of us will be there to help. I know you are afraid, but this is what has to be done! Please let them perform the exorcism and let's get rid of this thing.

Dr. Raymond: I will contact the church and have them meet us there at four thirty. Anne, you arrange for the group to be there the same.

Corey: Wait … don't they have to run this by the diocese or bishop or something?

Mrs. Delaney: We don't have time.

Corey: *(Sobbing.)*

Dr. Raymond: Corey, there are more and more cases of possession in the world today than ever before. The Catholic Church has been assembling individuals for the past several years on the practices of exorcisms. Anne has already been in contact with Father Joseph at St. Paul's Church.

Mrs. Delaney: It's time to prepare now, Corey. I will bring the group to your home this evening after I speak with Father Joseph when I leave here today.

Corey: *(Sobbing.)* Logan, please don't go. Please stay with me until everyone arrives. I don't want to go home alone.

Mrs. Delaney: Yes, Logan, please take her home. We will gather everyone together and be there by four thirty.

April 22, 2010, Exorcism

Father Joseph: In the name of the Father, and of the Son, and of the Holy Ghost. Amen. Most glorious prince of the heavenly armies, Saint Michael the archangel, defend us in our battle against principalities and powers, against the rulers of this world of darkness, against the spirits of wickedness in the high places. I want to speak to the entity that is tormenting this child of God.

Corey: *(Laughing.)*

Father Joseph: What is your name?

Corey: *(Laughing.)*

Father Joseph: By the power of God, I demand that you tell me your name.

Corey: *(Laughing.)* I have many names, Priest.

Father Joseph: I demand you to tell me your name. Why you are tormenting this child of God?

Corey: *(Laughing.)* She invited me in, Priest.

Father Joseph: Tell me your name.

Corey: I am many. I am many. I am many.

Father Joseph: Release her as she prays to have you removed from her body.

Corey: She prays for nothing and no one! She has no faith, Priest. *(Laughing.)* Ring around the rosy, pocket full of posy, ashes, ashes, you'll all fall down! *(Laughing.)*

Father Joseph: I know who you are. You cannot torment this child or her family anymore. She knows what you did, and you will enter into the eternal flames of hell for your deeds.

Corey: Hahahahahahahah! You have no control over her, Priest. She invited me in, and she has no faith in your so-called God.

Father Joseph: In the name of Jesus Christ, I command you to tell me your name.

(Note: Patient is being scratched by unseen hands. Bruising on face and arms are evident as body is thrashing around in chair. Patient lips are cracking at the corners and tearing healing scars of reconstructive surgery. Vomit is choking patient as exorcism progresses.)

Logan: You have to stop this! Look what this thing is doing to her! It's going to kill her! Please make it all stop!

Mrs. Delaney: Logan, you have to back off and let us do what needs to be done.

Logan: But it is killing her!

Mrs. Delaney: If you don't let us finish, it will kill her. It will kill all of you! Please let us handle this.

Corey: Logan, please help me! Don't let them do this to me. It hurts! It hurts so bad!

Father Joseph: Don't listen to it. It's not Corey talking with us now. Please don't look at her.

Corey: Logan, please! Help me! I love you! Don't you love me?

Logan: Please just do as they say.

Corey: Hold me, Logan. Hold me and please don't let them hurt me anymore.

Father Joseph: Don't listen to it. It's not Corey that you are dealing with. It is trying to trick you.

Mrs. Delaney: Logan, please be strong. Let him finish.

Father Joseph: Everyone, please recite the Lord's Prayer with me.

Our Father, which art in heaven, hallowed by thy name, thy kingdom come, thy shall be done, on earth as it is in heaven. Give us our daily bread and forgive us for trespassing as we forgive those who trespass against us and lead us not into temptation, but deliver us from evil.

(Note: Patient is resisting as she continues to fight the exorcism. Limbs are bruising as she continues in an attempt to break free from the restraints.)

Father Joseph: Unholy spirit, I command you to leave this child of God now!

(Note: Patient is vomiting violently.)

Father Joseph: Tell me your name, demon!

Corey: I am many. I am many, I am *custos animae perit!*

Father Joseph: Custos amimae perit, by the power of the Almighty God, you are cast down to the flames from which you came. God, whose nature is ever merciful and forgiving, accept our prayer that this servant of yours, bound by the fetters of sin, may be pardoned by your loving kindness. Holy Lord, Almighty Father, everlasting God and Father of our Lord Jesus Christ, who once and for all consigned that fallen and apostate tyrant to the flames of hell, who sent your only begotten Son into the world to crush that roaring lion, hasten to our call for help and snatch from ruination and from the clutches of the noonday devil this human being made in your image and likeness. Strike terror, Lord, into the beast now laying waste to your vineyard. Fill your servants with courage to fight manfully against that reprobate dragon, lest he despise those who put their trust in you, and say with Pharaoh of old: "I know not God, nor will I set Israel free." Let your mighty hand cast him out of your servant Corey Michaels so she may no longer be held captive by this negative entity. A servant whom it pleased you to make in your image and to redeem through your Son, who lives and reigns with you, in the unity of the Holy Spirit, God, forever and ever. Amen.

Corey, I am going to place this cross around your neck. You must wear it every day. It is a medallion of St. Michael. It will protect you.

April 22, 2010, Journal Entry

When I awoke, the straps on my legs and hands had been ripped apart. The chair I had been sitting in was in pieces on the floor. I was sweating profusely and lying in a pool of vomit. My arms and legs had been scratched. A pool of blood trailed from my frail body to the drain of the basement floor. It was if I had fallen asleep and when I awoke, I felt stronger than I had in a very long time. Something was different. I was different. I felt alive. I felt lighter. I thanked them all for staying by me. Father Joseph blessed the group then walked upstairs and out the door.

Chrissie began to burn sage and placed salt in each of the four corners in every room. I felt a sense of calmness as we began to walk from the basement to each floor above us. We worked our way up to the first floor, then the second floor. Alessandra went from room to room, telling stories of the previous owners and what had transpired in the house. Yet she knew nothing about my home or its history. She told us that the original owner was highly regarded and a well-respected individual in the community. She said he also had a twisted profession. Walking up the stairwell, Alessandra leaned back and took a deep breath in and began telling the original owner's sick tale. I could not believe what I was hearing. There were three spirits in the house, and they were all being restrained by the original owner of the property. They were confined to the attic, she said. They were tortured, hung by the joists and beaten. There was something else in the attic as well, and Anne stated that it had been waiting for me. Waiting for me to arrive.

When we made it to the second floor, all the bedroom doors violently slammed shut. Logan grabbed my hand and gently kissed my lips before stepping another foot forward. We all slowly walked down the hallway toward my son's room. Crossing the threshold, the attic door slowly swung open. Something was expecting us.

Chrissie turned and told me that the entity had followed me from one place to another over the course of my life. It had found me in the grove when I was a child. It meddled when it had to, but no one would have ever known that something evil was responsible for it. All of my trials, tribulations, and misfortunes were caused by this one nasty entity. It followed me everywhere, and it led me to this house.

We all proceeded up the stairs toward the attic. Suddenly, Chrissie began to cry out in pain. Her body buckled over, and it was obvious something was inflicting it on her. Alessandra continued with the ritual as she quickly stepped in front of Chrissie. Alessandra was suddenly thrown back against my son's wall with such force she collapsed on the floor. Logan and I got her to her feet and removed her to my bedroom. She lay in my bed motionless.

Logan remained by Alessandra's side and I head for my son's room. I knew this thing fed off of my fear, and as long as I was afraid of it and of my gift, I would never be able to protect my family. I trusted Anne. I trusted all of them and at that moment, I felt stronger than I have in a very long time.

The group and I proceeded to walk up the stairs to the attic. This time, I was leading the group. The anxiety consumed me. When I approached the last step going up into the attic, a small figure began to appear in the corner. We all saw it. It was negative, and it frightened me. I felt nauseous, my head was cloudy, and my gut turned with disgust as it spewed a putrid smell of burning flesh. The entity appeared as a small troll-like figure with a grimacing face and sharp teeth. Chrissie stated that it was hiding something. Anne reminded me that this was my house, and everything in it was mine. She stated that there was something that it was hiding in the attic, and we needed to find it.

I closed my eyes and imagined George up in the attic with us. I begged George to guide me to where this secret was being kept. I trusted George. He was my protector and I knew he would never put me in harms way. He gave me confidence that I could beat this thing and so I began to slowly walk in the direction where I was feeling the warmest. It was time to play the "hot and cold" game once again. Each step drew me to the corner where the entity hovered. The group could not believe my courage, nor would I if I had seen me do it. I put all my trust in God that day. And I relied on my guide George, to help me.

I concentrated on surrounding myself with the warmth of the God's embrace as I continued to approach the corner of the attic. Quickly, a malevolent presence took over the room and the atmosphere began to change. The attic grew pitch black, and the temperature dropped instantaneously. Anne and Chrissie began to recite prayers that they had taught me. I continued to slowly walk into the darkness of the room. I was not affected by the coldness, nor the darkness that surrounded us. However, I felt the presence of the evil entity and soon I began to question my strength.

The darkness was endless and I felt as I was no longer in my attic, rather in some infinite space, lost and alone. Pulling me deeper and deeper into an abyss that I had no way of knowing whether I would return. My feet were lifted off of the ground and I found myself looking down into nothingness. A space filled with emptiness and despair. It was dark and I was alone waving my hands and feet in mid-air trying not to fall. I allowed my fear to weaken me. I felt oppressive and defeated as I saw images of those that I loved around me dying. My children, Renee, my parents, and Logan would die terrible deaths. And then there were the others. The lost souls that slowly floated by me. I recognized them from my dreams. Men, women, and children all reaching out for me to help them. They too, were trapped in the darkness. And it was the doctor that held them there after he tortured and killed them. There were hundreds of them crying out for someone to save them. George was there too. I found comfort that he hadn't left me. But it was his tortured soul floating with the others. I have to help him. I have to help them all. *I will not let you win. I will not let you meddle in my life any longer! I know who you are!* I yelled.

I dropped to the floor as the darkness began to disappear. George appeared before me and was pointing in the corner. The entity was crouched over, rocking back and forth as if it were a dog ready to jump out at me. "Warmer, warmer, you are getting hot, hotter, and hotter, boiling," I heard George whisper. I felt the entity was getting bigger as I was getting closer. I pressed on and I gathered the courage I needed to look into its piercing black eyes. I remained calm although the adrenaline racing through my veins kept me sharp and determined. I would not show any fear, or it would know that I was a coward.

Alessandra slowly rose to her feet and joined us in the attic. They continued to pray to St. Michael while spraying holy water through-out the attic. The entity was agitated by our presence. It knew we meant business and none of us were going to stop until it was gone. It refused to leave the corner. It was struggling to move, as if caught in a spider web. It refused to leave despite our efforts, and it occurred to me why. It chose to stay there: *It's protecting something. That's why it's always in the attic, and that's why it won't leave now. The entity had followed me everywhere, and now it won't leave the attic corner. There is something in this floor, and we have to find it.* I screamed at the group, "Start pulling up the floorboards." I heard them whisper it in my ear. The lost souls that I had seen in the darkness. They were speaking to me and I could clearly hear them. The others were holding on to the attic joists as a powerful wind encircled the attic. I told the entity that it had no control over me anymore. I told it that I was not afraid of it.

The entity took possession of Chrissie's body, and she stood straight up. It lifted her feet off of the floor and spun her around. Chrissie's body quickly contorted into that of an animal. She bent over like a dog, and her hair began to sway like in my night terrors. Her teeth were different too. They were pointy, and there was blood dripping from her mouth as she bit down, deep into her lips. Her lips ripped at the creases and she began to growl and spit at us. Chrissie looked at Logan and began to taunt him with memories of the tragic day when his friends were killed. "It's your fault, Logan! You killed them all! They blame you for not saving them!" It screamed. Logan fell to his knees and cried.

"Get up Logan! Don't listen to it!" Anne screamed. "It lies! Don't believe a word it says, Logan!" I yelled back. "I saw them Logan. I saw them in the darkness! I saw all of them and they told me every-thing. They don't blame you!" I said. Logan rose to his feet, wiped the tears from his face then began to tear up the floor boards before him. Anne and Alessandra grabbed Chrissie and held on to her as they continued to recite prayers.

The wind grew stronger and debris flew at us by hands of the unseen. A toy box lifted off the ground and crashed into the wall before me. I jumped out of the way as it came crashing down where I was standing. I noticed a broken floorboard when I got back on my feet. I quickly pulled back the boards, and hidden in the insulation were two leather-bound journals. I looked at them in amazement. "I did it. I found them! I found them!" I screamed. Holding the journals tightly to my chest, I looked up and discovered that the mist was now covering the entire ceiling of the attic. Once again, I felt the adrenaline rush throughout my veins. "You have no control over me anymore. Do you hear me? I have the ledgers now. Now everyone will know what you did!" I threatened.

The mist grew bigger and bigger as it hovered above us. It moaned and it screamed. The windows and doors in the house were opening and slamming shut, and the televisions were blaring in unison to nothing more than static. The light fixtures burned so bright the bulbs began to explode. The group continued on, reciting prayers as debris continued to fly in our paths. A piece of glass shot out across the room and became lodged in Anne's face. Anne's face was badly injured, but she kept praying. Logan escorted me around the attic as objects continued to fly as we head for the stairs. We ran down the stairs and swung open the attic door. Logan stopped at the bottom of the stairs, turned around then head back up. He yelled for me to take the ledgers away from the house. Logan then raced back up the stairs to the attic to help the others.

I was worried for the others, but I knew what I had to do. I raced down the hallway and head for the stairs with the journals in my hand. The house still rattling with anger, the walls began to bleed. I screamed and it screamed back. A loud ear piercing screech that forced me to cover my ears and drop the journals. "Save them!" George whispered. A Soft, angelic voice reassuring me that I was not alone. It was the encouragement I needed.

I uncovered my ears and jumped to the first landing. When I jumped, the stairwell chandelier fell from the ceiling and it nearly missed my head. I lost my balance and went tumbling down the stairs, landing on the first-floor. My body ached as I slowly reached for the banister to help me stand up. The journals were right in front on me on the floor. I looked up and there it was. It was him. It was the doctor and the journals were underneath him.

I screamed for the group to come help me, but they were all still trapped in the attic. I knew I would have to do this alone. I closed my eyes and began to pray. I felt George and others standing by my side. I couldn't see them, but I felt them as they continued to whisper to me. The entryway began to heat up, and I could feel the doctor changing into the mist. It grew larger and larger and its teeth were chattering as blood dripped from its mouth. Suddenly, the mist turned into a ball of flames before my eyes. Spiraling along the foyer and rising up to the ceiling. But I wasn't afraid anymore. It was time to stand up for myself, my family and the others.

Logan broke down the attic door and the group came running downstairs. Anne screamed from the top of the stairs. "Corey, it's time! Call him by name! Do it now!" Anne instructed. I took a deep breath in and yelled with everything I had, "Dr. Franklin Thomas, this is my home, and you no longer have power or control over me, my family, or those you hold captive from the poor farm. The crimes you committed will forever be known in paper, in stone, and in the county's memory. You will no longer hold the lost souls of my poor farm against their will. They are free to leave into the light. Justice will be served, for your punishment in death will be burning in hell where you belong."

Anne threw the bottle of holy water to me. I sprayed it on my hands and slowly stretched my arm into the flames and grabbed a hold of the journals. The house growled and the mist moaned as it began to latch out at me one last time. My back was slashed with a whip and my arms were cut profusely. My legs were scratched and my face was being slapped. Still I held on dearly to the ledgers. I refused to let go. The mist let out a terrifying scream and then began to swirl downwards into the floor. I stood in the center of it watching the burning flames, holding the ledgers tightly. Strangely, I felt no pain from the flames. The flames disappeared and the house became silent once again. I ran straight out the front door.

A few minutes later, the group emerged from the house. Logan embraced me and kissed my lips as tears of joy flowed down our faces. We had conquered this thing. All of us together. They all helped me fight for what was right.

Alessandra placed some salt at the bottom of the doorway of my front door. I had found the missing ledgers and unearthed the doctor's dark secret. This nightmare was finally coming to an end.

The journals were still smoking from being so near to the mist. I took a deep breath in and carefully opened the journals. Only the cover of one of the journals was burned off completely. The pages were all intact. I carefully opened the journals when the letters caught everyone's eyes. *County Poor Farm, secretary, Lulu Cooper.* I knew why the entity was protecting them, and now I knew why I was drawn to this house and why things happened as they did. It was Franklin's house that I had been living in. Thomas was the one responsible for my beatings, night terrors, the harmful incidents that occurred to my family, the injuries and death of Bear, the possession of Harley, and the death of so many people at the poor farm.

"Things happen for a reason. There are no coincidences!" I heard those words over and over again in my mind. George and the others had drawn me to this house. George had been with me my entire life, guiding me throughout my childhood, safeguarding my children, and making sure I would find the right path in life when at times I had lost my faith. I felt confident I was getting closer to the truth about my life, the research, this house, the terrors, and all of the trials and tribulations that had plagued my life. It was all coming to an end now. I was anxious to begin the healing.

Days prior to my cleansing, I had learned that a Dr. Franklin Thomas was the county physician assigned to the poor farm. He served for twenty-one years as the county physician. But I had yet to find anything else on him. I knew that back in the day, physicians were more regarded as fly-by-night medicine men. They would concoct serums and potions in hopes of getting rich overnight. Many of them went from town to town treating patients with toxic potions. Franklin was not a physician by any means. He was noted as finding a cure for colicky children. That's it! Suddenly, everyone looked up to him, and the majority of children grew up to be addicted to morphine.

I explained to the group that I had been searching for records on the poor farm's earliest operation, and until now, so many negative things had transpired to keep me away from discovering the truth.

Lulu's missing ledgers held the names of people who once resided on the property. It also exposed the truth about what happened to them. Finally, I had everyone's name that ever lived and died there. And I had every name ever associated with the doctor's experiments that were buried elsewhere. I felt a sense of release finding them in my attic. It was soothing and calming, and it felt good for a change.

April 26, 2010, Journal Entry

I have been so busy researching the ledgers that I have had little time for my journaling, let alone going to counseling with Dr. Raymond. I managed to write down all of the names of the individuals in the book and began pulling ancestry records on them. When I pulled an inquiry record for Mr. Thomas, I discovered an article written about him. It appeared that he was subject to investigation in the 1880s for performing inhumane experiments at the poor farm. I couldn't believe what I was reading. We were not prepared for what we discovered next.

Logan and I pulled up all of the articles online with the doctor's name on them and found another one dated September 8, 1883. It told the story of a young man appearing at the old Spurgeon farm wearing nothing but a blanket. He was cold, malnourished, and unable to speak. His tongue had been cut out. He would communicate by signing to the authorities. He claimed that he was taken from the poor farm and brought to a homestead in the township. He claimed that he and others were subject to heinous cruelty. The boy had stated that hundreds of men, women, and children were imprisoned on the property in Winchester Grove.

The boy led them to where he was held captive, but when they arrived, no one was there. Not a soul was found. When I did a property search on my home, I discovered that Dr. Thomas owned eighty acres of land in Winchester Grove. He had several outbuildings too. Today, they are no longer standing, just the homestead.

According to the article, the boy gave great detail of how each prisoner was given a number, and certain experiments were conducted on them. He witnessed the doctor tying an expectant women's legs together so she could not give birth. The men were lab rats of bloodletting in an attempt to cure insanity. Men disfigured in battle were subject to shock therapy. Children with disabilities were even tied up and whipped for bad behaviors. Some were starved to cure diseases, and some were forced to eat their own feces to survive. This was how he documented the experiments. And it was all there in the ledgers.

The article never mentioned the young man's name publicly, but I had a strange feeling that Logan had lived a portion of it. Court documents suggest the doctor was never brought up on charges. The doctor disappeared the day the young man went to the authorities, and soon after, the young man died of his illness. This young man was the only source to expose the truth about what happened on the poor farm while Thomas was the physician.

The journals were dated December 1850 through September 1877. There were over a hundred people discharged from the farm between May 1875 and 1877. Until now, no one knew what had happened to them.

I called a close friend of mine who was on the board of directors at the local library. I explained to her what we had found in the attic in the house. She met us at the library a few days later and began pulling articles pertaining to anything with Franklin Thomas's name on it. The only newspaper article that popped up was of the young boy from the Spurgeon farm and the talk of the charges.

Hundreds of resident charts were reviewed by the jury. No autopsies were completed on any of the deaths that occurred during his position because no one could find their bodies. I was amazed at what I was reading. There were no death certificates, no notations for their cause of deaths either. They were just removed from the poor farm, and no explanations for their deaths were noted in the available county records during the proceedings, but the journals said differently.

Thomas remained at large, and to this day, his whereabouts remain unknown. According to the lost journals, all the men, women, and children had suffered various diseases, neglect, malnutrition, and abandonment. In the corner of each name, "discharged" was listed as their last entry, and I knew what that meant. I knew what he had done.

May 19, 2010, Therapy Session

Dr. Raymond: Hello, Corey. I remained hopeful that you would continue with your therapy sessions.

Corey: There has been so much that has happened since that night after our last session. I just don't know where to begin.

Dr. Raymond: Anne has filled me in for the most part, but I would like to know how you feel about everything that has transpired.

Corey: Where shall I start, from that night or what is going on now? There is so much to tell you. I am overwhelmed. I don't know where to begin.

Dr. Raymond: Well, let's start with that night. It was quite an evening I hear.

Corey: I still have much to learn, but I am no longer fearful of it. Logan is helping me too. We are helping each other actually.

Dr. Raymond: That is great, Corey. So, are you still having night terrors or feeling anxious?

Corey: I am still having dreams, but I don't see the mist anymore.

Dr. Raymond: Would you like to talk about the dreams you are having?

Corey: Sure. I still see things happening to people around me. I am just having a hard time relaying those feelings to those in the dreams. I don't know how they will take them.

Dr. Raymond: Do you still have the dream about Renee?

Corey: Yes.

Dr. Raymond: So, my next question. How do you think Renee would react if you told him about your dreams and your gift?

Corey: I don't know. I still don't know if he would believe me or not.

Dr. Raymond: I do believe that you should work on your relationship with him. You need to begin rebuilding that trust with him. It would be in the best interest for your children. It would also help with letting go of your guilt for leaving him.

Corey: I am still trying to help him. He has to be able to admit that he needs help though. I cannot make him do that. I have tried. But

I know if I don't keep pressing the issue, something terrible is going to happen to him and my children.

Dr. Raymond: And how are your children doing?

Corey: They are doing okay. They don't know anything about the journal or whose house we are living in. They really have not said much since we last spoke with Anne though. I find them asking more questions that anything these days. I think they may be a bit inquisitive, but I don't believe they are frightened by my gift.

Dr. Raymond: I would like to talk to your children if it's okay with you. Perhaps I can help them understand your gift and why strange things happened to you.

Corey: Perhaps, but I am not sure I am ready to do that just now. Like I said, I have a lot of work to do, and tying my calendar up with more appointments is only going to delay my work even longer.

Dr. Raymond: I understand. It is very important that your children are getting counseling too. Perhaps it would help them adjust to their new surroundings and Renee's drinking as well.

Corey: Oh my goodness! What time is it?

Dr. Raymond: Four thirty. Why?

Corey: Oh, crap! I have to be at Sara's school tonight for a band concert. I have to go.

Dr. Raymond: Okay, well, call Judy when you have time, and we can reschedule.

Corey: Okay, I am really sorry. I totally forgot about her concert. How foolish of me to forget. I will call Judy tomorrow. I promise.

Dr. Raymond: Okay, I will see you soon. Goodbye, Corey.

Corey: Goodbye, Dr. Raymond.

May 19, 2010, Journal Entry

When I dozed off to sleep tonight, I had the dream again. Renee was driving the kids to his home for the weekend. His eyes became heavy as he continued down the interstate, not knowing what lay ahead in his path. The children looked frightened as Renee crossed over the yellow line repeatedly into oncoming traffic. My son yelled for Renee to stay awake, and just then, Renee fell over the steering wheel and passed out. The car swerved off the road into oncoming traffic. The impact was so hard the median cut the vehicle in half. My children were killed instantly. I know they are still in danger as long as he refuses help.

June 1, 2010, Journal Entry

This afternoon, Logan invited the group to come with us to the cemetery grounds. He wanted to say a prayer for them. They all joined him in prayer as we placed several floral bouquets in the ground and toys for the children. I wanted them to know that there were still people in this world who cared about them. I promised them that no one would ever harm or forget them again. I promised that I would be their steward for protecting their gravesite and accepted their invitation to be their new caretaker.

I left the cemetery grounds feeling as though a weight had been lifted off of my shoulders. I felt quite relaxed as I walked throughout the rows of the numeric markers. This day was a good day. It had been a while since I felt this relaxed and at ease. It felt really good.

July 1, 2010, Journal Entry

As we welcome the summer weather, Logan, Anne, and I have worked long hours to prepare the site for the dedication. All the grant dollars are being filtered in through the museum, and work is underway. I am excited to be playing an active role in a mural being constructed on the poor farm grounds. It was what I have dreamt of, and I am watching it happen right in front of me. We invited senators, township supervisors, mayors, and representatives from the county to share in the historic unveiling, just as I had dreamed, and they were all planning on attending.

July 18, 2010, Journal Entry

A crowd gathered once more on the poor farm grounds, but it wasn't to farm the fields or dig any more graves. They gathered to pay respects to those who had died there. The ceremony crew would arrive early to spruce up the cemetery grounds before the unveiling later in the afternoon. When the crew was gathering their rakes and cans to head back to the mural, Logan made a remarkable discovery.

He had been gathering his gear when he tripped over what he thought was a vine. It turned out to be the corner of a tombstone. It had been buried in the ground below the other markers.

I was summonsed to come quickly to the grounds, and when I arrived, Logan had fallen to his knees. I embraced him and asked him what was wrong. He began to cry as he pointed to the ground. There in the ground and partially sticking out of the dirt was a tombstone, but it was not like the others. This one had a name on it, and the name was George Miller, who died in 1883. "Agru23" flashed in my head. I remembered it being written on the chalkboard. Just then, a lightbulb clicked in my head, and the voices confirmed my suspicion. The George I saw as a child died with symptoms of Agru, but the number twenty-three was not something I was not familiar with until his marker was found. It was buried next to marker 23 in the poor farm cemetery.

Logan cried that he had seen this tombstone in his dreams. This moment had played out in his dreams for years, and he never knew what it meant until now. It was then we finally understood exactly what had happened and why George was in our lives. He knew our destiny even before we did. He knew what we would become. He was preparing me, preparing us. Ingrid, Charles, Lulu, George, Logan—they were all part of my life path.

Discovering the tombstone gave clarity on who George was and Logan's relationship to me. It was George who had survived Thomas's experiments and come forward to expose him for what he had done back in 1883. Logan regressed to life as George back in 1883, which explained his dreams and his connection to the poor farm.

We learned that George ended up at the poor farm by accident. He was sent to the county farm because he was an outsider and had nowhere to go or family residing within the state. He remained alive for three days to tell his story to the authorities, but he never lived long enough to see justice done to Thomas.

George breathed his last breath on September 21, 1883. He was buried on the poor farm with the others. It was something we learned the day we found the ledgers, yet Logan had dreamt about George and the cemetery for more than fifteen years.

George's tombstone was placed in the cemetery out of respect for what he was subjected to and how he had managed to escape. It was comforting to see Logan find George's tombstone. This was no coincidence. He was meant to find it. The angelic voices once again whispering our confirmation.

That afternoon, I acknowledged all of their lives in public. I began by telling their stories. "Innocent men, women, and children, veterans, first settlers, and various individuals in their own crisis lived, loved, and died here. Over three hundred people are buried in the area's potters' fields, and many unbeknownst to society. Today, we are here to acknowledge them. We glorify them by dedicating this mural in memory of them all."

After I gave a brief history of the poor farm, I read the names of those buried on the property. The ceremony concluded with the playing of "Taps," and the curtain covering the mural was then removed. After everyone admired the mural, I invited everyone to the cemetery for the blessing by Father Joseph. I was able to breathe a sigh of relief. It was at that moment I felt resolution, overwhelmed with joy that I had made someone else's wrong a right.

After the ceremony, Anne noted the orbs encircling the mural after the unveiling. She saw them dancing around me as I spoke from the podium. I didn't see anything, but I did feel them. It was gratifying that they were finally able to move on after being held captive for so long.

July 19, 2010, Journal Entry

I slept well last night, and I know things will begin to look up again. I dreamt the most wonderful dream last night. I saw myself back at the mural giving my speech, and every time I said a name, one of them would come up from beyond the cemetery entrance and float into the mural.

I saw the children dancing around me while I was speaking at the podium. They were singing "Ring around the Rosy." That familiar nursery rhyme I had grown to fear. It was different now. It was tranquil this time watching the children sing it. It was a wonderful feeling.

George was there too. He sported a vest and dress coat. He was handsome, confident, and full of life. He was a short, slender young man with dark, almost black hair. He wore an Irish cap, similar to the ones I collected over the years. He motioned to those who were lost to come across the field. They came from beyond the tree line. He told them their families were waiting for them and it was time to go home. As each one of them approached the mural, they would turn and smile back at me, until George was the last one. He paused as he headed for the mural. "Corey, thank you for listening. There is still more you must do. Carry your faith whenever you go exploring. I'll be with you always, for this is not goodbye for me. Our paths will cross again, and when you venture off your life path, I'll be there guiding you in the right direction."

July 23, 2010, Journal Entry

When I awoke this morning, I remembered having a vivid dream. The dream kept me from daily chores today, so I decided to venture out and do some exploring of some old city plats. I guess you could say I am testing my abilities still. I still continue to pull records on the poor farm, but this morning, my curiosity pulled me in another direction. And one thing that I have learned is to follow my instinct.

I headed to the library to view some of the old articles and plat books. Only a few minutes into my research, I discovered a letter from 1866 that described a city cemetery that was not being maintained. The letter was from the son of the previous property owner, pleading with the city to take care of the grounds. He acknowledged the hundreds of men, women, and children who were buried there. Many of them were service men.

The cemetery was located in the city on a slope. The cemetery dated back to the 1830s. It was a city cemetery that housed thousands of diseased, orphans, veterans, and even our first settlers. It was a secret to the public, and the city was responsible for seeing that the grounds were forever protected from disturbances. A pest house was noted as being directly across the street for the convenience of burying the dead, unbeknownst to the townspeople.

I managed to pull records on the property where the article claimed to name the location. It was a needle in a haystack when I pieced the two together. And it made perfect sense now. It was now a children's park, and any signs of a cemetery were no longer evident.

Once on the property, I was overcome by déjà vu. Initially, I paid no attention to it, for I had grown up in the area and often played Ghost in the Graveyard in this park. This is true. Funny how things come full circle. You see, back then, it was known as a children's park, and I grew up playing in this park. Many times after dark too. It is where I first saw the mist. In the grove of timbers in my old neighborhood. This time, this visit was different. I was not thinking about my previous memories as a child playing on the grounds. The memories I was seeing were from a much earlier time. I remembered it. George showed it to me. He showed me pictures of men burying bodies and Thomas watching across the street from a house. It was the site of the old pest house! My house was two doors down from it.

I could not believe what I was seeing, but I was sure that this park held a secret buried underneath it. I wondered if this was where it all began. Did Dr. Thomas follow me from this park when I was a child? The more I thought about it, the more it made sense. Fortunately, I had guides to protect me—that is, until I invited him in permanently and opened a portal for others to come through.

Needless to say, I marked the spot on the plat map and contacted the local authorities on my suspicion.

August 1, 2010, Journal Entry

Logan received a call today from the city public works department, pertaining to that same children's park. Apparently it is being renovated, and while the construction crew was digging a trench for a sewer line, three tombstones were unearthed. The city knew of my research in potters' fields and contacted Logan when the stones were unearthed. Logan knew that I could find out who the tombstones belonged to, so I rushed down to the site and took photographs of the tombstones to begin my research.

One of the tombstones was that of the little boy who had died back in 1877. Only a portion of his tombstone was legible enough to determine that his name was Charles. He died the same day he was born. I assumed his mother's tombstone would be found nearby, but I was not allowed to physically dig to look for more tombstones.

August 18, 2010, Journal Entry

The mayor's office invited us to attend the land marking and grand reopening of the children's park today. I have been given the honor of placing a marker on the property to acknowledge its prior use as a cemetery. Once again I am excited to be playing a role in their preservation. There are still many unanswered questions though. I can't help but try to find others.

August 19, 2010, Journal Entry

Last night, I dreamt of a young, beautiful lady holding what appeared to be a small child wrapped in a blanket. She was there at the land marking, and she was motioning for me to follow her into the timbers.

She introduced herself as Alice. She then opened the blanket to show me her baby boy. He was a beautiful little boy. She named him after her father, Charles. She thanked me for finding her baby and for bringing them together again. I took his hand, and he gripped my finger tightly. I knew I was looking at Lulu Cooper.

The tombstone belonged to Lulu's son. No one had to whisper it to me. I just knew.

I was full of emotion at their reuniting. She motioned for me to walk to the edge of the grove. There standing in the morning dew were George and a small boy. "Go. Go speak with them. They are waiting for you," she said.

I knew George was there for a reason. "You still have work to do. This is not the end of your journey," he said. "Restore his faith and rid him of demons," he said. "More will come through the mirrors. Seal the portal, and he will be saved," he warned. I knew what he was talking about. Indeed, my job is not done.

I thanked George for helping me as I looked at the young boy who held his hand. He smiled up at me then reached for me to pick him up. I cried as he raised his little hands towards me. It was my boy. It was my son that I had aborted. "It's ok Momma. I'm with you always just like George." He whispered gently. "I'll visit you soon. In your dreams, Momma. Look for me in your dreams."

When I awoke, my pillow was soaked from my tears. I was not saddened; I was relieved that my son had forgiven me for what I had done while with Harley.

August 30, 2010, Journal Entry

I continue to visit Dr. Raymond to help me deal with the loss of my families. He has managed to help me cope with the feelings I receive from those who have passed. I have also decided to attend a support group at the hospital for those who have been subject to sexual assault.

I finally sat down and told Renee everything. I also explained the need to seal the portal I opened in his home and where the mist first came into our lives. I am not sure whether or not he believed me. Intuition tells me that I could never be labeled insane by someone struggling with personal demons they have yet to overcome. I pray that he will get help soon, and I pray that he will do what needs to be done to protect him and others who enter his life. Before I left him that day, I pleaded with him to reach out to Anne and the group. I am not sure that he will and I fear that if he doesn't, more harm will come to his life. I must do everything I can to protect my children until he does get help. It is the only way, for now.

October 15, 2010, Journal Entry

From this entire journey, I've learned that we all play a key role in God's plan. We may not realize it at the time, but our actions affect the reactions of others in this life and past lives. No one had ever taught me that. We all have the power to change our own lives and those of others that we meet along the way. You don't have to be sensitive to know these things. You don't have to go through what I went through to know that our loved ones are among us. There are guides that protect us and direct us to follow what God has planned for us. And sometimes there are negative things among us too.

And so, as one chapter ends, another chapter begins. I have a lot of work to do, indeed. I am anxious about my life ahead. I am no longer fearful of my abilities. I am no longer fearful of the unknown and things that go bump in the night. I have seen what is in the darkness. This is a new beginning for me and my family. For I know what my purpose is now. I know what I need to do to help those who become lost. I pray to God that the living will understand now too.

I continue to practice my faith each day. It has allowed me to become a stronger person. It has also provided me with a peace I have never experienced. I continue to pray for all of the lost souls that I saw while in the darkness that were left behind. There were so many of them reaching out for me. Those that were held there by the mist were able to move into the light. Others were held by something else. An evil so ancient, it terrified me. I caught a glimpse of the destruction of what it can do to the citizens of Winchester Grove. No this battle is far from over. The mist and Dr. Thomas was only the beginning.

For the dead continue to walk among us, guiding us, teaching us, and even wreaking havoc among us. Something evil is indeed coming to Winchester Grove and it wreaks like hell.

Special Note by
Dr. James Raymond

September 5, 2012

Corey Michaels's case was indeed a complex one. The discovery of her multiple past lives and the role they played currently has helped her understand why she suffered from night terrors, certain phobias, and fears. In addition, identifying her gift as a tool to help not only the living but also the deceased enabled her to resolve an injustice. I do believe my course of therapy provided her with a direction toward utilizing her spiritual sensitivity in order to return to her faith as a Christian.

Corey's night terrors stopped the day the journals were found. With Anne's teachings, Corey was able to learn how to use her gift to help others without being fearful of the unknown. I am fortunate to have been one of those individuals who witnessed her abilities firsthand during my sessions with other clients. Since the mural ceremony, Corey has worked with Anne and others within their group, with those suffering from similar possessions. In addition, she works with many of my clients that have past life regressions by researching ancestral lineage for validation. In her short time after the above events, she has been able to reconnect lost ancestors to the living as well as identify unrecorded burial records.

Harley Hillcrest was arrested in March 2010 for firing a weapon while driving. The bullet fired into the air unfortunately killed an innocent child playing in the park. I was assigned to evaluate him prior to conviction, due to Harley's irritability while being detained. When I began my interview process with Harley, it appeared that he had been subject to beatings. Hair was missing from his scalp, one of his ears had been partially bitten off, and pieces of flesh on his legs and arms were missing.

Harley confessed his intentions to harm Renee with little argument. He had planned to catch Renee off guard by sneaking up on him from the rear of his car. He was going to shoot him with a gun before Renee was able to step foot out of his vehicle. Harley claimed that voices in his head told him that if he killed Renee, he would no longer be subject to the doctor's treatments.

As a physician in psychiatry, it would be easy to diagnose Harley as suffering from some sort of a mental psychosis brought on by substance abuse. But again, that would be the easy thing to do. Due to Harley's mental state, he was not fit for a trial and was transferred to an insane asylum in southern Illinois where he continues with treatment.

I inquire with Corey as to Renee's well-being and her relationship with Logan from time to time.

Corey continues to encourage and support Renee as he battles his addiction. She has warned him of things to come if he does not get help soon. To this day, Renee has yet to seal the portal in his home at Corey's request.